EXPERIENCING T[...]
ESSAYS OF DIS[...]

For Keith Spalding

This volume, planned in June 2002 as a surprise to mark Keith Spalding's 90th birthday on 15 May 2003, brings together contributions by friends, colleagues, former Lektoren and students, united in their joy to honour a great scholar and good friend. Many others, unable to contribute, are listed in the Table of Supporters, originally intended as a *Tabula gratulatoria*. Sadly, after Keith Spalding's sudden death on 29 November 2002, the volume, almost ready to go to press, became a memorial. Our inability to invite contributions entirely without his help had made him aware of our secret, which was, however, never fully shared with him. Conscious of the nature of the discovery which Keith Spalding's students made in him the editors were preparing a collection of memories by students as a single copy to be presented. It will not appear now, but he lives on in his students.

The editors owe a debt of thanks to Tom Paulin, who readily agreed to write a preface; to Rachel Spencer, who designed the cover, and to Moira Tait who supplied many student addresses, and ensured that some typescripts became computer texts. Kristian Siefken listened and advised on many aspects of publication. The technical planning and production of the volume was greatly eased by Bob Sissons and his colleagues. Michael Johnson kindly helped us bring up to date the Tribute to Keith Spalding, originally published in *GLL* for the 80th birthday and used here with the permission of its editors. The volume would not have been possible at all without the generous support of the five institutions listed below. We are grateful to all who have made this volume possible.

Hinrich Siefken, Anthony Bushell - Bangor, December 2002

Printed with the support of

The University of Wales, Bangor
Blackwell Publishers
German Embassy London
Swiss Embassy London
Universitätsbund Tübingen e.V.

Experiencing Tradition
Essays of Discovery

*In Memory of Keith Spalding
(1913-2002)*

Edited by
Hinrich Siefken and Anthony Bushell

William Sessions Limited
York, England

© The Editors, Bangor 2003

ISBN 1 85072 294 3

Cover Design by Rachel Spencer

Printed in 11 on 12 point Plantin Typeface
from Editor's Disk
by Sessions of York
The Ebor Press
York, England

This volume could not have been published without the support of many.
Where possible, former students are listed with the years of their study; the maiden name is given in brackets.

Chris Allen, Epsom (1961-5)
Austrian Cultural Forum London
Nia Bagnall (Davies), Menai Bridge (1975-9)
George Barker, Bristol
Annelies Bednall, Chichester
Blackwell Publishers Oxford
Professor Elizabeth Boa, Nottingham
Dr Achim und Maria von Borries, Bremen
Dr Erich Brauch, Urbach (German Lektor, 1979-80)
Dr Charmian Brinson, London
David Bunday, Nishinomyia, Japan (1968-72, 1973-4)
Margaret Burgon (Dutton), Chandlers Ford (1962-7)
Professor Anthony Bushell, Bangor
Professor Alan Busst, Bangor
Caroline Camp (Rimmer), Hildenborough (1970-3)
Dr Elaine Canning, Bangor
Dr Rosemary Chapman, Nottingham
M L Clarke, Cholsey
Linda Coffey, Hawarden (1961-5)
Diane Collins (Simmons), Lowdham (1957-60)
Robert Cross, Cambridge (1976-80)
Valerie Cullen, Middleton USA
Rowland Davies (Romsey) (1960-6)
Dr Jo Desch, Bangor (German Lektor 1966-9)
Pauline Desch, Llandaniel
Deutsches Literaturarchiv, Marbach
Professor Martin Durrell, Manchester
John Elkington, Malvern (1958-63)
Dr Owen Evans, Bangor
Professor Dr Lothar Fietz, Tübingen (German Lektor 1959-60)

Olav Finne, Sandefjord (Norwegian Lektor 1971-3)
Professor John L Flood, London
German Embassy London
German Department, University College Cork, Ireland
German Department, Royal Holloway University of London
German Department, University of Leeds
German Department, University of Nottingham
German Section, SOLCCA, University of Keele
Professor George Gillespie, Cardiff
Professor Hans-Joachim Hahn, Oxford (German Lektor 1967-9)
William Hanson, Exeter (1957-62)
Rev Professor John Heywood Thomas, Bonvilston / Bangor
Dr Ian Hilton, Chipping Campden
Professor Dr Karl Holl, Bremen
Institute of Germanic Studies, University of London
David W M James, Lightwater
Professor Peter Jentzsch, Metzingen
Dr Michael Johnson, Brighton (1961-6)
Professor W Gareth Jones, Bangor
Professor G L Jones, Aberystwyth
Roger Jones, Keele
Diana v. Klein (James), Geneva (1958-61)
Peter Leighton-Langer, Bensheim
Maureen Lofmark, Lampeter
Harry Long, Wokingham
Barbara McEvoy (Hill), Prestatyn (1965-8)
Professor Dr Hans Heinrich Meier, Schaffhausen
Professor and Mrs Tim Miles, Bangor
Kari Moen, Notodden (Norwegian lectrice 1965-6)
Professor Dr Gerhard Müller-Schwefe, Tübingen
Professor Idris Parry, Bangor
Professor Robert J Pascall, Bangor
Professor Siegbert S Prawer, Oxford
Peter Prochnik, London (Bangor 1954-9)

Professor J H Reid, Nottingham
Professor Hans S Reiss, Bristol
Professor Hugh Ridley, Dublin
David Rock, Keele
Professor Dr Lutz Röhrich, Freiburg
Dr Laura Rorato, Bangor
Stan Royden, Meols (1963-7)
Professor Dr Horst Dieter Schlosser, Frankfurt am Main
Marcia Siefken (Birch), Nottingham (1961-7)
Professor Hinrich Siefken, Nottingham (German Lektor 1965-6)
Swiss Embassy London
Carole Thomas (Bond), Stoneleigh (1974-7)
Karl Ernst Tielebier-Langenscheidt
Professor Witold F Tulasiewicz, Cambridge
Dr Carol Tully, Bangor
Universitätsbund Tübingen
University of Wales, Bangor
Dr Walter Voigt, Ismaningen
Professor George A Wells, St Albans
Dorothea Wilde, Pfungstadt
Professor Rhys W Williams, Swansea
Professor Roy Wisbey, Cambridge
Dr Dietmar Wünschmann, Gerstetten (German Lektor 1964-6)
Professor W E Yates, Exeter
Professor Dr H Zirker, Kenn

Contents

	Page
Preface: Tom Paulin	xii
Introduction: Experiencing Tradition – Hinrich Siefken and Anthony Bushell	xiv

Karl Heinz Spalt - Keith Spalding
Biography and Tribute – Hinrich Siefken ... 1
Bibliography – Hinrich Siefken ... 18

Essays of Discovery (I)
My Six and a half Years in the Third Reich –
  Hans S. Reiss (Bristol) ... 24
Student Years – Harry Long (Wokingham) ... 30
Keith Spalding: From Pacifist to Soldier –
  Peter Leighton Langer (Bensheim) ... 31
'Kultur oder Vernichtung'? Karl Heinz Spalt and the
  Pacifist Dilemma – Charmian Brinson (London) ... 36
Wörter sind meine Werkzeuge – Walter Voigt
  (Ismaningen) [4 photographs] ... 45
Keith Spalding, Lifelong Lexicographer – Hans Heinrich
  Meier (Schaffhausen) ... 49
Changing Metaphors for Intellectual Activities in
  German – Horst Dieter Schlosser (Frankfurt) ... 55

Essays of Discovery (II)
Portrait Drawing Keith Spalding – Siegbert S Prawer
  (Oxford) ... 64
Muses on the Rhine – John L Flood (London) ... 65
George Berkeley: Rebel Against the Newtonian World
  Picture – T R Miles (Bangor) ... 73
Satire and Subversion: Nestroy and Paul de Kock –
  W E Yates (Exeter) ... 79

	Page
Musings on Muses: Poems by Goethe, Rilke and Bachmann and an essay by Anne Duden – Elizabeth Boa (Nottingham)	86
Musings on the Muses: *Goethe's Hermann und Dorothea* – Alan Busst (Bangor)	94
On the Unveiling of the Goddess: Some Observations on Schiller's *Das verschleierte Bild zu Sais* – Hans-Joachim Hahn (Oxford)	103
Mysticism, Irrationalism, and Existentialism – John Heywood Thomas (Bangor)	110
Saving the Self: Tradition, and Identity in Clemens Brentano's *Rheinmärchen* – Carol Tully (Bangor)	118
Scott's Edward Waverley and Tolstoy's Pierre Bezukhov – W Gareth Jones (Bangor)	126
Hereditary Keeper of the Crown – Idris Parry (Bangor)	133
'Der Frauen Zustand ist beklagenswert': Remarks on Two Plays by von Horváth and Goethe - Dietmar Wünschmann (Gerstetten)	138
Pacifism and Mysticism: Aldous Huxley's Rejection of Violence and Totalitarianism – Lothar Fietz (Tübingen)	145
Engaging Discovery: Inspirational Reading in Dark Times – Hinrich Siefken (Nottingham / Bangor)	151
Some Uses of Tradition: Heinrich Böll's and John Henry Newman – J H Reid (Nottingham)	159
Antikes Erbe in neuem Gewand: Johannes Bobrowki's 'Der Soldat an der Birke' – Peter Jentzsch (Metzingen)	166
The Break with Tradition in Literary Criticism and in Literature Today – George A Wells (St Albans)	174
Arnold Schönberg and Radical Guardianship – Robert Pascall (Bangor)	179
Hans Erich Nossack: New Beginnings – Peter Prochnik (London)	186
The Poet between War and Peace: Marie Luise Kaschnitz's Essays *Menschen und Dinge 1945* – Anthony Bushell (Bangor)	192
On Revering the Old and Espousing the New: F C Delius *'Die Birnen von Ribbeck'* – G L Jones (Aberystwyth)	200

	Page
Ludvik Kundera: A Question of Understanding – Ian Hilton (Chipping Campden)	207
'The most pain-ridden poetry I know': Uwe Saeger and Georg Trakl's 'Grodek' – Owen Evans (Bangor)	214
'Ungeist' in East and West: Representations of Ceaucescu's Romania and Pre-Unification Germany in Two Stories by Richard Wagner – David Rock (Keele)	220
'Er klammerte sich an alle Gegenstände': Büchner, Peter Schneider and the Uses of Germanistik – Rhys Williams (Swansea)	228
Spinoza and Post-Modernism: Some Reflections on Gianni Celato's *Adventure in Africa* – Laura Rorato (Bangor)	235
Uneasy Journey into the Past: Bernhard Schlink's *Der Vorleser* – Jo Desch (Bangor)	242
A (Post)Colonial Perspective on the Examination System – Rosemary Chapman (Nottingham)	250
Culture in Modern Foreign Language Education – Witold Tulasiewicz (Cambridge)	259

The Contributors 266

Preface

Tom Paulin

IN HIS AUTOBIOGRAPHY, *The Long March*, a courageous scholar, teacher and lexicographer tells the story of how Karl Heinz Spalt of Darmstadt became Keith Spalding. The story is, to adapt Nietzsche, 'word historical' – one of Keith Spalding's earliest memories was the ninth of November 1918. A man comes along the street, sets up a tripod, then screws the machine gun onto it, he stands there for a few minutes, then he packs the gun away. Two men come along the street, with a third man obviously in their power. They have a rope and are leading the third man to a street lamp. Keith Spalding's father runs out, speaks with the men, their prisoner runs away. Much later Spalding discovers the men were factory workers who wanted to hang their employer. The image of the factory owner running down Steinstrasse stays in his mind for the rest of his life. It was clearly one of the sources of his pacifism. Later Keith Spalding wrote a handbook of pacifism, *Kultur oder Vernichtung?*, which was one of the books burnt on Goebbels' orders in May 1933. He was only nineteen and was possibly the youngest author to have his work burnt. It was then that he began what he termed his 'long march', and it was at the start of that perilous journey across many of Europe's borders that he had an experience that stands out poignantly in the pages of his autobiography. He stops outside a pinewood thirty kilometres from Vienna and pitches his little tent. A Gypsy family in a caravan arrive, make a fire. From a parcel the Gypsy woman takes out some meat which she cuts into cubes and threads onto skewers:

> The skewers were then placed across the fire with their ends resting on the stones, and soon the air was filled with an aroma other than that of pine needles. The horse was fed, and then the whole family crouched around the fire, while the children had the job of turning the skewers. At last, everything seemed to be ready. The father took one of the skewers from the fire

and gave it to one of the children with a command in his own language, which was foreign to me. The child came to me, and handed it to me with a hunk of bread. I was honestly moved and didn't know what else to do than say 'Thank you', stroke the child's cheek and wave to the family. They took absolutely no notice of me, and devoted themselves to their meal. I enjoyed the hot, crisp meat, took the skewer back to them, and made my thanks, without receiving anything more by way of an answer than a nod of the head. Then the children played a little, looked for berries for their dessert, the father fetched a spade and covered up the fire with clumps of earth and sent the children into the vehicle. He then fetched out a violin, went and stood at the edge of the wood facing the setting sun and began to play. I had known Gypsy music only from the concert hall, or from pubs, where one would sometimes hear a wild czardas, but the music that I now heard had something so overwhelmingly moving, longing, melancholy. The violin seemed to weep and to complain, so sob gently and sometimes almost to sink into a slumber. There were fantasies and variations full of artistic skill obviously improvised depending on the mood of the moment. Then the man returned to his caravan.

Commenting on this spot of time as Wordsworth would call it – and we know it will be a dark spot of history – Spalding says that if he had seen a picture of this scene in a shop, he would have pooh-poohed is 'as rubbish, as a bedroom picture for people with simple tastes'. When he wakes next morning, he is alone in the wood. The Gypsy family 'must have decamped early and almost noiselessly.'

That disappearance we remember, when Spalding's Jewish girl-friend Marysia decides to marry a Jewish lawyer and not come to England as a refugee: 'So we made our farewells by letter, and I know nothing of what happened to her later. My fears must be that she was not spared by the holocaust.' Spalding's accounts of his visits to Marysia's family in Lodz are moving (a third of Lodz's population of 600,000 were Jews until the Nazis invaded Poland).

Keith Spalding, as his autobiography and these essays of tribute and commemoration make clear, was an exemplary figure. He moved from his youthful pacifism to fight in the British Army against the Germans. He crossed borders, had narrow escapes, and landed in this country as a refugee. He sought and was given asylum, and enriched the culture by his teaching, writing and gift for friendship.

Introduction

Experiencing Tradition

Hinrich Siefken, Anthony Bushell (Bangor)

> Being a historian means building bridges between the past and the present, watching both banks and being occupied on both of them.
>
> (B Schlink, *Der Vorleser*)

EXPERIENCING TRADITION, the life-giving validation of tradition by personal experience, suggested itself as the title for this collection of essays of discovery dedicated to Keith Spalding. His first publication, in 1933, had been an anthology based on the writing of the great European advocates of peace and harmony between people and nations. The young Karl Heinz Spalt had said in his introduction, that 'unfortunately, most human beings still allow themselves to be befogged by slogans. That is why those who use their heads have to intervene'. And that was why he 'compiled this collection so that you, my readers, may be able to resist the mindless pernicious ideology which is currently again flooding our poor Europe'. Quoting tradition, and making it relevant as personal experience, was highly dangerous, a provocation to those who were threatening to usurp German, and European, tradition in Germany.

Experiencing tradition, or 'Erfahrung und Überlieferung', is a title which owes a debt to Goethe's collection of aphorisms *Maximen und Reflexionen*. Goethe had written of the need of humankind to refer back to patterns of interpretation and understanding at moments of particular need when general issues of sublime importance are at stake:

Given the great needs of humankind with its limited judgment, the tradition of the experience of others, and of their judgment, is most welcome, particularly where matters of sublime importance and general issues are at stake. – Experience [...] is the touchstone of whatever the mind receives as a gift, of whatever the soul takes to be the truth.

Perhaps one way of measuring the success of teaching students, young and old, an understanding of the values, insights, experiences and discoveries buried in texts and artefacts of past and present, is to be found in the way in which these texts come back to life and open themselves up to us as ways of experiencing, and understanding, the bewildering and exciting richness of the world which surrounds us. That might be that secret of teaching others to read, of discovering the past in the present and the present in the light of the past, of which Milton wrote in *Areopagitica*:

Books are not absolutely dead things, but do contain a potency of life in them to be as active as that soul was whose progeny they are; nay, they do preserve as in a vial the purest efficacy and extraction of that living intellect that bred them.

Not all the essays gathered in this volume, did in the end quite fit that theme. Unexpectedly, some more biographical material came to light and had its own right to be included. Many friends wanted to contribute to this volume, and the range of disciplines and cultures represented is a reflection of a rich life, of friendships shared, and of lives enriched by shared experience.

Looking back at almost 90, from Gower House in Llanfairpwll on Anglesey, to Bangor across the Menai Bridge, was a unique view for Keith. We were occasionally invited to share it. It was and is worth celebrating.

Keith Spalding :
15 May 1913 – 29 November 2002

'Pacifist German scholar who fled Nazism
to become one of Britain's most distinguished
lexicographers'

Hinrich Siefken

KEITH SPALDING, Emeritus Professor of German and Teutonic Philology at the University College of North Wales, Bangor, former President of the Conference of University Teachers of German in Great Britain and Ireland, died suddenly some six months before his ninetieth birthday. His eightieth birthday had been celebrated at the University with a great number of friends and colleagues, and particularly with many of his former students. He had spoken with his usual wit and urbanity quoting Shakespeare. Ten years on he was as bright as ever, but in view of his physical frailty he had requested a very quiet marking of his forthcoming birthday when it became obvious that a volume of some sort, written by friends in his honour, would be presented to him on that occasion. – Some sixty friends gathered at the crematorium in Bangor on 11 December 2002. Idris Parry, his oldest colleague (at Bangor in 1950) spoke of the German-English professor of German who was most unlike the stereotypical academic – despite his beard and his pipe. His obituary appeared in *The Times* two days later; its heading is quoted above.

Born in Darmstadt as Karl Heinz Georg Spalt, the only child of a Protestant family, and educated at its Realgymnasium, he would have gone to university in the summer of 1931 had it not been for his keen interest in the 'Deutsche Friedensgesellschaft' and the 'Bund religiöser Sozialisten', and for his role as co-founder, with friends in France and England, of the small 'Internationale

1

Friedenskorrespondenz'. Instead he decided at the age of eighteen to take a year out in order to compile a handbook on the issue of international peace to remind the reader of the thoughts of important authors and philosophers through history. The manuscript grew over many late nights (his Bangor students never forgot the tale how he chewed the tea-leaves late at night to stay awake once the tea-pot was empty), till in 1932 it was published in Heide in Holstein by Paul Riechert, the publisher of the pacifist paper *Das andere Deutschland*, under the title *Kultur oder Vernichtung. Ein Handbuch des Pazifismus*. Louis Rufin, a French friend, had offered the author his savings to cover the required contribution to the printing costs.

By the time the book came out the passport of its author had already been marked, identifying him as a 'Landesverräter'. Keith Spalding had in a public speech drawn attention to secret German re-armament and arms depots at the German-Polish border, a violation of the Versailles treaty. Questioned two days later by the secret police about his speech he was given the choice of denying the truth of the allegation against him. He had chosen not to deny it. After the war, in 1946 and 1947, Heinrich Hollands reprinted the handbook in Aachen, under the new title *Der weite Weg*, from a copy given to him by Keith Spalding's parents in 1945. It went quickly out of print and was long forgotten. Thanks to Maria and Achim von Borries it became available again in a third edition (Darmstadt 1990) under its old title, together with documents about its own publication history and its courageous publisher Paul Riechert, who had been imprisoned and pilloried as a traitor in his hometown in June 1933 before his flight to exile in Denmark.

The book had a powerful impact on the future of its young author, who had decided in 1930 that he wanted to become a teacher of languages. His socialist and pacifist leanings had already disqualified him in the eyes of the Landeskirchenpräsident from work as a teacher and missionary for the Protestant church in Brazil. At the end of 1932 he rejected the strange offer made by a former school-friend, acting for the local NSDAP, of party membership with a low party number. In April 1932 Karl Heinz Georg Spalt began his studies of languages in English, French and Latin at the University of Frankfurt with Professors Immelmann and Erhard Lommatszch. However, after the 'Machtergreifung' of 30 January

1933 it became too dangerous for him to stay in Germany. Having spent a period sleeping in different places each night to avoid arrest, Keith Spalding escaped by train to Vienna, hoping to study German as his main subject, which he could then teach abroad. Meanwhile the pacifist handbook had come out in January 1933 but could no longer be reviewed. The publisher sent a box with two hundred copies to Darmstadt where it was stored in the attic of his parents' house, until it could follow Keith Spalding to Vienna, where selling copies to bookshops, using a letter of recommendation of its contents by Cardinal Innitzer, would help to finance his studies. A raid on Paul Riechert's firm in Heide on 3 May 1933 led to the confiscation of ninety copies of the paperback version and seventy-six bound copies. The book itself was banned, and probably also publicly burnt.

Today, the preface to the reader (like the author's various comments linking the quotations), dated September 1932, has lost none of its force:

> Warum nur wollt Ihr denn nicht einsehen, daß alle Tränen, die während eines Krieges vergossen werden, alle Klagen um die Gefallenen nach dem Kriege, alle Seufzer, Befürchtungen und das Gefolge des Krieges, Verzweiflung und Trauer, Wahnsinn, Hunger und Prostitution durchaus unnötig sind? Seid Ihr noch so barbarisch, daß Ihr von Zeit zu Zeit wieder einmal im Blut waten [...] müßt? Dann besinnt Euch darauf, daß Gott Euch den Verstand gab, um Euch vom Tier zu unterscheiden, dann arbeitet an Euch, um Euch vom Tier zu unterscheiden, dann arbeitet an Euch, um die Lust am Zerstören und Morden in Euch zu unterdrücken! Oder seid Ihr so verblendet, daß Ihr meint, Ihr brauchet den Krieg, um bessere Menschen zu werden?

He appealed to the memory of the tears shed over the loss of loved ones, of the despair, madness and misery of war to dispel the current obsession with revenge and aggression. Asking his readers whether they were really barbaric enough to need to wade in blood periodically, he appealed to their God-given powers of mind and reason. They are what distinguishes man from the beast, humankind from the animals, and suppressing the urge to destroy and murder will make then more not less human. Can they really be so blind that they believe war will turn them into better human beings? In 1932 that was a strong challenge to that mythical spirit of 'Frontgeist' the Great War, lost by Germany, was supposed to have engendered. According to that myth the war had turned boys mysteriously into men, forging them in the trenches into a fighting community of heroes. Publicly, and with recourse to a long European tradition, questioning that assumption now made Keith Spalding a stranger in his own country.

Few people who knew Professor Keith Spalding were aware of the story of his life which started here, until in retirement he told that story in his autobiography *33 – alles umsteigen* (Lübeck, 1992). The details, told with a light touch and humorous understatement, still have the power to amaze and surprise the reader. I had heard Keith Spalding tell some of the episodes over a bottle of wine and an occasional suck of the pipe when he was External Examiner in Nottingham in 1988. The autobiography tells of his long march through France and Italy in the summer of 1933, and back to Vienna for another semester's study, after a plan to teach in Algeria under the auspices of the Socialist Bureau had to be abandoned as too hazardous. It speaks of his long friendship, resulting in many visits to Poland in the years up to 1938, with a Jewish music student from Lodz whose parents enabled the young pair to travel widely outside Germany.

In 1934, as the political situation shifted further in Austria, Keith Spalding was told semi-officially in Vienna that he was now considered an undesirable visitor. President Masaryk of Czechoslovakia offered the author of the handbook on pacifism support and accommodation in his country should he be accepted by a university. The German University in Prague, however, considered him persona non grata – and so Karl Heinz Spalt, as he still was, tried England.

A friend from the 'Internationale Friedenskorrespondenz' who lived in Sheffield had put a small ad in the *Manchester Guardian*. A Baptist minister and his wife responded offering the pacifist refugee a home in Coventry. From that base contact with the University of Birmingham was not difficult, and so in October 1934 Keith Spalding began pursuing a daunting new course combining studies in German, French and History with Professors Sandbach, Ritchie and Hancock.

The story, told in his autobiography, of his lucky escape from the attention of Dr Hans Wesemann still makes chilling reading. Wesemann must have intended to abduct Karl Heinz Spalt, the enemy of the German people, in just the way in which Berthold Jacob had been dragged across the Swiss-German border into German jurisdiction. The likely involvement of Wesemann in the mysterious so-called double suicide in April 1935 of the two German exiles in London, Dora Fabian and Mathilde Wurm, was established in 1992 (*GLL*, 45 (October 1992), 324). Fortunately the student Spalt had travelled via Gdynia to Lodz after the December examinations of 1934 and was not in Birmingham when Wesemann, unfamiliar with student habits, called. He was safe.

His first year examinations resulted in the waiving of fees for the next session. Contact with the Quakers and other non-conformist churches led to his first sermon from the pulpit; the text was Matth. 5: 9 'Blessed are the peace-makers'. That was the beginning of many such invitations, culminating in an offer in 1939, not accepted, to act as minister to a Presbyterian congregation. For the session 1936/7 Keith Spalding was offered a place at Woodbroke College Birmingham by the Quakers, who were to give him much help and support in the years to come (his wife Phyllis, whom he met later, came from a Quaker family). The Easter vacation was spent with the Society of Friends in the Rhondda valley helping unemployed miners. He eventually graduated in June 1937 with an Upper Second class degree.

A Clayton scholarship for the following session made postgraduate work possible. Exceptionally he was allowed to submit his MA thesis of 275 pages on *Adalbert Stifter's Attitude Towards the State* for Professor Sandbach in October 1938, after only one year and one day. His empathy with Stifter never flagged after that. The subject – which made use of Keith Spalding's attendance at lectures by Professors Srbik and Bibl in the Department of History at Vienna (as he tells us in *33 – alles umsteigen*, p. 32) – allowed him considerable identification with his subject matter, despite a strongly critical attitude to Stifter's political ethics, based as they are on 'sentiments rather than convictions and logical conclusions' (p. 47). The quotation 'Hass und Zank zu hegen oder zu erwidern ist Schwaeche – sie uebersehen und mit Liebe zurueckzuzahlen ist Staerke' [to harbour hatred and aggression, or to return it, is weakness – to overlook them and to repay them with love is real strength] reminded him 'strongly [...] of the manifestoes of the Pacifist Parliamentary Group in England today' (p. 64). (The file of one of the Weiße Rose trials shows that Josef Söhngen, the Munich bookseller, used the same Stifter quotation on the 'Blätter der Stille' he sent at Christmas 1942 to his young customers fighting in uniform in Russia.) Keith Spalding wrote in 1938 that Stifter was 'a lover of peace, but not as a pacifist. [...] To him wars were a punishment, not imposed by God, but created by men themselves' (pp. 183-4). He pointed out that the novel *Witiko*, seen as 'the peak of Stifters's work as regards political ethics', contained the argument 'If each individual follows his conscience and the whole nation is governed by the moral law [...], force will disappear whether in the shape of revolution or war' (pp. 187-8). Altogether the unpublished thesis of 1938 with its informed attempt to locate Stifter in the development of political thought of his time still deserves to be read. Incidentally, one of the little anecdotes Keith Spalding used to share with his friends later may date from this period. Sitting in a railway compartment, dying to try out his English and frustrated by the formal silence, he grasped the opportunity offered by a casual 'O, what station was that?', and shared his knowledge of the sign he had just seen. 'That was Bovril, sir'. The ice was broken, and the rest of the journey was spent in lively, and probably humorous exchange.

Another scholarship, the A E Hills Postgraduate Scholarship, enabled Keith Spalding to embark on his Ph.D. thesis under the supervision of Professor Roy Pascal. The submitted copy of *Social Factors in German-Swiss Literature Since 1850* is dated May 1940, and after furious protests from Professor Pascal, and intervention of the British Academy, following Keith Spalding's internment on the Isle of Man as an enemy alien, the degree was formally conferred a few months later. (Many years later Keith Spalding contributed to the Festschrift for Roy Pascal who had also been invited to serve as External Examiner in the University of Wales in the early 70s.) The thesis surveys the work of some fifty prose writers between 1850 and 1939 against the social and historical background 'from as unbiased a standpoint as possible. Neither Marxist dialectics nor Nadler's theories are to be applied rigidly, which does not mean that the present writer objects to either or both' (p. 2). With this sentence the candidate acknowledges the influence of Roy Pascal's position on the left and his familiarity with Josef Nadler's work, whose lectures he had attended in Vienna, on the right, while skilfully detaching himself from both. The thesis itself digests an enormous amount of information into thematically organised chapters which do not disguise Keith Spalding's critical stance. He notes 'with surprise how little interest Swiss authors have taken in the guests of their country' (p. 231); he misses 'an interest in the surrounding world which at present does not exist' (p. 243), and writes in a splendid chapter on 'The Emancipation of Women': 'As long as Switzerland remains conservatively bourgeois, [...] woman will not be granted real equality, especially since under present conditions she does not think of asking for it' (p. 287).

During the period of the phoney war, and after submission of the Ph.D. thesis, Keith Spalding had written his first textbook, *An Introduction to the German Language through Lyric Poetry* (Harmony Press), which developed the idea, tried out in many hours of private tuition, of teaching German with the help of simple poems. The book was distributed, and even briefly reviewed in the *Manchester Guardian*, but is very rare today. Fifty-eight copies were sold, but almost the whole edition was destroyed in one of the German air raids on London. Nevertheless the idea it used was later taken up in Keith Spalding's next textbook *German Word Patterns* (1962/4), which would be praised in the *TES* as 'the most original and perhaps the most valuable aid for German studies that your reviewer has met for a long time' (25 January 1963, p. 119).

Parting with the Quakers in 1940 must have been a difficult and painful decision to make: Keith Spalding had come to the decision that his pacifism had to give way to an active role in the fight against Hitler. Little is known about his reasons; he was a private person and rarely, if ever, spoke directly about his convictions and beliefs. His decision compelled Phyllis, whom he would marry after the war, also to leave the Society of Friends, and there is good reason to believe that this caused her much pain, remembered decades later. Perhaps some of his change of attitude was foreshadowed in the sentence of his M.A. thesis of 1938 that 'Stifter always felt depressed in wartime – but nevertheless the State was right in defending its interests and citizens and enlisting the support of all its inhabitants for this defence' (p. 184). Although Keith Spalding had started naturalisation proceedings in 1939, after the statutory five years' residence in Britain, the outbreak of war stopped everything.

Instead, he was interned from June to October 1940. Fourteen days after the end of internment, in November 1940, he signed up for the British army, joining the Pioneer Corps at Bradford and Shipley, and spending the next two and a half years with the 246th Company, which consisted entirely of German refugees. In the summer of 1943, when under the influence of American practice the British army, reluctantly, allowed German refuges to join combat troops, Karl Heinz Spalt joined the infantry and was transformed, literally overnight, into Keith Spalding, retaining – as was standard practice – the initials of his German name. (According to an anecdote later shared with friends, Keith had on one occasion returned from Spalding in Lincolnshire with a tea-caddy spoon with the emblem of the town on it, presenting it with a grin on his face to Phyllis, with the words: 'How about this for our family crest?') After training with the Border Regiment at Carlisle he joined the Intelligence Corps with the rank of corporal. As NCO in charge of a leaflet unit (consisting of himself and a driver) he was given the task, jointly with a sister unit, of printing leaflets encouraging German soldiers to down arms and surrender. These leaflets were fired across the line in smoke grenades and supported by a loudhailer system. Six days after D-day he landed in France, eventually reaching Brussels.

Recalled to London for training for the press section in February 1945 he returned to Brussels as Staff Sergeant to produce the German newssheet *Mitteilungen*, first there, and later in Germany itself. From June 1945 he worked in Aachen on the *Aachener Nachrichten* with Heinrich Hollands, the first German publisher to be given a licence by the Allied Control Commission, who was also to reprint the pacifist handbook of 1933 a year later. With Dr Hanna Meuter, and with Professor Leopold von Wiese on the staff, Keith Spalding helped to set up a 'Schule für demokratischen Journalismus'. He incurred the displeasure of his superiors for using the authority of his high rank to issue and sign formal diplomas awarded by the school. The resulting reprimand led to his move to the film section at Lintorf near Düsseldorf. From there he was able to revisit Darmstadt: he had last seen his parents secretly at Cochem in 1936, when temporarily in possession of a legal and clean

German passport. In June 1946 Staff Sergeant Keith Spalding was discharged and his academic career began very soon after that. A large portrait painting of him in uniform, dating from those war years in Germany, would later be the only visible reminder at Gower House, his home in Llanfairpwll, and most visitors struggled to understand its true significance.

Called for interview on consecutive days in Swansea and Exeter, he was successful on the first day and obtained his first University teaching post as Assistant Lecturer in German at the University College Swansea from September 1946 (the Exeter post was not filled). He was offered British citizenship and given a British passport in November of that year.

He was married at Birmingham Registry Office on Christmas Eve 1946. His gifted and charming wife Phyllis, née Card, born on 30 June 1908 in Hollingbourne, Kent, of whose brilliant mind he used to speak with great warmth, became a very active partner in much of his work, and many of his editions acknowledge her contribution - which went far beyond correcting 'the clumsy syntax' of his introductions to which he draws attention in his very first academic book (*Der Ackermann aus Böhmen*, p. v). Although physically so frail, as the result of rheumatic fever at the age of 13 which had affected her mitral valve, that in 1946 the doctor told Keith 'She won't live beyond the year' and warned the couple not to have children, her active cooperation in his work continued until 1980 when angina, arthritis and deteriorating eyesight (she became blind after a fall) intervened. Her interest in his work continued unabated until her death on 21 September 1997. She was eighty-nine then.

After two years Keith Spalding was promoted to Lecturer; he resigned in 1950 to take up the post of Independent Lecturer and Head of Department at Bangor, where he stayed until his retirement in 1980 at the age of sixty-seven, living in Gower House, Llanfairpwll until his death.

As early as 1953, after only seven years in the profession, the University of Wales appointed him Professor with the title, first used in 1909, of Professor of German and Teutonic Philology. In the late fifties he served his College as Dean, was three times elected a member of its Council, which met in London, and eventually played a major role over many years in the College's committee structure as senior professor, particularly on the Selection

Committee of Council. For more than ten years the University School of Education benefited from his membership at its meeting in Shrewsbury. His sound judgment, combined with the standing of his seniority, made him a formidable and skilfully fair ally to colleagues from other colleges, like myself, who valued such support on the Academic Board and Court of the University of Wales.

When Keith Spalding joined the Department in Swansea F W Halliday was in charge; after his retirement in 1948 another exile, Erich Heller, took over. Keith Spalding's first publication in a journal was a paper on 'The Idiom of a Revolution: Berlin 1848' (*MLR*, 44, 1949) based on a collection of political broadsheets Halliday had left him. A paper on the poetry on the Rhenish author Paul Therstappen (*GLL*, 3, 1950) may have been the result of a discovery made in 1945: Hanna Meuter, who worked with Keith Spalding at the 'Schule für demokratischen Journalismus', was an ardent admirer of Paul Therstappen.

The first substantial academic publication, the first of a series of erudite editions, was the volume *Der Ackermann aus Böhmen*, which Keith Spalding described as 'the finest German prose text of the fifteenth century, the best example of the Early High German language and the clearest impact of Humanist thought on medieval tradition in Germany' (p. v). Spalding's edition was completed by December 1948, and published in 1950 in Professor James Boyd's distinguished series *Blackwell's German Texts*. Extensive and glowing reviews (by E A Philippson in *JEGP*, 50, 1951, 418-20; by W Fleischhauer in *Monatshefte*, 1951, 157-60; by J L Riordan in *MLQ*, 13, 1952, 416-7) established the lecturer's academic credentials beyond question. More established medievalists would have their work cut out to produce an edition of such learning. It traces many parallels in medieval literature whilst also continually making informed decisions on matters of textual emendation. Thirty pages of text are supported by some forty pages of introduction, some forty pages of notes, a glossary, appendices and a bibliography. The positive reception of this work indicated that a move to a position of academic leadership was now possible.

When Keith Spalding left Swansea for Bangor to replace Dr Cunningham, who had moved to Dublin to take up the mantle of her academic teacher, as Head of Department he joined Dr H M S Stuart, appointed in 1946 and continuing in the Department for some thirty years until her death. Idris Parry, appointed in 1947, and still only a probationary assistant lecturer, would be persuaded by him to continue his teaching of modern German literature, indeed he did not move until 1963 when he left for a chair at the University of Manchester. Gradually, over the coming years, Keith Spalding, whose own knowledge ranged over the whole syllabus, was able to build up the Department to a strength of ten staff. Since 1962-3 the syllabus included lectures on German history and culture, initially taught in one, later over two sessions.

Spalding's publications now began to bear the mark of the lexicographer and historian of the German language. Short papers in the *Modern Language Review* from 1950 onwards accompanied the two big projects which were to dominate much of his professional and personal life for decades: the revision of the Muret-Sanders English-German / German-English dictionary as *Langenscheidts Enzyklopädisches Wörterbuch*, whose four volumes appeared in 1962, 1963, 1974 and 1975; and the *Historical Dictionary of German Figurative Usage*, published by Blackwells, whose first fascicle came out in 1952 and which was completed in six volumes in January 2000.

The revision of the Muret-Sanders was a gigantic undertaking, funded by the Marshall Plan and headed by Professor Otto Springer at the University of Pennsylvania as Editor-in-Chief. Keith Spalding was the Associate Editor who checked every single one of 380,000 entries, before his corrections were approved by the Editor. By himself he compiled the letter P and part of the letter S, while his wife Phyllis was responsible for the phonetic transcription for the English and American pronunciations of every word in the English-German section. From 1952 to 1959 they both spent two months of every summer at the editorial offices at Berchtesgaden, training six to eight young lexicographers (many of whom later embarked on brilliant academic careers) and writing the detailed 'Richtlinien' for the huge team: 176 pages and 246 pages respectively for each part. On its completion the reviewers, myself included, welcomed the dictionary enthusiastically. The *Times Literary Supplement* said of the first part that it could 'confidently be regarded as the best large-scale English-German dictionary available to the student in either language'; *The Guardian* conceded of the second part that 'The work has been compiled with such truly Teutonic Gründlichkeit (thoroughness) that a goodly number of random tests have failed to discover any serious error or omission [...] the work will be easily the most comprehensive of its kind available'. Praise indeed for twenty-five years of time-consuming and patient labour.

The first fascicle of the *Historical Dictionary of German Figurative Usage* appeared in 1952 'after many years devoted to collecting notes' (Introduction, p. v.). In fact, the project goes back to an idea the budding postgraduate had put to Professor Sandbach in 1937 who rightly thought that Stifter's fiction was a more containable topic for a thesis. However, the proposal for such a dictionary did impress Basil Blackwell, although it was obvious from the beginning that the financial returns would not be impressive. Its aim was, and remained, to include 'those figurative expressions, established phrases, proverbs and quotations which are either still in use or to be found in German literature from ca. 1750 onwards', the vocabulary of which is 'still largely in use'. Characteristically, it is 'a dictionary which is largely compiled with the object of demonstrating the activity of human imagination in the realm of language' (*ibid.*), the English version after every German entry giving 'the nearest equivalent, not a literal translation' (p. vii).

The first fascicle was fiercely criticised in a review by Professor F P Pickering (in an earlier incarnation External Examiner at Swansea), who feared that 'scrutiny [...] suggests the need for thorough revision of what remains unpublished' (*MLR*, 48, 1953, 356-9, here 359). Although many years later Professor Pickering half conceded that he might have been rather harsh in his attack, at his and Professor Collinson's suggestions Kenneth Brooke was eventually appointed to assist. In December 1953 fascicle 4 listed the alterations suggested by reviewers and readers which had been introduced with the letter B. From fascicle 3 to fascicle 39, until his death in 1984, Kenneth Brooke of Belfast, later of Keele, scrutinised every page of manuscript before it went to the publishers; in later years this task must have become a more nominal one. Professor Gerhard Müller-Schwefe in Tübingen took over and assisted as friendly adviser until the work was completed.

In 1952 Keith Spalding described the work as 'an act of faith' and thanked those 'who have kept my faith alive' (p. iii): mentioning among them W E Collinson, F W Halliday, Basil Blackwell, and his own wife. He acknowledged the support of the Cassel Educational Trust and the Press Board of the University of Wales. Later the DAAD, the Volkswagenstiftung, the Geschwister Boehringer Ingelheim Stiftung für Geisteswissenschaften, the Leverhulme Foundation, the British Academy and UNESCO enabled Keith Spalding to employ assistants, to collect the necessary examples from the sixty-three dictionaries from which he compiled the entries. All financial support ceased in 1985; for a while a part-time assistant was paid by the lexicographer. After that he was constrained to carry on by himself, working at the little room of his old University in the morning, typing up the entries working late into the night at home. By 1993 he had started work on a German book, provisionally entitled *Phraseologische Streifzüge*, which would make the gist of the dictionary available to the German in a volume of about a hundred pages when it was published in 1996.

Keith Spalding's lexicographical work was complemented by the fine editions of selection from Stifter (1952), of Grillparzer's *Sappho* (1965), Stifter's *Abdias* (1966 – for Idris Parry's series for Manchester University Press) and of Goethe's *Hermann und Dorothea* (1968), which are all powerful evidence of his concern to offer his students the results of scholarship worn lightly and with easy authority. The *Selections from Stifter* attracted the attention of Max Stefl in Munich, the President of the German Stifter Society, affectionately known as Stifter-Stefl for his life-long editorial interest in Stifter, who also included the volume in the Stifter exhibition held in Vienna in 1955. Keith Spalding's very close links with Macmillan's, who highly valued his advice and cooperation over many years, also produced the well-known language-teaching textbooks *Advanced German Unseens* (1958 and 1961), the result of years of experience as a language teacher. All these volumes were based on the firm conviction that the classical heritage of German literature and thought since 1750 remains crucial and central both to any enlightened study of German and of the history of mankind, and to personal development, as Keith Spalding had first argued in the preface to his pacifist handbook of 1932. The teacher and scholar mediates between tradition and the personal experience of the reader in which the text comes to life.

In 1957 he wrote in *Advanced German Unseens* that his collection of passages from German prose works between 1760 and 1950 had a natural bias towards the 'vocabularies of literary criticism, philosophy, linguistics, the fine arts and music', 'in keeping with the character of the work required from students of modern languages at schools and universities' (p. vi). School and university courses have greatly changed since then, but the thought-provoking passages included in these editions represent a great treasure, collected by a catholic taste, which still deserves serious study: for example, excerpts from Börne's review of Bettina von Arnim's *Göthe's Briefwechsel mit einem Kinde*, from Schopenhauer's *Aphorismen zur Lebensweisheit* or Ernst Wiechert's *Der Totenwald*. Börne is one writer who appears repeatedly and Keith Spalding returned to him in the *Trivium* Festschrift for Peter Magill, *Erfahrung und Überlieferung*, on his retirement from the chair at University College Aberystwyth, with an essay 'Zum Börnebild der Gegenwart', which Herbert Heckmann, president of the Deutsche Akademie für Sprache und Dichtung Darmstadt would call 'eine Skizze [...], die ich zum Besten zähle, was über den Frankfurter geschrieben wurde' (*33 – alles umsteigen*, Vorwort, p. 12). *Worte sind meine Werkzeuge. Das kleine Börne-Brevier* of 1995 was an attempt to distil the aphoristic essence of Börne's writing, 12 volumes in the standard edition, into less than two-hundred pages, 'damit das immer noch Wertvolle seine Würdigung durch den Leser finde' (Vorwort, p. 8). The German critic Marcel Reich-Ranicki was so impressed that he sent Keith Spalding a copy of one of his books relevant here with the dedication 'dem Kenner der Materie'. Keith Spalding was delighted and liked to share the allusion with friends.

It was a well-kept secret that Keith Spalding was also the J G F Como who wrote the German readers *Der erste Astronaut* and *Kaspar Hauser* for Macmillan's in 1964 and 1969. The mysterious astronaut is Baron von Münchhausen; the delightful adaptation was reissued in Sweden in 1967 by the Magn. Bergvalls Förlag. With these little volumes Keith Spalding responded to the need for exciting reading material of limited vocabulary in schools. He wrote under the name of his old teacher in Darmstadt who had been a powerful formative influence.

The well-known editions of literary texts from the great German tradition were easy to use; they also assumed a demanding desire for reliable and detailed information on the part of teachers and students. The central role of the 'Goethezeit' and of Goethe's work was characteristic of the course Keith Spalding designed for Bangor, always contributing the classes on *Faust* himself. Students were expected to become familiar with the social and political history of the German-speaking countries. When the Austrian and Prussian parts of 'German' history, entrusted to John Bednall and Dr Ian Hilton respectively, got out of phase due to cancellation of classes, the confusion amongst baffled students produced much hilarity which they shared with this Lektor in 1966. A choice of Norwegian and Dutch had become part of the syllabus, a range of optional courses became available, an MA course in history of the language was established and exchange arrangements with German universities, particularly Tübingen, were from 1955 part of the teaching environment.

When Keith Spalding retired in 1980, after thirty years of distinguished service to his College and University, his last contribution to the Annual Report mentioned that the dictionary had now 'passed the middle of the alphabet'. He spoke with warmth of the 'enthusiasm of all members of staff' and was 'confident that the Department was flourishing and well equipped to overcome the difficulties which face all University Departments' (pp. 38-9). Sadly, the German section of the Modern Languages Department shrunk dramatically in the following years. Keith Spalding was delighted by the decision, when it eventually came, to fill the chair of German again. Tony Bushell became his successor in 1996; and two young colleagues helped to make a fresh start. The years of Professor Spalding's stewardship had been good years for German in the University of Wales and he was keen to see German continue to flourish at Bangor. The annual three-day gatherings of all German Departments of the University at Gregynog Hall, which he had helped to develop in its role as a conference centre, were highlights of the academic year for staff and final-year students, with distinguished speakers in attendance. I remember particularly well Siegfried Lenz, Friedrich Dürrenmatt, Golo Mann and J P Stern. Keith Spalding's casual but knowledgeable contributions on any topic under discussion were a legend annually confirmed; his room in 'dry' Gregynog (which later had its own bar) was often the focus of a preprandial drink.

The exchange with the University of Tübingen, set up in 1955 by him, was driven by that ethos of reconciliation between nations typical of that period. In its heyday it involved twenty-four students as well as staff. It provided Bangor with Lektoren – I came in 1965 for a year – and gave Tübingen a lively crowd of students enjoying a glorious summer term. Keith Spalding was very much the spiritus rector behind all this and, with the support of his able staff, his loving care and attention to the individual needs of all his students made their time rich and rewarding. He visited Tübingen repeatedly. His one-week seminar 'Deutsche Lexikographie und Sprachgeschichte im 18. Jahrhundert' in 1962, conducted at the Deutsches Seminar with Professor Wolfgang Mohr, whose 'wissenschaftlicher Hilfsbremser' I was at the time, was my first contact with him. Keith Spalding's lecture in the Auditorium maximum – one of many such lectures – was a revelation, both in style and in content. The conversational informality of a quite different university tradition was most refreshing and the audience produced a great deal more than just the customary polite noise of approval at the end of the hour.

In 1972 the Fachbereich Neuphilologie of the Eberhard-Karls-Universität awarded Keith Spalding the 'Grad und Würde eines Ehrendoktors der Philosophie'. The document cites his distinguished lexicographical work, his teaching and research in German language and literature and the importance of the links between the two countries, lauding the man 'der aus den Erfahrungen der Emigration die Folgerung gezogen hat, tatkräftig und mit hohem Einsatz die wissenschaftllichen, akademischen und menschlichen Beziehungen [...] zu fördern'. In 1975 he was awarded the Großes Verdienstkreuz der Bundesrepublik Deutschland. A generous supporter of the Institute of Germanic Studies at the University of London, he endowed the annual Keith Spalding Lecture, first given in 1994.

His colleagues and students remember him with much affection as the father of the Department with the gentle smile and the characteristic laugh. His splendidly humorous and yet carefully researched paper on 'Friedrich Stoltze, Frankfurt's Second Famous Son' at the Annual Conference of University Teachers of German of 1982 is unforgettable. Keith Spalding was a very private man whose personal kindness is remembered by those who got to know him. My wife and I treasure the memory of his joy when we told him on a flying visit to Bangor in March 1967 that his former Lektor was to marry his former student. The news of his sudden death, as we were planning how best to present this volume to him on his 90th birthday, brought together again many of his old friends.

Since Keith Spalding, himself a corresponding member of the Stifter-Gesellschaft, quoted Stifter as an inspiration at the end of his autobiography, we may now appreciate the personal element in the Stifter passage which fifty years ago opened his *Selections from Adalbert Stifter* (p. vi):

Mit Menschen menschlich sein, mit Höheren das Höhere lieben, an Gottes Schöpfung sich freuen, die festgegründete Erde nicht verachten, sich immer praktischem Handeln hingeben, es nicht verachten, selbst Gemüse zu düngen, und doch ein höherer, opferfreudiger Mensch zu sein, endlich mit fühlenden geistigen Menschen gleichsam einen unsichtbaren Umgang haben, das war ungefähr die Grundlage meiner Schriften.

Except that in his case a whole life, not just his writing, was inspired by this attitude.

Bibliography Keith Spalding

Compiled by Hinrich Siefken

1933 Karl Heinz Spalt, *Kultur oder Vernichtung? Ein Handbuch des Pazifismus* [Ein Handbuch über Gedanken bedeutender Menschen über die Friedensfrage, die Stellung der Frau, der Kirchen, des Sozialismus, der modernen Wissenschaft zum Friedensproblem, die geschichtliche Entwicklung der Forderung auf ewigen Frieden und Schiedsgerichtsbarkeit]. (Paul Riechert: Heide (Holstein) 1933), 224 S.

1938 Karl-Heinz Georg Spalt, *Adalbert Stifter's Attitude towards the State*, M.A. thesis, University of Birmingham [typescript] 1938, 275 pp.

1939 Karl Heinz Spalt, *An Introduction to the German Language through Lyric Poetry*. (The Harmony Press: London 1939), 198 pp.

1940 Karl-Heinz Georg Spalt, *Social Factors in German-Swiss Literature since 1850*, Ph.D. thesis, University of Birmingham [typescript] 1940, 333 pp.

1946 Karl Heinz Spalt, *Der weite Weg: Ein Handbuch über den Pazifismus*. (Heinrich Hollands: Aachen 1946), 176 S. [= 2nd edition of *Kultur oder Vernichtung*].

1947 Karl Heinz Spalt, *Der weite Weg:* .... (Heinrich Hollands: Aachen 1947), 176 S.

1949 Keith Spalding, 'Abraham a Sancta Clara: A philological note', *GLL* NS. 3 (1949-50), 64-9.

'The Idiom of a Revolution: Berlin 1848', *MLR*, 44 (1949), 60-74.
'Chronica Wiennensis', *MLR*, 44 (1949), 514-20.

1950 *Johann von Tepl, Der Ackermann aus Böhmen*, ed. (Blackwell's German Texts) (Basil Blackwell: Oxford 1950), xlviii + 118 pp.
'Paul Therstappen's Poetry. A Contribution to the Cultural History of the Rhineland', *GLL*, 3 (1949-50), 259-65.
'A Note on (g)rundgescheit', *MLR*, 45 (1950), 67-70.
'A Note on Later Traces of MHG berc', *MLR*, 45 (1950), 357-9.

1951 'MHG ran = slim > NHG rahn = subtle', *MLR*, 46 (1951), 64-6.
'A Theory concerning the 'Mad Hatter'', *MLR*, 46 (1951), 442-4.
'Adalbert Stifter', *Modern Languages*, 32 (1950-1951), 62-9.

1952 *A Historical Dictionary of German Figurative Usage*, Basil Blackwell: Oxford (fasc. 1 and 2; fasc. 52, letter T reached by 1993; completed 1999/2000).
Selections from Adalbert Stifter, ed. (Macmillan: London 1952), xiv + 210pp.
'Notes on the language of Wilhelm Serlin', *MLR*, 47 (1952), 529-46.

1956 'Lichtenberg's Use of heim-Compounds', *MLR*, 51 (1956), 570-2.

1958 *Advanced German Unseens*, ed. (Macmillan: London 1958), 182 pp.
'A German Account of Life in Wales in 1856', *Gwerin*, 2 (1958), 38-43.
'A Note on German "Dreck am Stecken"', *Archivum Linguisticum*, 10 (1958), 43-7.

1961 *Advanced German Unseens*, ed. (Macmillan: London 1961), 182 pp. [reprint].

'Bemerkungen zum Eisernen Vorhang', *Zfdt Wortforschung*, 17 (1961), 52-8.

1962 *German Word Patterns*, Macmillan: London 1962, 260 pp.
'Recent Writings on Adalbert Stifter', *Modern Languages*, 43 (1962), 100-3.
Langenscheidts Enzyklopädisches Wörterbuch, Teil I, *Englisch-Deutsch*, 1. Band: A-M. (Langenscheidt: Berlin 1962). [Mitherausgeber].

1963 *Simple German Unseens*, (Macmillan: London 1963), 118 pp.

1964 *Advanced German Unseens*, 2nd edition, (Macmillan: London 1964), 182 pp.
Langenscheidts Enzyklopädisches Wörterbuch, Teil I, *Englisch-Deutsch*, 2. Band: N-Z. (Langenscheidt: Berlin 1964). [Mitherausgeber].
J.G.F. Como [pseudonym], *Der erste Astronaut* [Freiherr von Münchhausen], (Macmillan: London 1964) [Die neue Lesereihe], 45 pp.

1965 *Franz Grillparzer: Sappho. Trauerspiel*, ed. (Macmillan: London 1965), xxiv + 122 pp.

1966 *Stifter: Abdias*, with introduction, notes and an appendix, ed. (Manchester University Press: Manchester 1966), 111 pp.

1967 J.G.F. Como [pseudonym], *Der erste Astronaut*, utgiven av Ake Palm. (Magn. Bergvalls Förlag: Stockholm 1967), 40 pp.

1968 *Johann Wolfgang von Goethe: Hermann und Dorothea*, with introduction and notes, ed.(Macmillan: London 1968), xl + 147 pp.

1969 'Some Aspects of Taboo and Up-Grading in Contemporary German', in *Essays in German Language, Culture and Society*

[Festschrift for Roy Pascal], ed. S. S. Prawer, R. H. Thomas and L. Forster. (London, 1969), pp. 110-122.
'Adalbert Stifter' in *German Men of Letters*, Vol. 5, ed. Alex Nathan. (Oswald Wolff: London 1969), pp. 183-206.
J.G.F.Como, *Kaspar Hauser. Die Geschichte eines Rätsels*. (Macmillan: London 1969) [Die neue Lesereihe], 55 pp.
'An Historical Dictionary of German Figurative Usage. Bericht über ein Wörterbuch', *Jahrbuch für Internationale Germanistik*, 1 (1969), 141-51.

1973 'Die sprachliche Aufwertung als neues Tabu', *Muttersprache*, 83 (1973), 185-95.

1974 *Langenscheidts Enzyklopädisches Wörterbuch*, Teil II, *Deutsch-Englisch*, 1. Band: A-K. (Langenscheidt: Berlin 1974). [Mitherausgeber].
'Gedanken zum Börne-Bild der Gegenwart', in *'Erfahrung und Überlieferung': Festschrift for C.P. Magill*, ed. Hinrich Siefken and Alan Robinson. (University of Wales Press: Cardiff 1974), pp. 88-99.

1975 *Langenscheidts Enzyklopädisches Wörterbuch*, Teil II, *Deutsch-Englisch*, 2. Band: L-Z. (Langenscheidt: Berlin 1975). [Mitherausgeber].

1990 Karl Heinz Spalt, *Kultur oder Vernichtung* – Ein Handbuch über Gedanken bedeutender Menschen über die Friedensfrage, die Stellung der Frau, der Kirchen, des Sozialismus, der modernen Wissenschaft zum Friedensproblem, die geschichtliche Entwicklung der Forderung auf ewigen Frieden und Schiedsgerichtsbarkeit. Mit zwei Zeittafeln. Dritte Auflage, neu herausgegeben von Maria und Achim von Borries. (Verlag Darmstädter Blätter Schwarz & Co: Darmstadt 1990), 226 pp.

1992 *33 – alles umsteigen. Eine Autobiographie.* (edition Outline: Lübeck 1992), 215 pp.

1993 *An Historical Dictionary of German Figurative Usage*, reprint of fascicles 1-50 in 5 vols. (Oxford: Blackwell Publishers 1993).

1995 *Worte sind meine Werkzeuge. Das kleine Börne Brevier.* (Droste Verlag: Düsseldorf 1995). 196pp.

1996 *Bunte Bilderwelt. Phraseologische Streifzüge durch die deutsche Sprache.* (Gunter Narr Verlag: Tübingen 1996).
Der lange Marsch Erinnerungen 1913-1946. [2nd edition of *1933 – alles umsteigen*]. (Gunter Narr Verlag: Tübingen 1996). 210pp.

1997 'The Bone of Contention: a Note on Goethe and Merck' in *Schein und Widerschein. Festschrift für T. J. Casey*, ed. Eoin Bourke, Roisin Ni Neill, Michael Shields. (Galway University Press: Galway [1997]), pp. 44-53.

1999 *The Long March* [translation of *Der lange Marsch* by Pauline Desch]. Sessions of York. (The Ebor Press: York 1999). 197pp.

2000 *An Historical Dictionary of German Figurative Usage.* Vol. 6. (Oxford: Blackwell Publishers). (January) 2000.

The many reviews by Keith Spalding are not included in this bibliography. He has reviewed for *GLL, MLR, Muttersprache, Erasmus, Archivum Linguisticum, New German Studies,* and *Revue Belge de Philologie et d'Histoire.*

Essays of Discovery (I)

My Six and a half Years In the Third Reich

Hans S Reiss (Bristol)

MY TIME IN the Third Reich lasted for just over six years and a half years. It left a deep mark, however fortunate I have been since. Nine years younger than Keith Spalding, I cannot tell a tale of courageous opposition to that evil regime which he so movingly recorded. I had no choice but to leave; for my father was a Jew.

I remember 30 January 1933 vividly, although I was then not yet ten and half years old. My mother was in bed suffering from a migraine. My father and I were at lunch alone. As always, if my mother was absent, we ate without speaking. Suddenly, my father rushed to the radio which announced Hitler's appointment as Chancellor. Since there were only two other Nazi ministers in the Cabinet, he was relieved. Like many, he, a non-political man with a liberal attitude of mind, believed Hitler would be powerless since the overwhelming majority of ministers were Conservatives. Moreover, he would not last long. Finally, he added quietly: 'The food is never eaten as hot as it is cooked'. Sadly, he was mistaken.

I heard of the attacks on Jewish shops and the arrests of Jews on 1 April 1933, but it did not affect my life. Sport, especially soccer, interested me far more than politics which was rarely discussed at home. My father was very taciturn; my mother, who had been an actress before her marriage, talked mainly about the theatre. She had acted in most of the German classical women's parts – Goethe's *Iphigenie* was her favourite - in many theatres, among them Hamburg, Basle, and Mannheim, my native city. But I read about politics in the papers, though at first events, even the Röhm massacre of 30 June 1934 or Hindenburg's death, did not make much of an impact on me. Only from 1936 onwards did I discuss politics with my closest school friend, a very bright 'Aryan' (that dreadful word has to be used in this context) baker's son.

I was not unhappy all my time in the Third Reich. I was living in a happy home. I liked school, had good friends to play with, hardly any of them were Jews. An only child, I loved reading, mainly history, the German classics and Shakespeare. Until 1937 I went to the theatre where I enjoyed operas, mainly by Wagner, and plays by Goethe, Schiller, Kleist, and Shakespeare. I was able to see films even longer.

Admittedly, in school an unfortunate orthodox Jew was sorely teased. In 1935 another Jewish boy, who as a first-rate soccer player was very popular, was expelled because he had replied cheekily to the worst of our teachers, whom all of us despised. The *Stürmer* reported the incident. The school had no choice but to act. But I cannot recall ever being harassed. Indeed, I was liked because I always did my home-work which others copied in the breaks between classes. All my teachers were kind to me. On the annual class-photograph I am usually standing next to the form-master, even though two of them were ardent Nazis. Even a young SS man never treated me badly. Because he won a Gold Medal at the 1936 Berlin Olympic Games he had been appointed to teach us Mathematics and Science, which he did not know well. Probably my teachers had been flattered that my 'Aryan' mother, a distinguished-looking, beautiful woman, well-known in Mannheim as a former actress, went to see them. Moreover, she had lived in the same Hamburg street as Hermann Göring's wife Emmy, who had also been an actress, and could show them a letter of invitation from Frau Göring which she had accepted to gain privileges for my father and me, but to no avail.

That Olympic champion also taught *National-Political Education* all Saturday morning and told us about the different races, the superior ones, Nordic and Langobardic , and the inferior ones, Semitic, Hamitic and others. Even I believed that unscientific nonsense until my eyes were opened in Dublin by Julian Huxley's *We Europeans*. When in puberty sexual feelings arose I was ashamed and attributed them to my Jewish heritage.

In summer we still spent our holidays in fine hotels, for currency reasons in the Black Forest, and no longer as before in the Swiss Engadine. However, political conditions probably caused my mother to fall ill for more than a year. My father suffered from a perforated stomach-ulcer.

Even the Nuremberg Laws meant little to me. Like many young boys, I was not interested in dating girls. Since our maid was older than forty-five, life at home did not change. In 1937 on a summer holiday in Garmisch my father by chance became friendly with the US Commercial Attaché, who strongly advised him speedily to leave Germany because Hitler had evil plans for Jews. My father considered it unrealistic to heed this advice. The sale of his large printing works would not bring him enough money to live abroad, except in severely straitened circumstances, if not in poverty, for the German Mark was worth little when changed into a foreign currency. Moreover, a 25% exit tax introduced in 1931 would have to be paid. Above all, it would have been very difficult to find a country to go to. He knew French but no other languages. Worn out from life-long hard work, at sixty-two he felt too old to start a new life. An inveterate optimist, he always hoped for the best. My mother, though eighteen years younger, knew no foreign languages at all, which barred her from a career in the theatre abroad, apart from Switzerland where there were no vacancies. Nor did they have well-to-do relatives or friends abroad to turn to for help.

After the Berlin Olympics life slowly grew worse for Jews. Many restaurants displayed signs forbidding Jews to enter. The theatre and cinema were out of bounds. I became increasingly depressed. The future began to appear bleak. I thought it wise to wait until I had passed the *Abitur* before taking a decision about my future.

In April 1938 came the decree compelling all Jews to sell their firms within six months. It was a terrible blow for my father to give up his life's work after forty-seven years in the firm. It was most difficult to find a buyer, but eventually the business was sold. My worries about the future escalated. My foreboding proved correct. In the afternoon of 10 November 1938 at the tail-end of the infamous *Reichskristallnacht*, our flat was vandalised. That morning, while I was waiting for the tram to take me to school, the newspaper salesman, from whom I bought my weekly sports magazine, came up to me, urged me to buy another one and warned me not to go to school. I heeded his words and stayed at home. My father, who was still working as a consultant for his firm's new owner, went to work, insouciant as always. After lunch, the bell rang. About twenty angry men, looking like the scum of the earth, burst into our flat and destroyed or damaged all glasses, crockery, clocks, works of art, mirrors and furniture. Books were thrown into the street to be burnt. I was sent into the kitchen; our maid had to take our angry Alsatian dog, wanting to counter-attack, into her upstairs room. My father, who had almost been hit by a large clock which had been hurled across two rooms, joined us. A former maid of ours suddenly appeared at the back door to warn us, sadly too late. My father gave her money to keep safe for him. Eventually, a storm-trooper marched us to the local police station. Quite a few Jews were there, one, an old man, was in great pain - a gall-bladder colic. The police superintendent was aghast to see my father, well-known as a generous benefactor to the police charity. He took him aside, apologised, explained that the police had been forbidden to intervene, and asked what he could do for him. My father gave him some important papers to look after. Suddenly, an SA officer appeared and ordered everyone to march to the railway-station. Since I was only sixteen I was told to clear out. I raced back to the house, but found our flat guarded by an SA man. Our maid sat crying on the stairs. So did an 'Aryan' widow who lived below us. I ran to my father's former firm to phone my mother who was visiting her sister in Hamburg. The office staff was silent, scared but appalled by the outrage. I told my uncle my tale of horror and pleaded for my mother's urgent return. I spent the night at the house of my best friend. His parents, fervent anti-Nazis, were horrified.

I thought I would never see my father again. But next morning our former driver came to tell me that my father was back in the flat. He had been taken to Karlsruhe, where those who were older than sixty were released. The others were sent to the Dachau concentration camp. My joy knew no bounds. Soon my mother arrived, tearful and outraged. 'Aryan' friends came, horrified by the vandalism. The firm's new owner told my father that he would have used his contacts with the Nazi authorities to have him immediately released from the concentration camp claiming that his work as a consultant was essential for the firm. Inevitably, that dreadful experience left me with a deep trauma that haunted me for many, many years.

I then heard that I, who was still nominally registered as a Jew, had been expelled from school. I knew I had to leave Germany. My parents, their relatives and friends thought so, too - all young people should go, the older people, too, if they could. But where was I to go? My father, a shattered man, was at a loss. My mother, ever resourceful, explored many avenues. One of her Basle friends, a good Christian, was willing to give me shelter, but the Basle City Canton forbade me entry for two years. Meanwhile, I decided to learn a craft and enlisted as a glazier, not my choice, but the masterglazier who hated the Nazis was the only craftsman glad to take me on. I also took French, English, and Spanish conversation classes at a Berlitz school. One kind English teacher and his wife sought to find a place for me in Britain, to no avail. One day, a Quaker friend asked my mother to give lunch to a modestly dressed Quaker visitor from Birmingham, whose name was Brandon Cadbury. His name meant nothing to us, although he told us that his father, who had something to do with chocolate, knew Neville Chamberlain quite well. He tried to find a place in Winchester College for me. But it did not work out.

Eventually, help came from Hermann Maas, who had been removed by the Nazis from his post as Pastor of the Heiliggeistkirche, the principal Heidelberg church. He was a great man, a true Christian; after 1945 he, a friend of Ben Gurion, was the first German to go to Israel where a forest is named after him. A railway bridge commemorates his name in Heidelberg. His preaching opened the gate to Christianity for me, who had never taken to the Jewish religion. With a friend's help he found a committee of Irish Protestants to take me for one year to continue my schooling in Ireland before I was to take up a scholarship at Duke University, North Carolina. Meanwhile, clothes were bought to last me for years and packed into trunks. For each item my father had to pay 100% duty. I was not allowed to take any German currency abroad but the statutory ten Marks; however, my mother cajoled a senior civil servant to grant me another hundred Marks.

Since I was convinced that war would break out any time, I decided to leave as soon as I had received the Irish visa. Waiting for the visa was agony. Eventually, it arrived and I was able to depart on 22 August 1939, three days after my seventeenth birthday. To leave my parents whom I deeply loved was terrible. I worried about their safety, especially about my father's, throughout the war. Fortunately, I saw them again, just over seven years later.

Crossing the border was frightening. I had gone to the dining-car, in which my father had thought I would be safer than in a compartment. Suddenly an excited guard rushed in and ordered us to pull down all blinds. The lights were dimmed. Fear overcame me. I thought war had broken out. Twice the train stopped. I expected to be ordered out and then to be sent to a concentration camp or shot straightaway. I was waiting for a third examination by SS men; for after paying for my meal I had still some small change left lying on the table to hand over. But no German official came. Finally, after what seemed an eternity, the train rolled on again. A new, friendly-looking conductor came to check the tickets. I asked him anxiously when we would get to Holland. He smiled and said: 'We are in Holland'. My relief was enormous. I had left the Third Reich for good.

Student Years

Harry Long (Wokingham)

I ENROLLED AT Birmingham University in September 1934 having selected a series of courses known as Grouped Honours. It was described as a new idea which allowed students to study three subjects up to Honours standard, an exacting undertaking which attracted about eighteen students. I selected French under Professor Ritchie, German under Professor Sandbach and History under Professor Hancock, an Australian. One other student chose this combination - Keith Spalding or, as I knew him, Heinz Spalt. It goes without saying that we became firm friends from the outset. In addition to attending the same lectures I recollect exchanging notes in order to economise on background reading, Keith specialising in German and I myself in History. I seem to remember the odd game of snooker among other activities. I spent the summer of 1935 in Germany during which time I paid a brief visit to Keith's parents in Darmstadt. The grim signs of military preparations for war were only too apparent including the recently opened autobahn where Keith's father took me for a drive.

We graduated together in July 1937 after which our ways separated for different studies although we met occasionally at University.

On the outbreak of war I joined the army and was eventually commissioned in the Intelligence Corps. On hearing that Keith had joined the Pioneer Corps I wrote to my Commanding Officer suggesting that better use could be made of his talents and qualifications in Intelligence work. I doubt whether my letter carried much weight but I was delighted to read in *The Long March* just how valuable his service was in Intelligence activity.

To my intense regret we have never met since our days at University but we kept in touch over the past 50 years or so, largely by the exchange of Christmas cards. I am happy and privileged to have been associated with a distinguished scholar and friend.

Keith Spalding, from Pacifist to Soldier

Peter Leighton-Langer (Bensheim)

MY MEETING Keith Spalding for the first time was the result of my decision to write about the 10,000 Germans and Austrians who served in the British forces during Word War II. He was one of them and so was I. By 1996, when his letter arrived, hardly anyone outside our families and some of our close friends knew that the King's Own Loyal Enemy Aliens had ever existed and that in spite of a book that came out in 1950. This had been forgotten quickly.

This state of affairs had annoyed me. As soldiers we were as good as any and as to our courage, I quote, 'in joining His Majesty's Forces each individual took the full risk, which being an enemy alien member of these Forces constituted, not only the risk of being killed or maimed, but also that of being taken prisoner and, being recognised, held to be a traitor, and finally, the risk that Britain might have lost the war with all the unthinkable consequences such a contingency would have brought about. Having taken the oath of obedience there was little any of us could do to minimise any of these risks. A soldier - and a member of the women's services - has to go where he or she is told. One can protest, one can volunteer, one can try to steer one's fate, but in the end one obeys orders, one goes where one is sent, into danger or away from it, and always with one's eyes open. None who joined up could ignore them, none was not afraid of them and everyone knew these risks. Yet all took them upon themselves. In the end, whether an individual covered himself in glory or remained an obscure member of an obscure unit, whether he or she was an officer or a private soldier, whether he or she was a commando, a pioneer or an ATS orderly, at the time one joined and throughout one's period of service, the risk which one took, knowingly and voluntarily, was the same.'

This is what made me write the book from which I quote, *X steht für unbekannt*, the story of these 10,000 (Berlin: Verlag Arno Spitz, 1999). Keith Spalding heard about my intentions and wrote to me to say that he agreed with them. We met when he visited Darmstadt and as I live within twenty miles of where he used to stay we have met quite frequently ever since.

I have read and condensed the biographies of hundreds of men and women who served. Many have distinguished themselves after leaving the services. But Keith Spalding is the only one of whom I know that he had been a leading pacifist from his early youth. Yet he volunteered for service in 1940, joining a fighting regiment in 1943. How come? Did he change his mind? Did he recant?

He himself was very reticent. In his 'Postscript, 1990' to the third edition of *Kultur oder Vernichtung*, the work of his younger days, he mentions his early pacifism almost apologetically. 'It was an error', he seems to say. 'I was wrong. It took me a long time, but in the end I realised what I ought to do.' And that seems to be all he is prepared to say on the subject. But is it all that is to be said?

I have never been a pacifist. My family is full of them, but my cousins have held me to be a militarist pure and simple. I admit to having enjoyed my pre-military training in Austria and I have always pleaded for a credible defence. I still do.

Yet, reading *Kultur oder Vernichtung* today I find little that I can disagree with and indeed I find it ridiculous that any non-pacifist should ever have held that first book by Karl Heinz Spalt, as he then was, to be any danger even to a militarist state. What, after all, did this precocious young man try to say?

Kultur oder Vernichtung is an anthology of poems and prose writings by many authors from about 500 BC to 1931 AD, almost all of whom say that war is terrible, that it brings pain, death and sorrow to everyone involved, that it is an irrational, stupid and suicidal exercise, and that one should do all one can not to let it happen. Many, and not only the most recent, are clear that war may bring about the end of mankind, indeed of the world. They oppose the glorification of war and stress their desire for peace. Amongst all these quotes, there is indeed one contribution which offers a credible method of avoiding war and that is Ghandi's instruction to his satyagrahis, which however refers to civil war against the British, a very law-abiding nation. But Karl Heinz does not appear to have recognised the unique character of the Mahatma's teaching, and apart from this there is nothing that should allow anyone to neglect the saying *'si vis pacem para bellum!'* And did he really think, fourteen short years after the end of World War I that his elders did not know?

In his selection of quotes Karl Heinz included many writers who were highly regarded by everyone as representing the best in German thought, writers who on other occasions had written texts which the Nazis were proud to use. Even some of the poets, whose odes to peace he had quoted, had on other occasions written texts which glorified war and death. Two hearts beat in many a breast.

Most probably the authorities in Darmstadt took objection to the connecting texts, more than the quotes. There Karl Heinz showed himself to be a rebellious type of person and there is little that annoys officials of an authoritarian regime as much as a young man who knows everything better and tells his elders they are wrong. But perhaps young Karl Heinz really did think that others did not know. He lived in a society in which many had lost their bearings.

History, as it had been presented to him by the liberal teaching establishment of his home town, seemed to indicate that wars resulted from lack of understanding, failure to communicate, greed and ambition by men in high office. It over-emphasized the influence of misguided individuals and under-estimated the forces of hate, of injured honour, of lust for revenge. It believed it could explain almost everything by recourse to economics and failed to take into account the psychology of the masses and the subconscious herd instincts.

I could imagine that in taking his stance he was not out of sympathy with many in his environment. Darmstadt was a city with liberal traditions. Relative to the number of people living there, more Darmstadters joined the British forces than people from any other town in the Reich.

It was only after many years of persecution and exile that he realised the truth of the old German adage *'Es kann der Beste nicht in Frieden leben, wenn es dem bösen Nachbarn nicht gefällt'*. (Even the best can't live in peace, when ill willed neighbours don't permit it.) He had had plenty of evidence that the country he had left, and its allies, were to the nation he had joined *böse Nachbarn*, and in the end he found he could not reason with them.

In volunteering for service in the Pioneers he joined a corps which did not have the highest reputation, but it was the only one open to him as an enemy alien. It consisted of A, C and Q companies: A for Alien, C for Criminal and Q for Queers. It has since changed its image, but that is how it was in 1940. The War Office did not trust us. A proposal to allow German refugees to join the army was approved by the Cabinet in September 1939, but it took the army till December before it enrolled the first volunteer. The structure of the alien companies was based on the colonial forces, that is to say, all officers were British and so was the sergeant-major: half the sergeants were British and only the other half came from amongst the men; the British were armed, the others were not. The men had truncheons as weapons and these were not under their permanent control. After all, the refugees might have been waiting their chance to give the nasty Nazis a hand. In the meantime we were set to work building camps and roads, handling supplies, digging ditches and doing other work suitable for unskilled labourers. This did not strengthen our self-esteem, but we accepted it, because we wanted to wear the King's uniform and we wanted to show where we stood.

It took till 1942 before the unison reports of all the alien company commanders that their men were trustworthy and in fact keener than any others to fight against the common enemy, overcame the prejudices of the War Office and even of the otherwise so well-informed Secret Service.

246 Company PC, which Pte. Spalt joined, was formed at Bradford on 29th November 1940. Then it was moved to Saltney, near Chester, thence to Stoke and lastly to Shrewsbury. There it was disbanded and that or just a little earlier must have been the time when said Pte. Spalt, now under the brand new name of Keith Spalding, transferred to the Border Regiment. There at last he was allowed to carry arms and feel that he was a real soldier, ready to take his proper place in the fight against Hitler and his minions. This was in the summer of 1943.

In his communications to me about his time with the Borderers Keith Spalding was as reticent as he has been about his conversion from the pacifism of his earlier days. Knowing him, however, and knowing what infantry-men had to go through in the run up to D-Day, I would imagine that he had a tough time. Perhaps it was even more unpleasant than his time in the Pioneers.

In 1942 a little more than one hundred German and Austrian refugees had been accepted into the Commandos and the Parachutists. They were formed into the 21st Independent Parachute Company and No. 3 Troop, 10th Inter-Allied Commando. Both were used in the forefront of operations and particularly the commandos immediately showed their usefulness in interrogating prisoners, reading and understanding captured documents and even more important, understanding the minds of the enemy. The people running the Intelligence Corps showed some intelligence and decided they wanted more of these people who had such wonderful gifts. It took them quite a time to persuade the War Office of this solution to their needs, but by the beginning of 1944 they were permitted to recruit suitable German refugees into their ranks.

No doubt, Keith Spalding's transfer to the Intelligence Corps in 1944 was the result of this. He was given the rank of Corporal and as time went on he was promoted Staff Sergeant. Although a staff sergeant is a very senior NCO, it is nevertheless amazing that in the army of occupation he was given charge of important German newspapers, first *'Die Mitteilungen'* and later *'Die Aachener Nachrichten'*. But he was not the only one and almost all the people, who were concerned with the re-establishment of the German press after the end of the Nazi regime, were German and Austrian refugee NCOs. None were commissioned. That is a measure of the importance the army attached to communicating with the people it had to administer. These NCOs did a wonderful job and Keith Spalding went beyond what was required of him. He started a school for German journalists and all went well, until he had the effrontery to sign the testimonials which were handed to the successful pupils. For this high-handed action he was reprimanded and dismissed from his job in press control. To teach him what's what, he was transferred to the control of films. He left the army in June 1946.

He might have smiled a little at these words had he lived to read them. I can just see him doing so. There may be one or two things which he would have seen differently. But this is how I see it and I think it may not be far from the truth. So I'm sticking to it.

Kultur oder Vernichtung?: Karl Heinz Spalt and the Pacifist Dilemma

Charmian Brinson (London)

'IT WAS,' SO Keith Spalding recounts of himself, the 17-year old Karl Heinz Spalt, in the midst of the turmoil accompanying the end of the Weimar Republic, 'time to ally myself to some cause, and the obvious choice for me was the German Peace Society.'[1] The Deutsche Friedensgesellschaft (DFG), established in 1892, and the German Peace Movement as a whole had grown greatly in membership in the wake of the Great War and, despite internal divisions, had by the late 1920s become a serious political force. Instrumental in the DFG's foundation had been two of the young Spalt's political mentors, Alfred Hermann Fried and Bertha von Suttner, whose writings would play a significant part in the 224-page collection of pacifist quotations and facts that Spalt published in 1933 under the striking title *Kultur oder Vernichtung?* [*Culture or Annihilation?*]. Other sources for his collection, from all cultures and ages, were recommended by the DFG or suggested in the leading pacifist journal, Fritz Küster's *Das andere Deutschland*, that Spalt had begun to read at this time.

In his autobiography, Spalding recalls how, faced with the rise of National Socialism on the one hand, and the disunity of the Left on the other, he had conceived his plan:

> The idea of being able to show mankind a better way forward through logical argument had taken root in me, and it ruled my thoughts [...]. Why not put together a book, where I could appeal to common sense? I had already made many notes, ready to be used in talks and debates. Quotations from important people on the subject of peace and understanding were available [...] which I could track down with no great difficulty. I could arrange this chronologically. At the same time, I could

record by means of tables, the political development of endeavours on behalf of peace. It was also clear to me that I would have to go into contemporary history with facts and figures about the last war and the outlines of the armament industry. All together, on a personal level, addressing the reader directly, I could produce a presentable book and satisfy my urge to do something for peace.[2]

The 'eighteen-year-old with more idealism than a sense of reality', as Spalding describes himself in hindsight,[3] then set about the work with great commitment, even deferring his entry to university in order to devote himself to the task.

Kultur oder Vernichtung? carried a subtitle that indicated the project's ambitious scope: *'Ein Handbuch über Gedanken bedeutender Menschen über die Friedensfrage, die Stellung der Frau, der Kirchen, des Sozialismus, der modernen Wissenschaft zum Friedensproblem, die geschichtliche Entwicklung der Forderung auf ewigen Frieden und Schiedsgerichtsbarkeit'* [A Handbook of the Thoughts of Eminent People concerning the Peace Question, the Attitude of Women, the Churches, Socialism, and Modern Science to the Peace Problem, the Historical Development of Demands for a Lasting Peace and Systems of Arbitration]. Indeed the range of quotation Spalt selected is little short of phenomenal: proceeding from primitive peoples, the work encompasses India, China, Greece and Rome; reflects on the particular part played by Christianity in pacifist thinking (the Religious Society of Friends, or Quakers, to whom Spalt was to find himself drawn during his first years of British exile, already receives a special mention here); considers the influence of European wars down the centuries on such thinking; and finally, approaching the present time, examines the movement for Franco-German understanding, the work of Suttner and Fried, the pacifists who spoke out even during the Great War, as well as those who had been making themselves heard since that time.

This last - contemporary - part is broken down into a series of interlinking subsections. One of them, 'Der letzte Krieg war schon furchtbar' [The last war was terrible enough], stresses the heavy costs involved, both in terms of lives lost and in material terms, then focuses on the horrors of gas warfare. 'Der nächste Krieg' [The next war] is made up of quotations from such leading figures as Winston Churchill and Lord Cecil on likely - and terrifying -

developments in chemical warfare. Finally 'Darum mehren sich die Stimmen' [Dissent is on the increase] comprises calls for peace both at home and abroad. German spokesmen here included men of the stature of Thomas and Heinrich Mann, Albert Einstein, Sigmund Freud and Hellmut von Gerlach who would shortly, like Spalt himself, be forced into exile; or Erich Mühsam who would end his life in a concentration camp.

Einstein would be one of the first of the high profile German pacifists to recognise the inadequacy of the pacifist response to National Socialism.[4] Another would be Ernst Toller, something of a role model to the young Karl Heinz Spalt.[5] However that still lay some way in the future. It is interesting to note that a long and powerful extract from a speech of Toller's from 1924, chastising German men, women and youth for failing to oppose the Great War, is included in *Kultur oder Vernichtung?* under the subheading 'Sozialismus und Friede' [Socialism and Peace]. Spalt exposes the tensions and inconsistencies within the German Labour Movement with regard to pacifism as he does, a little later in his work, to similar incongruities evident within the Christian churches, indicting those self-styled Christians not ashamed to defend war. In this latter section, 'Den kriegerischen Nazarenern' [To the war-loving Nazarenes], on the other hand, Spalt notably includes two statements by the Bund religiöser Sozialisten [League of Religious Socialists], a group with a membership of perhaps 20 000 to which Spalt himself belonged, who from their foundation in 1919 had set themselves to oppose the increasing militarisation of Germany and to combat the growing danger of Fascism. One of these, a poem entitled 'Wir wollen Frieden' [We Want Peace] from an appeal issued by the League on 1 May 1930, opens with the forceful line 'Darum Krieg dem Kriege!' [Wage War on War!], the watchword informing Spalt's entire purpose in compiling his *Kultur oder Vernichtung?*

In addition to the quotations, the volume carries at its heart two lengthy chronological tables relating to peace and pacifism, also compiled by Spalt himself. The second of these which charts important dates in the history of the Peace Movement, *inter alia*, ends confidently enough by recording the new lease of life taken on by the Movement since the end of the war. The first, which includes 'Plans for the bringing about of a lasting peace', runs through a long list of such endeavours, from St Thomas Aquinas to the foundation of the League of Nations and beyond, as well as citing the writings that Spalt considered vital in this connection: Count Coudenhove-Kalergi's *Pan-Europa*, of course, of 1922, and also two works by the leading German pacifist Otto Lehmann-Russbueldt, co-founder of the Bund Neues Vaterland and its successor organisation, the Deutsche Liga für Menschenrechte: *Die blutige Internationale der Rüstungsindustrie*, 1929, and *Die Revolution des Friedens*, 1931 [i.e. 1932]. Lehmann-Russbueldt, like Spalt, would soon be obliged to seek refuge in Britain.

Kultur oder Vernichtung? appeared in print very shortly before Hitler's advent to power. At the end of his preface, dated September 1932, Spalt defines his dual aims in compiling his collection as being to win over new converts to the pacifist cause as well as to provide his fellow pacifists with a work of reference to assist them in propaganda work. Earlier in the preface, however, Spalt had set out his purpose in markedly more passionate terms: he had put together his work, so he informed his readership, 'um Euch gegen den Ungeist, der auf das arme Europa jetzt wieder ausgegossen ist, zu feien' [to protect you against the evil that has yet again spread over our poor Europe].

The book was published in Heide, Holstein, by Paul Riechert, publisher of pacifist writings including the fortnightly *Deutsche Zukunft*. It was too late, however, for activity of this kind to have any effect. Riechert's stocks, including 2500 issues of *Deutsche Zukunft*, 76 hardback and 90 paperback copies of *Kultur oder Vernichtung?*, together with another 750 book jackets and, as it happened, 300 pamphlets by Otto Lehmann-Russbueldt, were seized by the National Socialist authorities in May 1933. Riechert and his family had to flee to Denmark where they managed to survive the war.[6]

Spalt himself was compelled to flee Germany even before Riechert, leaving his parents' home only an hour before the arrival of the SA there in search of him. After a period spent in Vienna and the adventures he describes in *The Long March*, he reached Britain in the spring of 1934. Interestingly, unlike the majority of his fellow exiles, Spalt appears to have spent little time in refugee circles in Britain, at least initially. Apart from his connections at the University of Birmingham, where he began to study, Spalt's most significant contacts in Britain at the time were with the Baptists - his first home in Britain was a Baptist Manse - and above all with the Quakers whom he found to be 'always open-hearted, convinced pacifists and representatives of a liberal humanitarian view of the world'.[7] The Quakers offered the young pacifist - and many other refugees besides - a great deal in the way of practical and spiritual support, such that during his final undergraduate year Spalt asked to be received into the Religious Society of Friends.

In fact, the sole meeting with a fellow German during his first British years that Spalt chooses to mention in his autobiography was with the former Social Democratic politician and Minister of the Interior Carl Severing whom he met in 1936 at the Woodbrooke Quaker College and who was not an exile. On the contrary, after a brief period of arrest in 1933 - and despite his reported contacts with the British Quakers in the mid-1930s - Severing was apparently invited to Woodbrooke to take part in discussions on international politics - he managed to live through the National Socialist years in his hometown of Bielefeld.[8]

There were, however, as already indicated, a number of leading German pacifists living in exile in Britain in the 1930s, among them Toller, Lehmann-Russbueldt and the lawyer and publicist Rudolf Olden, who between them continued to represent the banished Deutsche Liga für Menschenrechte. The young Spalt would have had little occasion to meet exiles of this eminence; yet he was linked to them - and others - in a curious manner by the interest of the Gestapo agent Hans Wesemann. In 1935 and 1936, Wesemann would briefly achieve international notoriety after his abduction of the German pacifist and publicist Berthold Jacob over the Swiss/German border. Prior to that, however, during a period spent in Britain, Wesemann was paid by the German Embassy in London to gather information from and report on the activities of the German political refugees there, including Lehmann-Russbueldt, of course, whom he judged 'die intellektuelle Seele des Londoner Hetzkreises gegen Deutschland' [the intellectual heart of the London-based agitators against Germany]; Gerhard Seger, former General Secretary of the DFG and ex-Reichstag Deputy who, having himself managed to escape from a German concentration camp, was in Britain to campaign for the release of his wife and child from another; Rudolf Olden who, among other things, had offered a home to Rosalinda von Ossietzky, daughter of the imprisoned editor of *Die Weltbühne*, Carl von Ossietzky; and Ernst Toller, like Olden and the others a vociferous critic of Nazi Germany.[9]

At the end of June 1934, Wesemann attended the National Peace Congress in Birmingham where he attempted to build up his contacts with British and foreign pacifists (trying though failing to persuade the ill-fated Berthold Jacob to come over from France for the occasion). It is likely to have been while he was in Birmingham for the Congress that Wesemann turned his attention to Spalt, calling on him at the University in the guise of an old fellow Socialist who wanted 'to meet me and have me show him something of England'. Fortunately for Spalt, he was by then no longer in Birmingham, having left for the vacation.[10]

Most of the German pacifists, as Karl Holl and others have documented, when confronted with the unprecedented evil of National Socialism, gave up or at any rate modified their pacifism in exile.[11] Ernst Toller, Spalt's role model, was among them, as has already been noted. Toller came to regard absolute pacifism as incompatible with the demands of political action and was in fact, by 1936, resigned to the prospect of a new European war.[12] In Spalt's case, the decision to play an active role in the fight against Hitler does not appear to have been taken until after the outbreak of war when he first began to donate blood, then applied for entry to a British medical unit. Though rejected for the latter, Spalt would before long go further and join first the Pioneer Corps, as a military unit accepting 'enemy aliens', and later the British Infantry, ending his army career in the Intelligence Corps. It was, however, a source of some considerable pain to him to have to abandon the pacifist ideals that had guided his life to that point and also, more specifically, to break with the uncompromisingly pacifist Quakers. He explains his 'conversion' as follows:

> It was now my conviction that the Nazis represented the 'quintessence of atavistic evil' as Kerr once expressed it, and that this evil, with its appeal to the primitive instincts, threatened all that culture had achieved in the whole of Europe. If I were to arrive at a logical conclusion, I would have to put forward other alternatives than those named in my book *Kultur oder Vernichtung?* It would no longer be pacifism to preserve culture,

but destruction of the Third Reich to rescue culture which came to mind as the imposed task. Once I reached this point, my pacifism disintegrated.[13]

It is interesting, in the light of this statement, that when the possibility arose in 1946 for his book to be republished - this time under the title *Der weite Weg* [*The Long Road*] - Spalding should still continue the venture worthwhile - 'selbst wenn das gewählte Thema der unpopuläre Pazifismus ist' [even if unpopular pacifism is its chosen theme] – on the grounds that 'ein Zeitraum von 14 Jahren ändert nichts an ethischen Grundtatsachen' [a period of 14 years has no effect on fundamental ethical premises]. Moreover, most of the friends, so Spalding would write in his preface to the 1946 edition, who had supported him in his original efforts to publish *Kultur oder Vernichtung?* were now dead, victims of National Socialism. 'Ihrem Gedächtnis,' he continued, 'sei diese zweite Fassung gewidmet' [may this second version be dedicated to their memory].[14]

The new edition remained very similar to the original, though the chronological tables were extended to include such events as the Peace Ballot of 1934/35, a manifestation of the prevailing British mood at the time, as well as Carl von Ossietzky's death in a concentration camp in 1938, both of which would have made a great impression on Spalt during his first years of British exile. The tables end, appropriately enough, with the recent foundation of the United Nations and the re-emergence of the Deutsche Friedensgesellschaft in Cologne.

The 1946 edition, which was distributed to school libraries in the Rhineland, soon sold out as did a subsequent edition in 1947. 'Money was not important in those days and reading material was in short supply,' Spalding recalls.[15] And nor does the story end there, for in 1989 - significant year - the work was rediscovered in Germany and its author traced to Wales. Thus, in 1990, *Kultur oder Vernichtung?* reappeared, under its original title once again, accompanied by material relating to its extraordinary publication history. Spalding himself, persuaded to contribute a 'Nachwort' to the 1990 edition, looked back over the 59 years that had elapsed since he had originally conceived the idea of his pacifist volume, the first appearance of which was to have such critical consequences for author and publisher. Then, conscious of the 'geschichtliche

Wendepunkt' [historical turning-point] at which the world stood at that time, November 1990, Spalding greeted his book's reappearance and ended in optimistic vein:

> Alte Fronten zerbröckeln, manche Konfrontationen der Vergangenheit verlieren ihre Existenzberechtigung, und neue Verfassungs- und Lebensformen sind im Entstehen. Eine friedlichere Welt darf erhofft werden – Grund genug, ein Dokument aus der Vergangenheit abzustauben und noch einmal anzusehen.[16]
>
> [Old fronts are crumbling, many a past confrontation is losing its raison d'être, new forms of constitution, ways of life are emerging. There is hope of a more peaceful world – reason enough to dust down and take a fresh look at a document from the past.]

Since 1990 world events have taken a significant turn for the worse. *Kultur und Vernichtung?*, though the work of a nineteen year old and dating from 1933, delivers a message that is every bit as relevant, as powerful, today as it was 70 years ago, while posing much the same pacifist dilemma. As Karl Heinz Spalt exhorted his readership in his original preface: 'Wollt Ihr alle ruhig mit zusehen, wie auf der ganzen Welt die Mittel zu Eurer Vernichtung hergestellt werden?' ['Do you all intend just to stand by and watch as, all over the world, the means are produced for your annihilation?'].

NOTES

1 Keith Spalding, *The Long March*. (York: 1999), p. 27.
2 *Ibid.*, pp. 40-1.
3 *Ibid.*, p. 41.
4 See Einstein's letter, published in *La Patrie Humaine* on 18 August 1933, reprinted in *Peace*, October 1933, p.14, admitting that, were he a Belgian, he would not refuse to take part in military service but rather 'accept it with my whole conscience, knowing that I was contributing towards the salvation of European civilisation'.
5 *The Long March*, p. 153.
6 See Maria von Borries, 'Der Verleger und Pazifist Paul Riechert', in Karl Heinz Spalt, *Kultur oder Vernichtung?* (Darmstadt: 1990), pp. 207-25.
7 *The Long March*, p. 114.

8 On this, see Carl Severing, *Mein Lebensweg*, vol. 2: *Im auf und ab der Republik* (Cologne: 1950). Severing makes no mention of a visit to England, however.
9 On this, see Charmian Brinson, 'The Gestapo and the German Political Exiles in Britain during the 1930s: The Case of Hans Wesemann – and Others', *German Life and Letters*, 51: 1 (January 1998), 43-64.
10 *The Long March*, p. 123. The situating of this episode in June 1934 rather than in the following Christmas vacation, as Keith Spalding has suggested, is more in line with Wesemann's known activities in Britain.
11 See, for example, Karl Holl, 'Deutsche Pazifisten im britischen Exil', in Charmian Brinson, *et al.*, eds., *'England? Aber wo liegt es?': Deutsche und österreichische Emigranten in Großbritannien 1933-1945*. (Munich: 1996), especially pp. 81ff. See also the strikingly entitled Rolf von Bockel, 'Wer kann Pazifist bleiben, wenn Hitler an die Macht kommt? Zum Wandel der politischen Überzeugungen deutscher Pazifisten nach 1933', in *Das Argument*, 165 (1987), 688-97.
12 See Richard Dove, *He Was a German: A Biography of Ernst Toller*. (London: 1990), pp. 220-1.
13 *The Long March*, p. 153.
14 Karl Heinz Spalt, 'Vorwort', *Der weite Weg: Ein Handbuch über den Pazifismus*. (Aachen: 1946), pp. 1-2.
15 *The Long March*, p. 182.
16 Keith Spalding, 'Nachwort 1990', *Kultur oder Vernichtung?* (Darmstadt: 1990), p. 205.

Wörter sind meine Werkzeuge

Walter Voigt (Ismaning)

IN EINER SEINER zahlreichen Publikationen bietet Keith Spalding dem Leser ein ungewöhnliches Umschlagbild:[1] die Titelseite von Grimmelshausens *Der Teutsche Michel*. Man erblickt dort einen Maler, dessen Leinwand der folgende Spruch ziert: 'Wie des Mahlers Färb-gemeng, So ist unser Sprach-gepräng'. Extensives 'Sprach-gepräng' hat Keith Spalding nicht nur in seinem *Historical Dictionary of German Figurative Usage* vor uns entfaltet - auch seine Arbeit am größten zweisprachigen Wörterbuch, dem *Neuen Muret-Sanders*[2] ist unvergessen; sie gehört zur Geschichte der deutsch-englischen Lexikographie im zwanzigsten Jahrhundert.

Der *Muret-Sanders* wurde ursprünglich in den Jahren 1869-1901 kompiliert. Er setzte in der zweisprachigen Lexikographie durch seinen enzyklopädischen Umfang, die exakte semantische Darstellung und eine ausgefeilte Typographie, neue Maßstäbe; er ist auch ein schönes Zeugnis der Gründerzeit. An den vier Bänden des *Neuen Muret-Sanders* wurde von 1950-1975 gearbeitet und in diesem Zeitraum war Keith Spalding als Mitherausgeber aktiv tätig - häufig in den Räumen der Langenscheidt-Redaktion in Berchtesgaden und immer in kollegialer Zusammenarbeit mit dem Herausgeber Professor Dr Otto Springer (University of Pennsylvania). Für die Lautschrift des Britischen Englisch im englisch-deutschen Teil zeichnete überdies seine Frau Phyllis verantwortlich.

Wer die beiden großen lexikographischen Arbeiten Keith Spaldings kennt, kann nicht mehr behaupten, dass die zweisprachige Lexikographie ein in der Germanistik kaum beachteter Forschungsbereich der angewandten Sprachwissenschaft ist. Selbstverständlich baute der *Neue Muret Sanders* auf den bewährten

Grundsätzen auf, denen der Vorgänger seinen Ruf und seinen Nachschlagewert verdankte. Keith Spalding sorgte aber bei der genauen Durchsicht des Wörterbuch-Manuskripts dafür, dass der *Neue Muret-Sanders* mit den neuen Erkenntnissen und Forderungen der Sprachwissenschaft und der modernen lexikographischen Praxis im Einklang stand.

'Daß die Reichtümer der deutschen Sprache, wie wohl jeder, nicht oben liegen, sondern daß man darnach graben muß [...]' - dies schrieb Ludwig Börne, dies zitierte Keith Spalding, und danach handelte auch der große Lexikograph Keith Spalding.[3] Noch immer hängt ja die Qualität eines Wörterbuchs von den Kenntnissen und der Zuverlässigkeit des Lexikographen ab, ganz gleich, ob das Wörterbuch auf einer Tontafel (wie in vorchristlichen Zeiten) oder im Internet zur Verfügung steht.

Eine sehr umfangreiche, sehr positive Rezension des *Neuen Muret-Sanders* in einer großen deutschen Tageszeitung[4] trägt die Überschrift 'Sisyphos schuftet am Wörterberg'. Damit wollte der Rezensent die schwere Arbeit der Herausgeber und Redakteure dieses Wörterbuchs in den Mittelpunkt rücken. Keith Spalding ein Sisyphos? Ja, aber mit dem großen Unterschied, dass die Bemühungen des Sisyphos in der griechischen Mythologie nie - die lexikographischen Arbeiten Keith Spaldings aber immer ans Ziel kamen.

NOTES

Anmerkung der Herausgeber: Herr Dr Voigt war bis 1991 Leiter der englischen Redaktion des Langenscheidt-Verlags.

1   Umschlagbild in *Bunte Bilderwelt. Phraseologische Streifzüge durch die deutsche Sprache*. (Tübingen: Gunter Narr), 1996.
2   Heutiger Titel *Der Große Muret Sanders. Langenscheidts Enzyklopädisches Wörterbuch*. [Zwei Einzelbände Englisch-Deutsch und zwei Einzelbände Deutsch-Englisch].
3   Zitat nach Keith Spalding, *'Worte sind meine Werkzeuge': Das kleine Börne-Brevier*. (Düsseldorf: 1995), S. 92.
4   *Die Welt* vom 18. April 1974.

Press Reception of 2nd October 1975.

*Celebrating the completion
with Dr Walter Voigt, the English Language Editor (above),
and with the publisher Karl Ernst Tielebier-Langenscheidt.*

Keith Spalding, Lifelong Lexicographer

Hans Heinrich Meier (Schaffhausen)

IT WAS AT Berchtesgaden in 1954 that I first met Keith Spalding and his charming wife Phyllis. The editorial staff of the English-German part of Langenscheidt's new *Enzyklopädisches Wörterbuch*, published in 1962/63, were spending some summer weeks on a working holiday. For me, who had got his Ph.D. in English and German the year before and accepted assistant editing to eke out his pay as assistant teacher at various Zurich schools, this was a great and, as it should turn out, a decisive experience. It was my first real acquaintance with 'German professors', and I found them as singularly un-professorial as Keith had found English ones. For many years, until his autobiography *33 - alles umsteigen* appeared in 1992, I had no idea of the story of Keith Spalding's life. He was far too modest to talk about his background, the long march that took him across Switzerland, the escape to England, the doctoral thesis on German-Swiss authors, or his war service, let alone his religious and political convictions. In my naivety I greatly underrated his sly sense of humour when, on my wondering about his name, he told me that both were quite familiar in Germany: 'Spalding' was a well-known Darmstadt surname, and 'Keith' (pronounced 'kite') was the name of a Prussian general who had been of the principality of Neuchatel in Switzerland. How lucky, I thought, to have settled in Britain with such a name. And I told the story to everybody.

In fact, both are names of Scottish families who emigrated to Germany (as I learnt from the *Allgemeine Deutsche Biographie*, 1882). Of highest repute was the theologian Johann Joachim Spalding (1714-1804), the dean at St. Nikolai's church in Berlin, a mild, optimistic religious thinker, avoiding all extremes of doctrine. Then there was Peter Karl Christof von Keith (1711-1756), lieutenant colonel under Frederick the Great, of whom it is said that he had a 'sanftes, mitfühlendes Gemüt' [a mild, sympathetic disposition]. I find both characterisations fitting Keith Spalding nicely.

At lunchtime the various dictionary workers converged from their quiet desks on the dining-hall amid exchanges of the odd German greetings of 'Mahlzeit!'-'Mahlzeit!' Langenscheidt provided us with hearty meals, too heavy for brainworkers, really. The meals were the social highlight of the day, where a lot of small as well as shoptalk went on. I remember a controversy about whether the word 'like' was an adjective, a preposition, or an adverb (the dilemma found its way into the dictionary). I remember telling them that the Swiss-German slang for a (temperamental) cigarette-lighter was 'es Pöötééterli' (a 'peut-être' thing), and also Phyllis Spalding, the dictionary's phonetic transcriber, always charming, outspoken and commonsensical, once remarking, with strong level stress: 'I think the Germans are héalth mád!'

The Berchtesgaden bunch were a serious, hard-working lot, but in retrospect none of them seem to have been experienced lexicographers, except Professor Spalding, who was already engaged in his magnum opus, of which the first fascicle was to appear five years later. At these meals the editor, Professor Springer, occasionally gave us one of his briefings, which were indeed sparing and brief. By suddenly ordering basic shifts in styling and arrangement, however, he sinned against a lexicographer's first principle: never to change horses in midstream.

The Langenscheidt lesson was decisive in making me turn to lexicography in earnest the following year. I had accepted a job as assistant editor of the *Dictionary of the Older Scottish Tongue*, and was to be a university tutor in Early English. So I moved to Edinburgh where, getting married to a Swiss girl in 1956, I plunged deeply into historical dictionary work and became quite professional. Though profoundly satisfying, I found the work very exacting, self-effacing, and careerwise a dead end, and we left in 1959. After four years of schoolteaching back in Switzerland, I was offered a position as Reader in English Philology at the Vrije Universiteit in Amsterdam. So we moved abroad again; after four years I became full professor there.

During these years I had no regular contact with Keith and Phyllis, but in 1971 my wife Elsbeth and I were to visit them. The

University College of North Wales at Bangor was the last stage of a tour of inspection that took us up and down Britain through beautiful spring scenery in the second half of May. I was sent by the Dutch Students to Britain Committee, and the Ministry of Education, to meet Dutch students on scholarships at the Universities of Hull, Leeds, Nottingham, Durham, Edinburgh, and Glasgow, on the so-called 'Harting beurzen'. These scholarships had been instigated by Harting, a very demanding Dutch professor, who used to pay calls personally every year. The British were still so much in awe of him that we were splendidly received and entertained everywhere, and in Bangor even by the Principal himself, R.C. Evans, of immortal Mount Everest fame (1953), then, sadly, in a wheelchair. As in some other places, our students were allowed to teach some Dutch, and they were all well content and looked after. For them our visit was perhaps superfluous, but the hearty welcome from the Spaldings at Gower House, in Llanfairpwll, across the Menai Strait, is unforgotten. Keith's photographic (or rather phonographic) lexicographer's memory for the oddest words was apparent when he reminded me of the 'Pöötééterli' of so many years ago. I learnt about their continued 'working holidays' in Berchtesgaden: they now shouldered the main task of completing the German-English part of the Langenscheidt dictionary (LGE), and that the *Historical Dictionary of German Figurative Usage* was progressing steadily. Phyllis seemed to me as vigorous as ever, and Keith struck me as quite unchanged, with as modest and mild-humoured a liveliness as years before.

After our memorable visit to North Wales my contact with him was never interrupted, and although we did not keep up an extensive correspondence, we at least exchanged succinct Christmas cards with reports on our professional work. It was sad and moving to hear of Phyllis's long illness and of the unceasing care he bestowed on her while keeping up all his other activities, including his persevering labour for the *Historical Dictionary of German Figurative Usage.*

When one hears about a comprehensive, historical, critical representation of all figurative expressions in a language, one's mind boggles at such a tremendous undertaking. Why, every current full word in any language, verbal as well as nominal, will have a number of non-literal, 'figurative', i.e. transferred or metaphorical, meanings. All of these, many for most people no longer conveying their sense in an image, must be accounted for. Then there are masses of phrases, familiar or rare, turns of speech, locutions, proverbial sayings, proverbs, quotations and house-hold words, that contain metaphors. Typically, the more lively sayings are authentic elements of folk-speech, and Keith had early tuned his ear to these, as at home they always spoke the dialect of Darmstadt. He was fascinated by the metaphoric wealth and raciness of Hessian speech with is popular comparisons and allusions and nicknames.

It must have been no small compensation for the long drudgery that dictionary making entails, to be aware of the wide popular appeal that this lively, picturesque element of language enjoys. No wonder there are marketable dictionaries of German 'Redensarten', like those by Duden and Mackensen, which, it is true, now and then remark on possible origins, but Spalding made his own purposeful extracts from literature, and tracing the history was for him no mere side-show.

Beside the great achievement of the *Historical Dictionary of German Figurative Usage*, Keith Spalding has merited homage paid to him for the German-English part of Langenscheidt's dictionary. Moreover, as Professor Rudolf Jud has suggested, he deserved a prize from the Deutsche Akademie für Sprache und Dichtung [German academy for language and literature] in Darmstadt. Professor Jud edits the review journal *Erasmus* there, to which both Spalding and I have contributed. Such a prize would then not have been for any particular performance, but for his life's work and all he stood for. 'Das ist schon ein bewundernswertes Leben! [If that isn't a life to win our admiration!]' Professor Helmut Schrey, founding Rektor of Duisburg University, reader of *Der lange Marsch* and a former visitor to Woodbrooke, once wrote of its author in a letter to me. The Akademie might thus have honoured a man who, like Darmstadt's most famous son, the dramatist Georg Büchner (1813-1837), publicized his youthful humanitarian ideals, was persecuted by the authorities, and driven into exile.

I amused myself by making notes of all the figurative expressions used in his autobiography, and these amounted to about 90 on 200 pages. His tone throughout is lively but matter-of-fact. All his metaphors are completely appropriate but hardly ever out of the ordinary. Of the few more colourful ones, all tinged with his inimitable irony, I noticed these: 'ein wenig trunken im Irrgarten der Liebe herumstolpern' [to stumble around a bit drunk in the maze of Love], 'da knisterte etwas in meinem Gehirnkasten' [then something crackled in my brain-pan, i.e. 'rang a bell'], 'meine Moselfahrt hatte einen herberen Geschmack, wenn auch etwas Süssigkeit eintropfte' [my trip to the Moselle had a more acid taste (sc. than the local wine), even if some sweetness trickled in].

I have just received the English version of the autobiography, *The Long March*. The translator shows the highest respect for the original while successfully combining empathy and accuracy. At the same time her method is variable and resourceful. Let me illustrate this with five well-chosen renderings. *'Zusammenhänge, welche sich einprägten'* becomes 'links which were so impressive and lucid that they stayed in one's mind'. *'Zeichnete sich ab an ihrer Geistesverwandtschaft'* appears as 'became perceptible through many signs of spiritual affinity'. *'Süssholz raspeln'* is 'to ooze charm'. *'Der Austro-Faschismus erschien ungeschminkt auf der Bildfläche'* is translated as 'Austro-Fascism showed its face in all its ugliness'. *'Mühsam nährt sich das Eichhörnchen'* ['a squirrel feeds the hard way' (a proverbial saying that was new to me)] becomes 'Great oaks from little acorns grow'. And *'auch Stifter war wegweisend'* corresponds to 'even Stifter nudged me in this direction'. Thus Pauline Desch has turned the impressive Spalding saga not just into English but into good Anglo-Saxon.

Going back, however, to the great work of the *Historical Dictionary of German Figurative Usage*, we shall find that, whichever way one looks at it, it will stand the test of criticism as well as the test of time.

On what would today be called a metalexicographical level, let me conclude by first observing that Spalding's dictionary should be a basic resource, in time to come, for all explorers of the metaphor, a subject that has emerged in recent decades as an important field of study. It is a splendid interface, too, for traditional philologists like him and me, who refuse to accept a division between linguistics and literature. Spalding had in fact once before bridged the gap between the two sides with his German course based on simple German poems.

Most people seem to think that a dictionary grows by itself, like fruit-trees at the Creation, each 'yielding fruit after his kind whose seed is in itself' (Gen. 1: 11; AV). The last thing people are thinking of are the editors behind the dictionaries. The great Scottish lexicographer David Murison once mused with me about the fame and fortune of dictionary makers, their thankless task, little rewarded toil, and obscure status. When I applied this to the other great Scottish lexicographer, Jack Aitken, remarking how true of him, too, all this was, David said: 'Ah, but then the lexicographer's immortality is assured in his dictionary.' And this is perhaps as good a note to end on as our friend Keith Spalding, essentially a one-man lexicographer, might have wished.

Changing Metaphors for Intellectual Activities in German

Horst Dieter Schlosser (Frankfurt am Main)

KEITH SPALDING deserves much praise for his work exploring the German language, especially the figurative usage in German. So I wanted to dedicate to him some remarks about a special field of linguistic figures in German: about old and recent metaphors for thinking, understanding, and remembering. My modest contribution will now appear on his 90th birthday as a memorial saved on a computer disc, but we remember him in our hearts without electronic help.

It seems that a suitable denomination of intellectual activities is very difficult in any language, because these activities themselves are extremely abstract phenomena. Even specialists in phrenology or psychology are obliged to paraphrase these phenomena and have to use various metaphors, like *neuronal architecture, cerebral network, carpal tunnel syndrome, cortical tissue, clasp knife reflex* etc., in order to imagine the more or less invisible procedures of thinking and understanding. The common language is even more dependent on metaphors to denominate intellectual processes. If one looks at English and German vocabulary one will find some examples of an early transfer of concrete actions into the field of special terms for intellectual activities. One only has to think of German terms for comprehension like *begreifen* (> *Begriff*), *auffassen* (> *Auffassung*) or *erfassen*. These words let us yet see the original 'physical', obviously manual work, by which human beings became familiar with their environment in early times. But also the German words *erfahren / Erfahrung* (*to come to know / to experience*) let us see how in former times men enlarged their conception of the world by running, riding, driving, sailing (German *fahren*). The special morphology, i.e. the secondary formations like compositions (e.g.

auf-fassen or *über-legen*) and derivations (e.g. *be-greifen* or *er-fassen*) demonstrate the subsequent origin of those German terms, when the older words like *denken* (*to think*), *lernen* (*to learn*) and *wissen* (*to know*) were no longer sufficient to denominate intellectual activities (in pre-historical times these words were metaphors, too, but now they have become so-called 'dead metaphors').

The number of English words which are comparable to the German 'physical' metaphors seems smaller, because many English terms, after the displacement of an important part of the Old English vocabulary, are French (originally Latin) loan-words and their former meaning can only be recognized by knowledge of the Latin language, e.g. *consider* (< *considerare*), *imagine* (< *imaginare*), *reflect on sth.* (< *reflectere*). Only a few English words show an origin in 'manual work', similar to the German *begreifen, auffassen, erfassen*: One of these isolated examples is *to catch*. Clearly the English verb *remember* also attests a metaphorical transfer from concrete action to abstract conception: to make a passed experience a part (*member*) of mine again. The German equivalent *sich erinnern* has gone a step further to announce that intellectual activities cannot be described sufficiently by transferring external acts into metaphors; the reference to internal abilities (here: *er-inner-n*) opened the way for abstract denominations, suitable to invisible actions.

1. The coexistence of abstract terms and 'physical' metaphors

This way was, however, not straightforward either in English or in German. In principle the change of vocabulary by insertion of new terms and new meanings, or the vanishing of obsolete terms, does not take place systematically. It depends on various cultural, social and political conditions. In German, the way to specific denominations of internal abilities has been greatly enriched by the meditative efforts and the corresponding usage of language of the medieval mystics. Terms like *einsehen, einleuchten*, but also *begreifen*, were attempts to apprehend mystical activities of spiritual understanding. Today, a word like *sich einbilden* has acquired a pejorative meaning (similar to *to be conceited*), but in mystical usage it meant to form a man's soul by a godlike image. Another German word with a mystical background, almost identical to *sich einbilden*, has retained the original positive meaning: *sich einprägen* (*to imprint into the mind*). Less 'mystical' are the German variants *be-halten* and *sich merken* (= *to retain*). Originally, these words meant retaining information and knowledge by 'holding fast' (*be-halten*), or by creating 'marks' in our memory (*sich merken*) - both terms demonstrate again the general tendency to use 'physical' images. But both became 'dead metaphors' a long time ago. In this connection it may be interesting that the English term for memorising complete texts like poems reflects the idea of simultaneously activating intellect and emotion: *to learn by heart*, whereas the German counterpart, *auswendig lernen*, exemplifies a more mechanical conception of learning. The coexistence of rather abstract and 'physical' metaphors in mystical usage shows that even within the scope of a homogeneous line of thinking the invention of new terms cannot be systematic.

Although after the medieval mystics the terms for intellectual activities developed in various directions, some former motives of denomination seem to be preserved. One of these may be the attempt to comprehend the internal dimension of understanding in a manner similar to mystical inventions. But if we look at a recent term like *verinnerlichen* we recognize that this word is a case of loan-formation. Its origin is the technical term of modern psychology: *to internalise* (in German also *internalisieren*). Here we have another condition which ensures that the vocabulary cannot develop systematically: the influence of other languages (some German mystical terms had similarly been stimulated by a foreign language, by Latin). In a similar way to *internalisieren* the English lexical model *to realize* has broadened the meaning of the German loan-word *realisieren* within the last decades. At first, *realisieren* has only meant 'to translate something into reality' (*verwirklichen*). Just like the second semantic aspect of English to *realize*, German *realisieren* now also means 'to imagine or picture something' (*sich vorstellen*) - a new German metaphor for an intellectual activity.

2. Jugendsprache as a source of new metaphors

There are always new impulses for lexical differentiation coming from colloquial language, sometimes even from dialects. In colloquial German the word *kapieren* has long been used for an act of comprehension. Originally, *kapieren* had been borrowed in the 17th century from Latin *capere*. For a long time, though, *kapieren* has not been a metaphor anymore, although the original Latin word *capere* in non-figurative usage had the same 'physical' meaning as *to catch*. More important to our subject is the social aspect of the early usage of *kapieren*. It had been borrowed, and used, by students and thus by young people, who are more interested in denominating subjects without complicated paraphrases than in doing so with 'scientific' balance. A generally careless, but at the same time creative usage of language is a special characteristic of the younger generation. There has long been discussion in linguistics, whether this usage is a particular, even homogeneous subsystem of language or not. Using the German term *Jugendsprache (juvenile language)* in this context is very misleading. Be that as it may, the linguistic usage of young people certainly has some special features, but more often these are only common tendencies rather than steady elements. One of these marks is the intention to express opinions and feelings very directly.

Jugendsprache has in recent years imparted some new terms for comprehension to the German colloquial language, which share the familiar tendency to describe intellectual activities with physical concepts. Perhaps the new German metaphors for understanding are only variants of the conventional 'physical' metaphors, which no longer satisfy the general inclination of young people to denominate subjects, especially abstract phenomena like thoughts and ideas, in a very clear and direct manner. Nevertheless, at first sight the following examples seem to be shibboleths, elements of a secret language. Indeed, the language of young people also has the function to shield their communication against the older generation. However, even German 'oldies' are now familiar with the meaning of words like *checken, raffen* or *schnallen*. All three words are used by young people to paraphrase the term *verstehen (to understand)*.

raffen and *schnallen* are recent examples for the old, almost archaic manner of naming abstract subjects by concrete 'physical' images. *raffen* means non-metaphorically *to snatch up*. As a metaphor the word denotes the intellectual procedure of mentally *snatching up* information (cf. the older *sich auf-raffen*, English *to pluck up one's spirit, courage*). In a similar way *schnallen* denotes understanding as an act of saving perceptions by a buckle (German *Schnalle*). Both words represent the characteristic tendency of young people to express their experiences by striking formulations, which are not yet as worn out as the utterances of adult people.

checken has been taken from the language of engineering. One must think of testing (*checking*) motorcars, aeroplanes and other machines. Today though, Germans can paraphrase an examination of their state of health by a physician as '*Ich lasse mich durch-checken*'. But *checken* as a juvenile term no longer means the procedure, but the positive result of a test. Whoever has 'checked' a piece of information, has already verified it and comprehends its content. Therefore this verb is used only in the past tense. Usual juvenile utterances are: '*Hast du das gecheckt*'? (correspondingly, *gerafft, geschnallt* - in standard language: *verstanden*) - '*Ich habe das gecheckt*'.

3. The influence of technical concepts

The borrowing of figures from engineering is no longer a special mark of juvenile language only. In many domains of life technical concepts are advancing more and more, into our consciousness and into the German colloquial language. Here we need only quote a few examples from various technical domains, which have produced a wide spectrum of metaphors.

The domain of railway has given figures e.g. *Schiene* (*rail*) for the direction of a certain development, or *Weichenstellung* (*throwing the switch*) for a certain decision. The employment of electricity has produced many metaphorical formulations for the denotation of emotions, like *unter Spannung* (*voltage!*) *stehen* for being under strain, or *auf Draht* (*wire*) *sein* for being very attentive. Air traffic has given figures like *Bruchlandung* (*crash landing*) to paraphrase a fiasco, or *Überflieger* (*a plane which flies over sth.*) for a person who outdistances his rivals. The motor industry has produced metaphors like *bremsen* (*to brake*) for going slow or *Gas geben* (*to step on the accelerator*) for speeding up in any action.

The displacement of older, pre-industrial figures for non-technical situations and actions by technical metaphors, is more than a superficial modernisation of linguistic usage. This change transfers fundamentally new concepts to our view of life and consciousness. After many examples of former 'physical' images for intellectual activities (e.g. *be-greifen, er-fahren, er-fassen*), which have become 'dead metaphors' mostly because of their coexistence with more abstract denominations (e.g. *er-innern, ver-innerlichen*), one must expect new perspectives of our comprehension of those activities, if new metaphors from fields of new experiences will become accepted, especially if the figures are still so recent that everyone is aware of their real source. Our first example for the penetration of technical metaphors for understanding was *checken*. Indeed already other technical metaphors beside *checken* are beginning to spread, at first in juvenile language, but more and more in the linguistic usage of adults, too. The computer term *speichern* (*to save*), which at first was a metaphor in the language of computer technology itself, has become a new figure for holding on to any information by a human being, like *behalten* or *sich merken*, since the spread of computer technology in Germany in the late seventies.

Behind this usage of words one can detect a new estimation of learning, which is understood as a nearly mechanical fixation of data. If one names the 'reactivation' of such data (in older terms: *Erinnerung* or *remembrance*) with another computer term like *abrufen* (*to call off*), the human memory seems to lose its creative function, because data saved in a computer memory chip (German *Speicher*), are in fact dead elements without any intellectual activity between input and output.

It may not be surprising that other (provisionally ironic) metaphors begin to complete this conception. In contemporary German colloquial language one can hear that the attempt to forget useless thoughts and impressions is called *'Ich muss meine Festplatte räumen'* (*I have to wipe my computer hard-disc*). The deliberate change of subject in discussion can be described by a formulation like *'Wir wollen ein neues Fenster öffnen'* (*Let us open a new window* - in this case *window* is the well-known computer term, already a metaphor in this technical language). And commonly young people will paraphrase an intellectual break with words like *Chipinfarkt* and *Systemabsturz* (*infarct of a computer chip* resp. *crash of the computer program*).

The preliminary culmination of this development to give intellectual activities a new interpretation is represented by an official term: In the late nineties the Federal Ministry for Research and Technology of the Federal Republic of Germany pleaded that Germany had to be prepared for the coming *Wissensgesellschaft* (= *society of knowledge*). At first sight this term did not seem very exciting; extensive knowledge must be good for any society. But *Wissen* here has another semantic dimension. It means the software of computers (the growing quantity of data and the programs to process them) and the hardware, computer systems, which must become more and more powerful.

The term *Wissensgesellschaft* thus attests that the German verb *wissen* could, like English *to know*, change its meaning by degrees from a denomination of personal experience to a term of technological processing of any information. The Indo-European etymological root of *wissen*, in Greek *oida* = *ich habe erfahren* (*I have come to know*), has to be forgotten completely. Instead of the acquisition of knowledge by personal intellectual work, *wissen* can now mean the quantity of digitalized data stored in computers.

Yet this development must not simply be criticized by arguments of a conservative conception of culture. It must be seen against the background of two various, but related phenomena of cultural and social change. On the one hand, life today generally demands from us the control of ever-growing quantities of data, which nobody can retain without technical help. On the other hand, we have to recognize the growing influence of technology over almost any domain of life. We have explored only a few examples of new metaphors besides the figurative colloquial denominations of intellectual activities. Phrenology in particular operates more and more with electronic models of brain activity, as we saw at the beginning (cf. *cerebral / neuronal network*). Even theories of language production describe the internal procedures as a cooperation of various *modules* in our brain.

It may not surprise us that these factors work together to change the colloquial vocabulary, too. But we need not be anxious that the new technical metaphors for intellectual activities will replace the traditional denominations completely. Perhaps after a certain time the new terms and formulations will be dead metaphors. At least there will be a coexistence of traditional and new technical terms, in a manner similar to the former coexistence of 'physical' and abstract terms. In any case, the increase of terms increases our competence to differentiate in our understanding of the way we understand.

BIBLIOGRAPHY
Keith Spalding, *A Historical Dictionary of German Figurative Usage*. (Oxford: Blackwell, 1959-2000).

Keith Spalding, *Bunte Bilderwelt. Phraseologische Streifzüge durch die deutsche Sprache.* (Tübingen: Gunter Narr, 1996).

F. Dornseiff, *Der deutsche Wortschatz nach Sachgruppen.* (Berlin, 1965).

M. Egerding, *Die Metaphorik der spätmittelalterlichen Mystik.* Vol. 1-2. (Paderborn, 1997).

K. Jakob, *Maschine: mentales Modell - Metapher. Studien zur Semantik und Geschichte der Techniksprache.* (Tübingen, 1991).

F. Kluge, *Etymologisches Wörterbuch der deutschen Sprache.* (Berlin/New York, 1989).

F. Maurer, H. Rupp, (ed.), *Deutsche Wortgeschichte.* Vol. 1-3. (Berlin, 1978).

H. D. Schlosser, 'Technikmetaphern und Technikbewertung'. In: Axel Satzger, (ed.): *Sprache und Technik.* (Frankfurt am Main, 1999).

W. W. Skeat, *An Etymological Dictionary of the English Language.* (Oxford, 1963).

J. Trier, *Der deutsche Wortschatz im Sinnbezirk des Verstandes. Von den Anfängen bis zum Beginn des 13. Jahrhunderts.* (Tübingen, 1931/1973).

Essays of Discovery (II)

FOR MY DEAR, WISE COLLEAGUE, KEITH SPALDING, WITH ADMIRATION AND RESPECT.
SIEGBERT PRAWER,
2002

Muses On the Rhine

John L. Flood

EXACTLY FIVE hundred years ago, in 1503, the teacher and poet Jacob Micyllus (1503-1558) was born at Strasbourg. After being in charge of the Latin school at Frankfurt am Main since 1524, he was appointed, on the recommendation of Philipp Melanchthon, to teach Greek at the University of Heidelberg in 1533. The appointment had not gone entirely smoothly: the Elector Palatine, whose blessing was necessary, had suspected Micyllus of Lutheranism, but he was able to reassure him: 'Ich hab bissher mich der theologeien nichts vnderzogen vnnd mit keynerley sect umbgangen, allein bonis literis vnnd meynem fürgenommenen studio angehangen, wie ich auch fürther zu thun gedenck' [I have had nothing to do with theology hitherto and have not consorted with any sect, but I have devoted myself exclusively to good letters and my chosen subject, as I intend to do henceforth also]. He was indeed devoted to *bonae literae*, and though forgotten now, he was in his day a respected poet. In one of his poems, he laments how uncongenial the present age was for poetry and why there were so few poets.

> Non bene conveniunt trepidae cum carmine cunae,
> non eadem versus cura lucrumque facit.
> Pierides silvas atque otia libera quaerunt
> et tacitas inter flumina sacra vias.
> at fora sollicitae curae populosa frequentant
> et strepitus vulgi iudiciumque colunt.
> hinc est quod raros aetas habet ista poetas
> et nostra nullum carmen ab urbe venit.
> divitias quando solum spectamus et aurum,
> curarum fontes et caput omne mali,
> nec studium recti nec fas laudatur, et omnis
> a pretio virtus famaque victa iacet.[1]

[A rocking cradle does not harmonize with songs, making verses is not consonant with earning money. The Muses need woodlands and leisure and quiet paths between sacred streams. Worries and cares frequent the crowded market-places and they follow the din and opinions of the masses. This is the reason why poets are rare in this age and why no poetry comes from our town. When we focus only on riches and gold, the source of cares and root of evil, the study of what is right and proper is ignored, and virtue and fame are felled by money.]

In another poem, too, Micyllus lambasts the greed of the present 'golden age':

Lucrum est, quod petitur, magnique salaria census,
  Aureaque ista licet saecula iure voces.
[People seek lucre and high salaries, and this age may truly be called a golden age.]

Ironically, for all his high-minded sentiments about preferring good letters to filthy lucre, Micyllus was to quit his professorship at Heidelberg in 1537, finding his salary of sixty, and later eighty, Gulden inadequate to support his large family.

Micyllus dreamt of the tranquil woodlands and quiet paths by sacred rivers for his Muse to flourish. He does not specify a location for this idyll, but there can be little doubt that he sought it in Germany. A few years earlier Conrad Celtis (1459-1508), writing in the warm glow of the rediscovery of Tacitus's *Germania* which gave Germans a real pride in themselves, had spoken of his desire to bring the Muses to Germany, and Sebastian Brant (1458-1521), too, had a vision of them taking up residence on the Rhine.

Celtis, the first German to be crowned imperial poet laureate, by Frederick III in 1487, set his heart on seeing classical tradition take firm root in Germany. His vision of a Roman Empire of the German Nation in cultural and intellectual terms brought him into contact with some of the leading figures of his day, not only a wide range of scholars and writers such as Konrad Peutinger and Hartmann Schedel but even Emperor Maximilian I himself, who proved to be especially receptive to the ideas of this son of a Franconian peasant, involving him in many of his grandiose plans.

In one of his most famous poems, Celtis dreams of Apollo and the Muses coming to Germany:

Ad Apollinem repertorem poetices ut ab Italis ad Germanos veniat

Phoebe, qui blandae citharae repertor,
linque delectos Helicona Pindum et,
ac veni in nostras vocitatus oras
    carmine grato.

Cernis ut laetae properent Camenae
et canunt dulces gelido sub axe.
tu veni incultam fidibus canoris
    visere terram.

Barbarus quem olim genuit, vel acer
vel parens hirtus, Latii leporis
nescius, nunc sic duce te docendus
    dicere carmen

Orpheus qualis cecinit Pelasgis,
quem ferae atroces, agilesque cervi,
arboresque altae nemorum secutae
    plectra moventem.

Tu celer vastum poteras per aequor
laetus a Graecis Latium videre,
invehens Musas, voluisti gratas
    pandere et artes.

Sic velis nostras, rogitamus, oras
Italas ceu quondam aditare terras,
barbarus sermo fugiatque, ut atrum
    subruat omne.[2]

Here, Celtis invites Phoebus, i.e. Apollo, to leave Greece and, summoned by poetry, to come to Germany where the native German muses sing sweetly under a cold sky. May the barbarian learn the art of poetry under Apollo's guidance as Orpheus had once done before the ancient inhabitants of Greece. After all, Apollo had deigned to come to Italy, bringing the Muses with him, so will he please now set foot on German soil to put barbarism and darkness to flight.[3] Indeed, in his poem requesting the laurel from Frederick, he flatters the emperor by asserting that, under him, the Golden Age (*aurea saecula*) has arrived and the Germans are now the heirs of Greece and Rome:

> Te vivo lyricos iam canimus modos
> Et laudata viris plectra prioribus
> Concinnis fidibus pollice tangimus.[4]
> [Under your rule we are singing lyric airs and pluck the harmonious strings with our fingers as the ancients used to do.]

This rosy view contrasted with that of the Italian Humanist Bartolomeo Fonzio (1445-1513) who, dedicating a manuscript to Matthias Corvinus, King of Hungary, in 1488, praised him for granting a safe refuge there to the Muses 'who long ago were driven out of Greece, forsaken by our [Italian] princes, neglected by the French and the Germans'.[5]

At about the same time as Celtis, Sebastian Brant, too, had a vision of the Muses in Germany. This is found in his eulogy of the German invention of the art of printing, a poem addressed to Johannes Bergmann de Olpe, printer of the *Narrenschiff* (1494).

> Quid sibi docta cohors, sibi quid studiosa caterva
>   gratius, utilius commodiusve petet,
> quam sanctum et nuper compertum opus atque litturas
>   quo premere edocuit grammata multa simul?
> quodque prius scripsit vix ullus mille diebus,
>   nunc uno solus hac aget arte die.
> rara fuit quondam librorum copia doctis,
>   rara, inquam, et paucis bibliotheca fuit.
> singula perque olim vix oppida pagina docta:
>   nunc per quasque domos multiplicata iacet.
> nuper ab ingenio Rhenanae gentis et arte
>   librorum emersit copia larga nimis,
> et qui divitibus vix regi obvenerat olim,
>   nunc liber in tenui cernitur esse casa.
> gratia diis primum, mox impressoribus aequa
>   gratia, quorum opera haec prima reperta via est.

quae doctos latuit Graecos Italosque peritos,
    ars nova, Germano venit ab ingenio.
dic age, si quid habes, Latialis cultor agelli
    quod tali invento par sit et aequivalens?
Gallia tuque adeo recta cervice superbam
    quae praefers frontem: par tamen exhibe opus!
dicite si posthac videatur barbara vena
    Germanis, quorum hic prodiit arte labor?
crede mihi, cernes (rumparis, Romule, quamvis)
    pierides Rheni mox colere arva sui,
nec solum insigni probitate excellere et armis
    Germanos: orbis sceptra tenere simul.
quin etiam ingenio, studiis, musisque beatis
    praestare et cunctos vincere in orbe viros.
iam pridem incepit doctos nutrire Platones
    Theutonia: invenies mox quoque Maeonidas.
mox tibi vel Celsum dabimus, iurisque peritum
    Messalam, aut quales Roma vetusta tulit.
iam Cicero in nostra reperitur gente Maroque;
    novimus Ascraei et caecutientis opes.
nil hodie nostram prolem latet atque iuventam,
    Rhenus et Eurotae fert modo noster aquas.
Cyrrha Heliconque sacer nostras migravit ad Alpes,
    Hercynium ingressa est Delphica silva nemus.
iure igitur pineta ferunt laurumque hederamque,
    Rhaetica tellus habet nectar et ambrosiam.
idque impressorum processit ab arte operaque
    nostrorum, hoc fruimur quippe beneficio.
namque volumina tot, totque exemplaria, libros
    praestiterant nobis: gratia multa viris.
magna tibi hos inter debetur gratia, nostra
    fragmina qui multis fors placitura premis;
Religiosa cohors grates aget usque pudicis
    Plus elegia nostris carminibusque piis,
Luxuriosa procum dederit quam turba Catullo,
    Vel tibi, quem pepulit Musa petulca Gethos.[6]

What is more useful to the scholarly world, Brant asks, than the recently invented art of printing. What used to take scribes a thousand days to write, can now be printed in a single day; books, once rare, can now be found in modest homes, thanks to the achievements of Rhinelanders.[7] Germany's genius invented what had remained hidden from Greeks and Italians. What can Italy offer to match this? What has proud France to compare with it? Will she still call Germans barbarians now? Surely Rome will burst with envy when it sees the Muses dwelling on the banks of the Rhine, when it sees Germany not only excelling in loyalty and valour but also ruling the world, surpassing all with its talents and learning and its devotion to the blessed Muses. We have excellent poets and scholars. The Eurotas [the river on which Sparta stood] now mingles with the Rhine, the Helicon [the mountain sacred to Apollo and the Muses] is now part of the Alps, and the sacred grove of Delphi has joined up with the Hercynian Forest of central Germany. There are pinewoods with laurel and ivy,[8] and nectar and ambrosia flow in German lands – all this our printers, whose praises we sing, have made possible.

In a prefatory poem to his *Stultifera navis* (Basle 1487), the Latin translation of Brant's *Narrenschiff*, Jacob Locher (1471–1528) suggests that Brant's skill as a poet is a sign indeed that the Muses have arrived in Germany. (Brant held, after all, the lectureship in poetry at Basle,[9] and his *Narrenschiff* was, in terms of its European impact and thanks to Locher, the most important work of German literature before Goethe's *Werther*.) Locher adds (fol. a3^v):

Iam modo plaude: tuis foelix Germania nymphis
   Quas fontes Rheni Danubiique fovent
Non sumus aversi a musis & Apolline dextro:
   Tangere iam didicit Theutona terra lyram.
[But now, happy Germania, rejoice in your nymphs [i.e. poets], nurtured by the sources of Rhine and Danube; we are not deterred by the Muses, and Apollo is on our side; our German land is now learning to play the lyre.]

An *epigramma* by Thomas Beccadellus, a Fleming who had studied at Bologna, appended to the second 1497 Basle edition of Locher's version, asserts that Italy and Greece must cede the palm to Germany, where the Muses now dwell. Though there are now many laurelled heads there, Brant outshines them all.[10]

Idyllic though the German setting described by Brant may seem, the Muses found it less than congenial – that is, if Hans Sachs (1494-1576) is to be believed: he saw them trailing dejectedly home to Greece. In verses written in 1535 for a broadsheet entitled *Clagred der Neün Muse oder künst vber Teütschlandt*, with a woodcut by the Nuremberg artist Georg Pencz showing the Nine Muses, pale, hungry and bedraggled, emerging in their sandalled feet from a dark, wintry German forest, Sachs has them tell a huntsman they meet that whereas once they had been celebrated and honoured in Germany, they were now unwanted and neglected and so were going home to Greece. The arts are thought worthless, they complain, because they do not generate wealth:

Wer gelt hat / der hat was er will
Derhalb so gilt die kunst nit vil
Weil sie nit treget brot ins hauß
Des seint wir gar gestossen auß
Das vnser fürthin niemandt gert.[11]
[Anyone with money can get what he wants, so learning is held in low esteem because it doesn't bring in the necessities of life. We are utterly rejected so that no one wants anything more to do with us.]

It seems that the complaints that Hans Sachs puts into the mouth of the Muses reflect the general sense of malaise in German humanism in the 1530s, occasioned in part by the Reformation and the unstable political situation of the time, but also by what was seen as the rampant materialism of the Germans and the neglect of the humanities. Although Hans Sachs is unlikely to have had direct knowledge of Micyllus's lament and his unhappy circumstances at Heidelberg, it is almost uncanny how the state of affairs he describes in his verses mirrors the demoralisation so intensely felt by Micyllus and other humanists at the time.

But are things any different now, in Germany or in Britain? *Plus ça change, plus c'est la même chose.*

NOTES

1. Cited after Harry C. Schnur (ed.), *Lateinische Gedichte deutscher Humanisten*. (Stuttgart: Reclam, 1966), p. 298. Micyllus's collected verse was published by his son Julius as *Iacobi Micylli Argentoratensis Sylvarum libri quinque*. [Frankfurt am Main:] P. Braubach, 1564.
2. Felicitas Pindter (ed.), *Conradus Celtis Protucius, Libri odarum quattuor, Libri epodon, Carmen saeculare*. (Leipzig: Teubner 1937), Odes, IV, 5.
3. A similar conceit is found more than two centuries later in a poem submitted to the Teutschübende Poetische Gesellschaft at Leipzig in 1723. Here Apollo, driven out of Greece by barbarians, takes up residence in Germany where he delights in this society at Leipzig. See Detlef Döring, *Die Geschichte der Deutschen Gesellschaft in Leipzig. Von der Gründung bis in die ersten Jahre des Seniorats Johann Christoph Gottscheds*, (Frühe Neuzeit, 70).(Tübingen: Niemeyer 2002), p. 190, n. 2.
4. Odes (ed. Pindter), I, 1.
5. This is Cod. Guelf. 43 Aug. 2° of the Herzog August Bibliothek, Wolfenbüttel. See Wolfgang Milde, *Die Wolfenbütteler Corvinen*, Wolfenbüttel: Herzog August Bibliothek 1995, p. [20].
6. Friedrich Zarncke (ed.), *Sebastian Brants Narrenschiff*. (Leipzig 1854, reprint Hildesheim: Olms 1961), p. 192.
7. He is presumably thinking not only of the inventor Johannes Gutenberg, from Mainz, but also of his successors like Johann Mentelin at Strasbourg and Johann Bergmann at Basle. Celtis, too, was full of praise for 'that German skill which has taught us to write with printed letters' (Odes, I, 1); see also Odes, III, 9.
8. The laurel and ivy, plants mentioned in Virgil's *Eclogues*, were the symbols of the poet.
9. See Joachim Knape, *Dichtung, Recht und Freiheit. Studien zu Leben und Werk Sebastian Brants 1457-1521*, (Saecula spiritalia, 23). (Baden-Baden: Koerner, 1992), pp. 161-72.
10. Fol. 156[r]. See Aurelius Pompen, *The English Versions of 'The Ship of Fools'*, (London: Longmans, 1925), pp. 276-77. Pompen describes the edition in question (which I have not seen) on p. 17.
11. The broadside is reproduced and analysed in my article 'Kultur auf einem dürren Ast. Zu einem Einblattdruck des Hans Sachs.' In: Alan Robertshaw and Gerhard Wolf (eds), *Kultur und Natur in der deutschen Literatur des Mittelalters*. (Tübingen: Niemeyer, 1999), pp. 279-92.

George Berkeley, Rebel Against the Newtonian World Picture

T R Miles (Bangor)

BERKELEY WAS a rebel, and he is therefore an appropriate subject for this volume. It was his fate, like that of many rebels, to be misunderstood during his lifetime. As is clear from his writings, he believed that once people had read them carefully they would be immediately persuaded by them.[1] However, in this he was mistaken - 'some thought him insane, and some that he could not be wholly serious; some thought he was corrupted by an Irish propensity to paradox and novelty'.[2]

As a result of the scientific revolution which took place in the West about the time of the 17th century, educated thinkers had come to accept a particular view as to what the world was like. This was the 'Newtonian world picture' referred to in the title. Sir Isaac Newton (1642-1727) had been influential in shaping it, and it is a view which, more especially, found expression in the writings of John Locke (1632-1704), whose influence on Berkeley was considerable.

Some of the central beliefs of the time were as follows: the world was made up of solid bodies - 'material substances' - which interact with each other in accordance with the laws of Newtonian mechanics. Moreover, when they impinged on an observer's sense organs, they were the cause of 'ideas' in that observer's mind. The qualities inherent in these material substances could be *primary* (extension, figure, shape and motion), and *secondary* (colour, warmth, taste and smell); the latter did not themselves inhere in matter but were the consequences of the ways in which the particles of matter (atoms) were arranged.

Berkeley, who lived from 1685 to 1752, took the view that this world picture was fundamentally flawed. In particular he believed that it could give comfort to the opponents of religion and that it led to scepticism about the possibility of knowledge. If the world was a self-contained structure operating in accordance with mechanical laws, there was no room for the activities of a Divine Providence or for belief in immaterial souls; and if the 'material substance' of the physicists - 'philosophers' in Berkeley's terminology - was the source of ideas in our minds, it seemed to follow that this 'material substance', in that it lay behind or beyond our ideas, must remain for ever unknown.

Berkeley believed that the solution to these difficulties lay in the formula *esse est percipi* - 'to exist is to be perceived'. (He makes clear that this formula applies only to objects of sense and not to the percipient). 'The table I write on, I say, exists, that is, I see and feel it; and if I were out of my study I should say, I might perceive it, or that some other spirit actually does perceive it'.[3]

In addition, 'Besides that endless variety of ideas or objects of knowledge there is likewise something which knows or perceives them [...]. This perceiving active being is what I call *mind, spirit, soul*; or *myself*. By which words I do not denote any one of my ideas, but a thing entirely distinct from them.'[4]

Berkeley maintains that the only causal agents are spirits: 'the fire which I see is not the cause of the pain I suffer on approaching it, but the mark that forewarns me of it'.[5] 'It is the searching after and endeavouring to understand those signs instituted by the Author of Nature, that ought to be the employment of the natural philosopher and not attempting to explain things by corporeal causes'.[6]

Berkeley proposed what we would now call a programme of *conceptual revision*. 'We are not deprived of any one thing in nature';[7] it is rather that we need to talk about the world in a different way. Because the things around us are not causal agents but are passive, Berkeley proposes that they be called 'ideas' rather than 'things'; the investigations into them are then said to be carried out 'by way of idea'.

In choosing this terminology Berkeley was well aware that it might be misunderstood;[8] and there are in fact various substitutions which may be helpful to a modern reader in clarifying Berkeley's intentions. For 'spirit' or 'soul' it may be helpful to substitute 'observer'; for 'ideas' one can quite well substitute 'things', with the proviso that they are not considered as causal agents. By the expression 'existing in the mind', as he himself makes clear, is meant only that the mind perceives them.[9] 'Existing in the mind' could be understood to mean 'illusory'; this was not Berkeley's intention, though even Kant misunderstood him on this point.[10]

Berkeley believed that his views provided a refutation of both scepticism and an anti-religious view of the world. If we dispense with the concept of *material substance* lying behind or beyond the things which we perceive, there are no longer any grounds for concern about how we would ever come to know about such things. As for religion, it follows on his view that there is a place for design and intelligence in the world, for free will, and for belief in the immateriality of the soul.[11] 'When the corner-stone [i.e. belief in material substance] is once removed the whole fabric cannot but choose to fall to the ground'.[12]

His claim that there has to be an omnipresent observer to ensure the continuity of things when no one else is observing them has not, in general, found much favour. This, however, does not detract from the value of his other insights.

Similar issues to those in the *Principles* are also discussed in the *Three Dialogues Between Hylas and Philonous*. Hylas is the spokesman for the educated scientist of the day, Philonous the spokesman for Berkeley himself.

The theme of scepticism runs through all three dialogues. Philonous maintains that it is his own views which represent common sense and that it is those of Hylas which lead to scepticism. At the start of the First Dialogue both agree that 'that view shall be taken as true which is nearest to common sense and furthest from scepticism'.[13] At one point, on the basis of recent physics, Hylas argues that sound is a wave motion through the air, and Philonous then gets him to agree that it is the senses of sight and touch which detect motion; this leads to the conclusion that 'real' sounds may be seen and felt but never heard. Philonous then says, 'I imagine myself to have gained no small point, since you make so light of departing from common phrases'.[14] In the Third Dialogue Hylas is led to the admission that about the 'real nature' of things he can know nothing at all.[15] Philonous then argues that these absurd consequences are the result of belief in *material substance*.

The First Dialogue also contains Philonous' arguments that primary qualities are observer-dependent no less than secondary qualities.

Berkeley's attack on the notion of 'abstract ideas' in the Introduction to the *Principles* is what we would now think of as an elucidation of the concept of *meaning*. If we consider the meaning of general words - man, triangle, motion, etc. - it is wrong to suppose that these words 'stand for' an abstract general idea; we learn their meaning by being exposed to particular examples; thus there is no 'abstract general idea' of a motion which is 'neither slow nor swift, curvilinear nor rectilinear'.[16] All this is part of Berkeley's programme 'to rid the first principles of our knowledge from the embarrass and delusion of words'.[17] 'He that knows he has no other than particular ideas, will not puzzle himself in vain to find out and conceive the abstract idea annexed to any name. And he that knows words do not always stand for ideas will spare himself the labour of looking for ideas where there are none to be had'.[18]

Berkeley also makes a contribution towards solving what has more recently been called the 'mind-body' problem. On the traditional view, which is formulated by Hylas at the start of the Second Dialogue, material objects acting on the brain give rise to 'impressions' (or 'ideas') in the mind. However, as Philonous points out, the brain itself, like any other object in nature, is investigated 'by way of idea', from which it follows that the causal relationship asserted by Hylas is impossible. In any case, as Philonous rhetorically asks, 'What relation is there between a motion of the nerves and a sensation of sound or colour in the mind?'[19] Finally, and more speculatively, it is possible to see in Berkeley the forerunner of modern behaviourism. At first glance this may seem an absurd suggestion, since the typical behaviourist[20] is thought to deny the existence of 'minds', whereas, on the contrary, Berkeley denies the existence of 'matter'. This 'denial of existence' idiom, however, is potentially misleading. Many conceptual reformers have found it difficult to rid themselves of the influence of the views which they are apparently rejecting. This seems to be true of both Berkeley and Watson. It was Ryle[21] who explicitly pointed out that to talk of 'two types of entity', 'mental entities' and 'physical entities', each having an 'absolute existence', can be called a 'category mistake'. To elaborate on one of his examples, someone ignorant of cricket might speak of 'bat' and 'ball' and then ask, 'Now show me the team spirit': it is not that team spirit does not 'exist' (it may or may not do so on a given occasion), but it would be a category mistake to put 'team spirit' in the same logical category as 'bat' and 'ball'.

What is interesting is that there is a foreshadowing of this idea in Berkeley. This is illustrated in particular by the following passage:

> After what hath been said, it is I suppose plain that our souls are not to be known in the same way as senseless inactive objects or by way of *idea*. *Spirits* and *ideas* are things so wholly different that when we say, *They exist, they are known*, or the like, these words should not be thought to signify any thing common to both natures. There is nothing alike or common in them, and to expect that by any enlargement of our faculties, we may be expected to know a spirit as we do a triangle, seems as absurd as if we should hope to *see a sound*.[22]

Some of the similarities between Berkeley and Ryle were noted in a paper by the present author; and the following passage is perhaps worth repeating:

> On this interpretation what both Berkeley and Ryle are attacking is a 'two-world' theory, in which we are required to believe in two separate *kinds of substance* or *kinds of existence*. It is this view which constitutes the 'category mistake' which both philosophers are attacking.[23]

Berkeley was, indeed, a rebel, but he was not the madman which he was alleged to be by some of his contemporaries. It is a sign of his greatness that one can continually return to his writings and find all kinds of new insights.

NOTES

Where page numbers are given they refer to the Collins Fontana 1962 edition of Berkeley's writings edited by G. J. Warnock.

1 *Principles*, Preface.
2 Warnock, p. 34.
3 *Principles*, section 3.
4 Ibid., section 2.
5 Ibid., section 65.
6 Ibid., section 66.

7 Ibid., section 34.
8 Ibid., Preface.
9 *3rd Dialogue*, p. 243.
10 I. Kant, *Critique of Pure Reason*, 'Refutation of Idealism'.
11 *Principles*, section 93.
12 Ibid., section 92.
13 *1st Dialogue*, p. 151.
14 Ibid., pp. 151-3.
15 *3rd Dialogue*, p. 216.
16 *Principles*, Introduction, section 10.
17 Ibid., section 25.
18 Ibid., section 24.
19 *2nd Dialogue*, pp. 193-4.
20 J. B. Watson, *Behaviourism*. (Kegan Paul, Trench Trubner & Co., 1925).
21 G. Ryle, *The Concept of Mind*. (Hutchinson, 1949).
22 *Principles*, section 142.
23 T. R. Miles, 'Berkeley and Ryle: Some Comparisons', *Philosophy*, xxviii, 104 (1953), 58-71.

Satire and Subversion: Nestroy and Paul de Kock

W E Yates (Exeter)

THE JULY revolution of 1830 in Paris generated shock waves throughout Europe. One effect was a turning-point in the political life of Vienna, a sharpening in discontent that would eventually culminate in the Revolution of 1848. A related turning-point can be observed in the theatrical culture of the city: not just in the Burgtheater, the court theatre, whose veteran guiding spirit and effective artistic director, Joseph Schreyvogel, was dismissed in 1832, but also in the commercial theatres. If the 1820s had been the decade of Adolf Bäuerle and Ferdinand Raimund, the engagement of Nestroy in 1831 by Carl Carl, the new director of the Theater an der Wien, signalled a more unsentimental and iconoclastic spirit both in performance and in playwriting. At the same time the predominantly inward-looking tradition of Viennese dialect comedy began to be opened up - part of a wider internationalization of cultural horizons driven by the expansion of the press and the increase in travel, the latter thanks not least to the spread of the railway network. It is indicative that when Grillparzer visited Paris and London in 1836, going to the theatre frequently in both and recording his experiences in a fascinating and detailed diary of his journey, he found familiar material in both cities. Increasingly Vienna too was open to international influence, and Nestroy drew sources both from the Parisian stage, which was regularly covered in Vienna in reports in Bäuerle's *Theaterzeitung*, and to a lesser extent also from the London theatre.

The influence of the Parisian stage in mid-century was so powerful that eventually, partly as a result of the inadequate protection of copyright, the London stage was practically swamped by adaptations from Paris.[1] The Viennese, jealous of the unique local tradition of comedy, also felt under threat. When Carl Carl took over the Theater in der Leopoldstadt, which had been Raimund's theatre, in December 1838, the Viennese press carried increasingly sharp attacks on his direction. Accusations that he was debasing standards were linked with accusations of indecency, which were levelled in particular against Nestroy both as author and as actor and were often associated with criticisms of his use of Parisian material. It is true that between 1840 and 1850 no fewer than eleven new Nestroy plays were based on sources that belonged to the genre of the *comédie-vaudeville* then fashionable in Paris; in fact, however, what can be observed in Nestroy's adaptation of French sources is a remarkable independence in spirit from the material he reworked.

French sources came to the notice of Viennese playwrights in various ways.[2] They could be available from a theatrical agency such as that of Adalbert Prix, whose office also acted as a translation bureau. The *Theaterzeitung* regularly carried reports of recent successes in Paris, including outlines of the plot. There were performances by touring French companies that could be visited in Vienna itself (this was how operetta came to Vienna in the 1850s and early 1860s). Or theatre directors could pick up tips on visits to Paris. Carl Carl undertook just such a journey of discovery in the late summer of 1840. One consequence was his introduction to Vienna of a local form of 'vaudeville', comedies with a number of songs, adapted from French originals for performance starring the singer and actress Ida Brüning-Wohlbrück. Carl's intention was different from Nestroy's; he saw this variety of 'vaudeville' as supplementing or even replacing traditional Viennese dialect comedy, which he judged had reached a dead end. This is spelt out in an unpublished letter written on 25 March 1844 by his wife, Margaretha Carl, to the actress and theatre director Charlotte Birch-Pfeiffer. Carl's purpose, she explained, was not to recreate the Parisian *vaudeville* but to take over an 'interesting' plot, add attractive songs, and so satisfy the craving of the theatre public for entertainment, in a way that would also contribute to improving the moral tone of the commercial theatre: 'Carl hat sich überzeugt daß die Posse zu sehr ausartete, und immer gemeiner wurde; er wollte ein Gegengewicht aufstellen, das ebenfalls Glück machen, und jene wieder nach und nach in sittliche Schranken heben sollte'[3] ['Carl has convinced himself that local farce was degenerating too far and was becoming ever more vulgar; he wanted to counterbalance it with something that would be equally successful and gradually elevate the moral level of local farce to an acceptable standard'].

Carl, whose fortune was underpinned by Nestroy's popularity, clearly underestimated him - or was anxiously conscious of the possible effects of any decline in that popularity. Five years later, when Nestroy had a brief run of box-office failures, Margaretha Carl - again presumably echoing her husband's view - was quick to inform Charlotte Birch-Pfeiffer that Nestroy had lost steam and that his time was past.[4] In fact the box-office successes kept coming; the letter of 25 March 1844, indeed, was written only a fortnight before the première of one of his most successful plays, *Der Zerrissene*. The source in that case was a *comédie-vaudeville* by two quite well-known minor playwrights, Duvert and Lauzanne, entitled *L'Homme blasé*. (This play also spawned an adaptation in London, *Used up*, a 'petit comedy' that was probably written partly by Dion Boucicault, partly by Charles Mathews junior, and was produced in the Theatre Royal, Haymarket, in February 1844, starring Mathews in the central part.)

The playwright whose work Nestroy most frequently mined, however, was one of the most popular authors of the time, Charles Paul de Kock (1794–1871), a prominent figure in Paris both as a playwright and as a novelist. One of the most widely read French novelists of the 1830s and 1840s (he was, indeed, one of the favourite novelists of no less a reader than Karl Marx, who was in Paris from 1843 onwards),[5] he was best known for his light and slightly risqué novels; and in collaboration with other authors he also wrote over two hundred plays for the commercial stage between 1818 and 1870. Gautier, one of the most astute and readable critics of the time, wrote of his popularity in his review of one of the plays that Nestroy drew on, a *comédie-vaudeville* entitled *Moustache*: Paul de Kock was 'the most popular writer in France', whose success outdid that of Hugo, Musset, George Sand and 'all the great geniuses of the age' ['l'écrivain le plus populaire de France, et dont le succès éclipse celui de Victor Hugo, d'Alfred de Musset, de Georges Sand et de tous les génies supérieurs de l'époque'].[6]

Kock's early novels appeared both singly and in a thirty-volume collected edition, *Œuvres de Paul de Kock*, published by Barba (Paris, 1835–1840), and further collected editions followed into the early twentieth century. Once issued, the novels would be recycled in dramatic form to provide light-weight entertainment for the Parisian commercial theatre. These plays were generally the product of collaboration between Kock himself and one or more other playwrights, a process of routine manufacture characteristic of the commercial theatre in nineteenth-century Paris.[7] Many of the novels were also translated into German, a familiar feature of the publishing scene in the first half of the nineteenth century.[8] The German versions are often very shoddily written, but they too enjoyed considerable popularity and appeared in several collected editions,[9] most notably published by two rival firms, Rieger (Stuttgart) and Nübling (Ulm). They brought Kock into disfavour with critics suspicious of portrayals of loose living in the French capital.[10] Nestroy had from the early 1830s onwards been subject to repeated criticism for his aggressively suggestive acting; his use of this suspect source material attracted further criticism, especially at a time when critics were looking nostalgically back on what they extolled as the edifying comedy of the Raimund years and were eager to defend indigenous dialect comedy against the influence of foreign traditions.

Nestroy based at least four plays on works by Paul de Kock. The first was *Glück, Mißbrauch und Rückkehr* (1838). The plot derives from a novel *La Maison blanche* (1836), which was available in two German translations under the title *Das weiße Haus*. It was one of Nestroy's biggest hits, both in Vienna and on tour, but was inevitably criticised because of its provenance: it would have been preferable, one critic wrote, for Nestroy to have 'drawn his material from a purer source' especially since Kock's reputation was 'not particularly good even among the French' ['Es wäre wohl zu wünschen gewesen, wenn Hr. Nestroy aus reinerer Quelle seinen Stoff geschöpft hätte, als aus dieser, selbst bei den Franzosen nicht besonders im guten Geruche stehenden'].[11] Later the same year, *Gegen Thorheit giebt es kein Mittel*, much less successful at the box-office, was based on another novel, *Ni jamais, ni toujours* (1835), which was available in a German version, *Weder: Nie! noch: Immerfort! ist der Liebe Losungswort*. It can be assumed that Nestroy used the German versions in both these cases.

In 1841 another of his biggest hits, still one of his most-performed plays even today, *Das Mädl aus der Vorstadt*, was based on what had originally been a novel, *La jolie femme du faubourg*, the first German translation of the novel appeared in 1840. In this case, however, the version he used is known to have been the *comédie-vaudeville* composed in the same year and under the same title by Kock and Varin; a draft, half paraphrase, half adaptation, in

Nestroy's hand has survived. The final play derived from Kock, *Die beiden Herrn Söhne*, was written in 1844 and performed early in 1845 - this time unsuccessfully. That Kock was named as Nestroy's source on the theatre-bill was a hostage to fortune: the critics, especially the reviewer in M.G. Saphir's journal *Der Humorist*, pounced on the connection, asking what else one could expect of a playwright who sought his material in the novels of Paul de Kock.[12]

As with *Das Mädl aus der Vorstadt*, Nestroy used not the novel (*L'Homme de la nature et l'homme policé*, 1831), which in this case had not been translated into German, but the dramatic offshoot, a comedy first performed and published in 1832, on which Kock collaborated with Charles-Désiré Dupeuty. Moreover, this was not Nestroy's sole debt to Kock in the play: there are borrowings both from the novel *Moustache* (1838) and from the dramatization by Kock and Varin which was performed and published the same year. It was not the first time Nestroy had used material drawn from Paul de Kock over and above the main source: a comedy *Un bon enfant* (1833) by Kock and the brothers Cogniard seems to have served as a secondary source for *Glück, Mißbrauch und Rückkehr*.[13]

The critics - how could it have been otherwise under the strict censorship imposed in Metternich's Austria? - were for the most part both politically and aesthetically conservative. They were watchful of the theatre's role as a 'moral institution', committed to a notion of moral comedy that upheld rather than disturbing the social fabric, and nostalgic for the less aggressive popular comedy of the 1820s.[14] There was every reason for their suspicion of Nestroy: he was a satirist in a new mould, and the impact of his voice would later be reflected in the later claims of Laube and others that his influence helped to make possible the Revolution of 1848. But Paul de Kock's novels were not the stuff of revolution; the critics' charge that Nestroy was using 'impure' material masks political fears, dressed up in terms of moral outrage.

What Nestroy did was to use material drawn from Kock, whether from his novels or from his comedies, and fashion it to the needs of Carl's company, shaping plots to the players at his disposal; an example is the significant addition in *Das Mädl aus der Vorstadt* of the figure of the draper Knöpfl as a role for the actor Louis Grois. In the process he transformed his material into satire - at best, sharp satire - of mid-century Vienna. *Das Mädl aus der*

Vorstadt provides, indeed, the clearest illustration of how, far from corrupting the Viennese stage with imported immorality, he transformed his sources into moral comedy.

Even in 1841, however, he was criticised for using immoral material: the second act, which is set in Knöpfl's workshop and shows seamstresses awaiting male visitors and angling for suitors, was described by a prominent critic, Emanuel Straube (who after the Revolution would serve as a censor) as 'bordering on the lascivious' ['obwohl die Situation [...] ziemlich hart an das Lascive streift'].[15] The situation was indeed risqué: that was the point, for what Nestroy is satirising is the double standards of morality rife in Vienna, which underlay the exploitation of the seamstresses and their like - a point enforced by a solo scene (I, 13) inserted for the sparky actress Elise Rohrbeck in the role of Frau von Erbsenstein, who is given a satirical song precisely about double standards to add what one might almost call a proto-feminist perspective on the inequality that obtained between the sexes.

Nestroy was a natural parodist, whose adaptation of his sources is always informed by a parodist's critical watchfulness. In *Das Mädl aus der Vorstadt* he has transformed his source, as he did all his sources, satirising the hypocrisies of his time, which expressed themselves in the linguistic falsity and hollow clichés that he characteristically exposes. But the result is a subversion not of the original nor even of a tradition of comedy but of the society from which Nestroy's own theatre public, and his critics, were drawn.

NOTES

1. See John Russell Stephens, *The Profession of Playwright. British Theatre 1800–1900* (Cambridge: Cambridge University Press, 1992), pp. 102–03.
2. For more detail see my 'Paul de Kock und Nestroy. Zu Nestroys Bearbeitung französischer Vorlagen', *Nestroyana*, 16 (1996), 26–39.
3. Deutsches Theatermuseum, Munich: VIII 10274.
4. Deutsches Theatermuseum, Munich: VIII 10275 (letter of 12 April 1850).
5. See S. S. Prawer, *Karl Marx and World Literature* (Oxford: Oxford University Press, 1976), pp. 255–56, 318–19, 410.
6. Théophile Gautier, *Histoire de l'art dramatique en France depuis vingt-cinq ans*, 6 vols (Paris and Leipzig: Hetzel, 1858–59), I, 153.

7 See F. W. J. Hemmings, *The Theatre Industry in Nineteenth-Century France* (Cambridge: Cambridge University Press, 1993), pp. 247–56.
8 See Norbert Bachleitner, 'Übersetzungsfabriken. Das deutsche Übersetzungswesen in der ersten Hälfte des 19. Jahrhunderts', *Internationales Archiv für Sozialgeschichte der deutschen Literatur*, 14/1 (1989), 1–49; Bernd Kortländer, 'Übersetzen – "würdigstes Geschäft" oder "widerliches Unwesen". Zur Geschichte des Übersetzens aus dem Französischen ins Deutsche in der 1. Hälfte des 19. Jahrhunderts', *Forum Vormärz Forschung*, Jahrbuch 1995 (*Journalliteratur im Vormärz*, 1996), 179–203.
9 See Hans Fromm, *Bibliographie deutscher Übersetzungen aus dem Französischen*, 6 vols (Baden-Baden: Verlag für Kunst und Wissenschaft, 1950–53), III, 418–30.
10 See A. G. Polz, 'Paul de Kock', *Der Humorist*, 19 and 21 January 1839, reprinted in: Nestroy, *Sämtliche Werke*, hist.-krit. Ausgabe, ed. by Jürgen Hein, Johann Hüttner, Walter Obermaier, W. E. Yates [hereafter: HKA], *Stücke 17/II*, ed. by W. E. Yates (Vienna: Deuticke, 1998), pp.162–63.
11 ch l— [= Wilhelm Schlesinger], *Der Humorist*, 14 March 1838, reprinted in HKA, *Stücke 14*, ed. by W. E. Yates (Vienna: Jugend und Volk, 1982), p. 171).
12 —l—, *Der Humorist*, 18 January 1845, reprinted in HKA, *Stücke 22*, ed. by W. E. Yates (Vienna: Deuticke, 1996), p. 186.
13 See Friedrich Walla, '"Da werden doch die deutschen Affen nicht lange zurückbleiben" – Neue französische Quellen zu Stücken Johann Nestroys', *Etudes Germaniques*, 51 (1996), 283–305 (pp. 295–97).
14 See my *Nestroy and the Critics* (Columbia, SC: Camden House, 1994), pp. 2-9, and Martin Stern, 'Die Nestroy-Polemik des deutschen Vormärz - Vorspiel des "Poetischen Realismus"', in *Johann Nepomuk Nestroy: Tradizione e trasgressione*, ed. by Gabriella Rovagnati (Milan: C.U.E.M., 2002), pp. 43–60.
15 *Wiener Zeitschrift für Literatur, Kunst, Theater und Mode*, 27 November 1841, reprinted in HKA, *Stücke 17/II*, pp.179–80. On the satirical thrust of the play see more fully *Stücke 17/II*, 152–61, and my 'Sex in the Suburbs: Nestroy's Comedy of Forbidden Fruit', *Modern Language Review*, 92 (1997), 379–91.

Musings on Muses:
Poems by Goethe, Rilke and Bachmann and an Essay by Anne Duden

Elizabeth Boa (Nottingham)

IN AN ESSAY of 1823 Goethe writes of repeated reflections ('wiederholte Spiegelungen'): a youthful ideal returns reflected in memory later in life to the poet who externalises it in words, so creating an after-image which will radiate out to affect also the reader.[1] At the end, Goethe extends the idea from personal psychology to define tradition as a process of mutual reflection between life and art: literature arises as the heightened reflection of experience, distilling the essential from the contingent; conversely experience, as we reflect on it in imagination, is in turn heightened and given meaning by the cultural texts. Goethe's repeated reflections are a kind of quotation which is at the same time an act of transformation: citation of past texts transforms immediate experience and immediate experience in turn breathes new life into the cultural heritage. I want here to look at how repeated reflections of the Muse as a motif drawn from the Classical tradition appear in three modern poems. My concern is with the gendering of cultural creativity. As Christa Reinig once said, literature has for millennia been 'harte Männersache'.[2] Men have held up the mirror to nature to reflect woman in the mirror of the male imagination and have symbolised the inspiring power of the reflected image in the figure of a goddess.

As goddesses, the Classical Muses represent the Olympian realm which men aspire to in creating poetry or drama, music, dance, or astronomy. In modern love poetry, however, the mythic figure often overlaps with the beloved. The Muses are closely associated with Eros, the god of love: sexual creation requires the union of male and female; likewise the act of cultural creation requires an opening to the other or a coming together, whether of human and divine, of man and nature, of male and female. Creative man finds his complementary other in allegorical goddesses; the problems arise when the allegory becomes human. In Goethe's age, the humanisation of the Muse as the beloved reflects the rising status of women as bourgeois affective individualism undermined traditional patriarchy and young men resisted their fathers, claiming the right to marry for love. And as the late Enlightenment, *Empfindsamkeit* and the first stirrings of Romantic sensibility intertwine, the traditionally feminine values of emotion, intuition, and closeness to nature came increasingly to be seen as necessary to creativity. But this revaluation often took the form of a kind of colonisation as men claimed to discover the feminine side of their own nature rather than nurturing the cultural creativity of their daughters, sisters and wives by opening up education, the arts and sciences to women. The historical field is too complex to be summarised here and still leave time for poems. So let me turn to my first example, Goethe's Fifth Roman Elegy.

In this poem woman as beloved and woman as Muse overlap ambiguously. The beloved woman awakens the erotic vitality which will fuel artistic creation. But even in the midst, or is it the aftermath, of love-making, the woman begins to transmute into a marble statue under the poet's synaesthetically feeling eye and seeing hand. Aesthetic contemplation is still mingled with erotic desire, but to be fully effective as poetic Muse the woman must either be absent or at least asleep, for whereas sculpture requires the presence of the model, writing is a solitary activity: making love or even conversation ('es wird vernünftig gesprochen'[3]) cannot happen simultaneously with writing. In the latter part of the poem, the beloved is asleep, allowing her lover's thoughts to turn more decisively from the erotic to the aesthetic and from sculpture to poetry as the poet quotes the rhythmic measure of his chosen form on the beloved's backbone, turning her body into poetic text. At the end, however, as her breath glowingly penetrates the poet's breast, the statuesque or textualised figure turns back into a live woman whose breath literally inspires. Thus the poem discreetly cites the myth of Pygmalion and Galatea, the statue come to life. Pygmalion is an archetype of creative men through the ages who have made the images of women which the poet recalls in caressing his lover's marmorealised body. Thus tradition is handed down through a male artistic fraternity: men make images which they recall in imagination, so aestheticising the female body and heightening its beauty, which in turn inspires further creation in the spiral of repeated reflections. The woman's ambiguous value as Muse and beloved, as image and breathing woman, keeps tradition alive: she introduces life, *Originalität* as nature. In her bodily presence, she interrupts textual repetition, bringing refreshment and renewal to the Classical tradition and saving it from mere imitative academicism. The Muse as living woman *and* as image handed down is thus a key bearer of Goethe's poetic ambition to harmonise the Classical heritage with modern sensibility. Goethe's humanised Muse is a conservative device allowing the poet to side-step Oedipal struggle with his poetic fathers of the kind which Harold Bloom has written of and the poem ends on a statement of brotherhood with the triumvirate of Roman forebears.[4] The Roman Elegies mark a shift from the overweening defiance of the *Sturm und Drang*. Perhaps even reactionary if seen within the history of anti-patriarchal revolt of the sons, the cycle is more ambiguous within a history of the daughters in expressing a gentler mood with some space for relations with an actual woman, albeit one with marmoreal tendencies.

A less benign reading of Pygmalion and Galatea would suggest, however, that there is no real woman: the statue who comes to life, like Hoffmann's Olimpia in *Der Sandmann*, is perhaps just a further outgrowth of the male imagination. Any real woman would quickly cease to inspire after the first fine careless rapture. A surer way than relying long-term on a real woman as Muse is for the Muse to do her inspiring work and then die, so making way for a successor - the eternal feminine in serial instantiation. In *Die Wahlverwandtschaften*, Ottilie is not a statue come to life, but a woman turned post-mortem into a statuesque effigy.[5] As a writer of a journal *in* the text, she is a female alter ego of the male author *of* the text. But Ottilie's writing consists mainly of quotations from men, for as a woman she has no tradition as writing subject, only as the object of writing or painting by men. Ottilie also fails as a surrogate mother ('scheinbare Mutter') when she juggles with another woman's baby and someone else's book, dropping the former in the water to drown. A failed writer and woman, Ottilie turns post-mortem into a mythic goddess, her dead face repeated in the painted angels she has inspired a mediocre artist to paint. Thus Goethe disposes with bitter scepticism of the new Romantic ideals of creative woman and feminine creativity in man and unmasks the figure of the Muse as an instrumentalisation of woman as raw material for their art by male artists like himself.[6]

One last point about the Fifth Roman Elegy: until recently, biological creation required the injection of a substance from a male into a female body. Here the substance is breath entering a breast, presumably by way of the nostrils. Reversing male impregnation of the female, the woman's breath penetrates the male poet who will undertake the process of poetic gestation and suffer the creative birth pains. In the second poem in Rilke's first cycle of sonnets to Orpheus, not just her inspiring breath but the whole Muse, embodied as a girl, enters the poet through another orifice and curls up embryo-like in his ear. To turn from Classical Goethe to Modernist Rilke is to enter an age when gender discourse, an arena of new thinking in Goethe's time, had long been the field of battle between, but also within, the sexes as the shifting boundaries of sexual difference were blurred or re-asserted. Orpheus was the son of Calliope, Muse of epic poetry, and through his emblematic instrument, the lyre, is associated with music and the lyric mode in poetry. Dead Eurydice is the Muse of Orphic poetry as lament. Moreover, according to Hesiod, the Muses are the daughters of Zeus and Mnemosyne, the Goddess of memory. In memorialising the dead, the elegiac mode lends the dead a shadowy life in the poet's text and the reader's imagination. More gloomily, though, the myth also suggests that texts and statues can never really bring the dead back to life. The second sonnet conveys this tragic insight in the figure of the wraith-like almost-girl who is summoned up through the union of song and lyre, but at the end is falling away again. The almost-girl evokes both Rilke's immediate Muse, Wera Ouckama Knoop whose early death at the age of nineteen inspired the cycle, and her archetype Eurydice. A further intertext, evoked in the motif of the 'Frühlingsschleier', and the trees and meadows, is surely Botticelli's La Primavera. Thus like Goethe's evocation of classical statuary, Rilke too engages in ekphrastic quotation of visual art. The Primavera, and beyond her Persephone, evoke cyclic return so enabling Eurydice and the other dead girl to be summoned back, for a moment, to wraith-like existence in the poem. Thus like Goethe's Elegy, this poem too effects a reconciliation between originality and tradition, by way not of a live woman but of a dead girl. As composite Muse, Eurydice and the dead girl pass from the God to the poet as the god-created gift of poetry. Like Goethe's sleeping beloved, the imaginary girl is asleep. Better still, she does not go in even for sensible conversation: 'Singender Gott, wie hast / du sie vollendet, daß sie nicht begehrte, / erst wach zu sein? Sieh, sie erstand und schlief.'[7] As a woman reader, these beautiful yet irritating lines induce in me the squinting look which Sigrid Weigel has argued afflicts women as writers.[8] With the sleeping Muse as ear-plug, no distracting chatter from an actual woman can divert attention from the dream within in its double envelope of the poet's womb-like ear enclosing the embryonic girl who in turn is a second womb enclosing the dream. Thus the girl in the ear serves as birth-channel for Rilke's lyric subject in giving birth to his poem. To mix my metaphors, the girl, created from the Orphic union of song and lyre, provides the ear-trumpet, so to speak, through which male god speaks to male poet. Thus Rilke incorporates the feminine and mythologises a dead girl. But at the end, the almost-girl begins to sink away again for poetry cannot bring the dead back to life: the Muse cannot *be* the woman. This acknowledgement, a step beyond the illusory real woman returning to life in Goethe's poem, marks the sensibility of a later age when the instrumentalisation of woman as Muse was becoming more problematic.

Rilke is the paradigm androgyne poet in whom masculine and feminine mix. In 1971, just as the so-called second wave of feminist agitation was breaking, Ingeborg Bachmann published her novel *Malina* about a woman author and her male alter ego, the eponymous Malina, in an exploration from a woman's viewpoint of androgynous creativity. Here Eurydice claims the Orphic position of writing subject, perhaps in answer to Bachmann's own poem of twenty years earlier, 'Dunkles zu sagen' (1952). For in this earlier poetological meditation, the lyric subject identifies with Orpheus, and the beloved other is Eurydice: 'Wie Orpheus spiel ich / auf den Saiten des Lebens den Tod ...'[9] Goethe's Muse offers a double gift which the poet transmutes into poetry: her sleeping body recalls the Classical tradition and her breath inspires new feeling in his breast. This is subtly changed in Bachmann's poem: 'Die Saite des Schweigens / gespannt auf die Welle von Blut,/ griff ich dein tönendes Herz'. Here the emotion, which the poet turns into poetry, sounds first in the Muse's heart, so gendering Nietzsche's Dionysos/Apollo dualism as a feminine expressive core, the sounding heart, and a masculine formal impulse, the lyre strings. The division is similar to that in Rilke's poem between the dream in the ear to which the Orphic poet will lend form. Bachmann's poem laments the division - 'Und ich gehör dir nicht zu. / Beide klagen wir nun.' - but reaches a paradoxical resolution in that Eurydice's closed eye is yet blue like a sky within the lyric subject, an image similar to the springtime motifs in Rilke's sonnet. Twenty years on, Bachmann's novel ends on a less reconciliatory note, for the first-person female narrator - Eurydice-as-subject - after a musical exchange with Malina, is finally dispatched behind the wall and her Orpheus is one of the prime suspects in this murder of the feminine. 'Dunkles zu sagen' deploys ancient figures of masculine activity, intellect, creativity set over against the feminine passion which must be sublimated or even killed off to produce the poetic text, for writing and love, as even Goethe's poem shows, cannot happen simultaneously. Bachmann's poem exemplifies the invasive power of the masculine subject-position for a woman seeking to engage in the 'harte Männersache' of poetry, a power which Bachmann would later analyse in Malina's dominance of *Ich*.

Anne Duden's essay 'Vom Versprechen des Schreibens und vom Schreiben des Versprechens' (1998), may serve as an epilogue written in our post-modern time.[10] This meditation in praise of the poetic sentence draws not on Classical but on Christian iconography, thus entering into another resounding tradition of quotation and transformation. Duden takes an Annunciation by Jan van Eyck as her model of poetic inspiration.[11] If Goethe and Rilke use ekphrastic quotation of visual images in poetry, van Eyck's painting turns quoted words into images. The observer reads the painting from left to right: the Angel Gabriel, just arrived, is bowing before Mary on his right, just as the Dove is flying down towards her head along a beam of light from a window high above, to our left and behind. The picture is dialogic as the angel greets Mary, 'Ave Gratia Plena', and Mary answers, 'Ecce Ancilla Domini'. Mary's sentence emerging from her mouth is written back-to-front and in mirror-writing so that the Dove can read it. Whereas the depicted action moves from left to right, the mirror-writing moves in the opposite direction from right to left, making clear that the sentence is Mary's and suggesting a mirror world of movement from Mary towards the Angel and the Dove.[12] From a feminist perspective, Mary is an ambiguous figure: is it not reactionary at the end of the second millennium to symbolise female poetic creation in the virgin mother in whom two ideals of womanhood, that have so often been misused to subordinate women, impossibly combine in an unrealisable ideal? But on reflection it seems to me that the potentially terrifying arrival of the Angelic Muse with his sentence and the calm readiness of Mary's answering sentence, addressed to the Dove, evoke a conversation between masculine and feminine and spirit in a liberating re-valuation of ancient figures of creativity and its gendering.

NOTES

1 *Goethes Werke*, Hamburger Ausgabe, XII: *Schriften zur Kunst, Schriften zur Literatur, Maximen und Reflexionen*, ed. by Herbert von Einem and Hans Joachim Schrimpf, 6. Auflage (Hamburg: Christian Wegner, 1967), pp. 322-23.
2 Cited in Margret Brügmann, *Amazonen der Literatur* (Amsterdam: Rodopi, 1986), p. 198.
3 Römische Elegie V, *Goethes Werke*, Hamburger Ausgabe, I: *Gedichte und Epen*, ed. by Erich Trunz, 7. Auflage (Hamburg: Christian Wegner, 1964), p. 160.
4 Harold Bloom, *The Anxiety of Influence: A Theory of Poetry* (Oxford: Blackwell, 1975).
5 On the beautiful female corpse as literary motif see Elisabeth Bronfen, 'Die schöne Leiche. Weiblicher Tod als motivische Konstante von der Mitte des 18. Jahrhunderts bis in die Moderne', in *Weiblichkeit und Tod in der Literatur*, ed. by Renate Berger and Inge Stephan (Cologne, Vienna: Böhlau, 1987), pp. 87-116.
6 For a fuller version of this argument see Elizabeth Boa, 'Die Geschichte der O oder die (Ohn-)Macht der Frauen: *Die Wahlverwandtschaften* im Kontext des Geschlechterdiskurses um 1800', *Goethe-Jahrbuch*, 118 (2001), pp. 217-33.
7 Rainer Maria Rilke, Die Sonette an Orpheus, Erster Teil, II, 'Und fast ein Mädchen wars', *Sämtliche Werke*, 2, Insel Werkausgabe, hrsg. Rilke-Archiv (Frankfurt am Main: Insel, 1976), pp. 731-2.
8 Sigrid Weigel, 'Der schielende Blick. Thesen zur Geschichte weiblicher Schreibpraxis', in Inge Stephan and Sigrid Weigel, *Die verborgene Frau. Literatur im historischen Prozeß*, Neue Folge 6, *Argument-Sonderband*, 96 (Berlin, 1983), pp. 83-137.
9 Ingeborg Bachmann, 'Dunkles zu sagen', *Werke* I, *Gedichte, Hörspiele, Libretti, Übersetzungen*, ed. by Christine Koscher, Inge von Weidenbaum and Clemens Münster (Munich: Piper, 1982), p. 52.
10 Anne Duden, 'Vom Versprechen des Schreibens und vom Schreiben des Versprechens', in Robert Gernhardt, Peter Waterhouse, Anne

Duden, *Lobreden auf den poetischen Satz*, ed. by Heinz Ludwig Arnold, Göttinger Sudelblätter, (Wallstein: Göttingen, 1998), pp. 37-45.

[11] My thanks to Anne Duden who in conversation identified the work discussed in the essay as the Annunciation (1425-30) attributed to Jan van Eyck in the National Gallery in Washington.

[12] My thanks to colleagues attending the annual Women in German Studies conference in 2002, organised by Andrea Reiter, for an inspiring discussion of the mirror writing.

Musings on the Muses: Dedications in Goethe's *Hermann und Dorothea*

Alan J L Busst (Bangor)

AMONG WRITERS striving in later eighteenth-century Germany to reconcile tradition with modernity by combining classical Greek literary art with present-day preoccupations, Schiller and Goethe occupy a pre-eminent position. While Schiller concentrated on the field of tragedy, Goethe showed with *Hermann und Dorothea* what could be achieved in the epic. This remarkable work, often considered Goethe's most perfect poem, won enthusiastic acclaim for a variety of reasons, which included general admiration for its highly successful blending of the classical and the contemporary. However, although critics have generally been agreed on the excellence of certain aspects of this combination, such as the brilliant adaptation of Greek hexameters, various Homeric stylistic features, classical simplicity and clarity, which emphasized the typical, the ideal and the general, one procedure that has constantly caused dissension is the dedication of the Cantos to individual Muses. Virtually all critics have accepted that this was in imitation of Greek practices, and especially of Herodotus, but there has been little agreement about the effectiveness of the procedure, and in particular about the correspondence between the character of individual Muses and the Cantos which bear their names, and therefore about the appropriateness of the dedications. The views of critics have varied from the denial of any correspondence whatsoever in any Canto[1] to the assertion of a correspondence in every one, the vast majority of critics settling for correspondence in most Cantos, but failing to agree on which ones, or on the precise nature of this correspondence.

If it is maintained that it was in imitation of ancient Greek practices that Goethe sought to create these relationships, it is curious that over two hundred years of criticism seem to have ignored the fact that this effort was not only unnecessary, but also flagrantly anachronistic. Most editors observe that Goethe followed here the example of Herodotus's *History*; a few[2] add that the division of this work into nine books, each named after a Muse, was not carried out by the author himself but, three centuries later, by Alexandrian scholars; nobody, it appears, mentions that this reorganization not only often fails to establish the unity of a book's content, but creates absolutely no correspondence between the subject-matter of any book and the function of its presiding Muse. In making their breaks in Herodotus's work, of course, the editors had regard not so much to content as to the manageable length of a roll of papyrus and, in allotting names of Muses to the nine books, they merely followed the sequence of names first provided by Hesiod in his *Theogony* (77-79): Clio, Euterpe, Thalia, Melpomene, Terpsichore, Erato, Polymnia, Urania and Calliope.

That the Alexandrians did not here attempt to respect the particular artistic responsibility of each Muse is above all explained by the fact that, throughout Greek antiquity, into the Hellenistic period, and indeed right up to the Roman Empire, there existed virtually no fixed relationship between individual Muses and particular branches of the arts and sciences. If, despite an excellent classical education, Goethe did not know this, he may perhaps be forgiven in the light of the experience of Melchiade Fossati, a classical scholar of colossal erudition who in the 1820s carried out research on Greek and Roman literature and antiquities for writers such as Jean-Baptiste Dugas-Montbel, the famous French commentator and translator of Homer, and for wealthy collectors such as Lord Charles Kinnaird. Pursuing enquiries for Pierre-Simon Ballanche on Diodorus Siculus (IV,7), Fossati was very much surprised to find the Muses separated from individual responsibilities in the arts and sciences, noting for example, that 'Clio, whom later authors recognized simply as the Muse of History is here acknowledged to preside over poetic praise. And Urania presides over the sciences and education, which she extols to the heavens'.[3] It is now accepted that 'the differentiation, familiar to us, of the Muses according to their arts was foreign to Greek antiquity', which 'knew nothing of this division of roles and gave the Muses attributes at random', observing 'where individual Muses are named, complete independence and the greatest discrepancy in interpretation and in the allotting of occupations, even within the same work'.[4] Professor H. R. Rose, writing of 'the fanciful distribution of the individual muses among the different arts and sciences; *e.g.*, Clio as muse of history, Erato of love poetry, Urania of astronomy', points out:

> The lists which have come down are all late and disagree widely with one another; that they are without authority is clear from the way the names of individual muses are employed by classical authors. For instance, Apollonius Rhodius and Virgil called on Erato to inspire an epic poem, while Horace mentions Clio, Calliope, Euterpe, Melpomeme and Polymnia all in connection with lyrics.[5]

In classical Greece, distinctions between the Muses are based on the significance of their names, which indicate, not a responsibility for any particular art form, but the way they sing and celebrate the deeds of gods and men. It has indeed been convincingly argued that Hesiod, in his enumeration of the nine Muses in *Theogony* 77-79, merely invented names that reflected precisely those activities as set forth in the preceding desciption.[6] Although, in about 30 BC at the time he is completing his universal history, Diodorus Siculus, who reproduces Hesiod's list, recognizes that each of the Muses is commonly assigned a special aptitude for one of the branches of the liberal arts, he himself, examining the obvious etymologies of their names, underlines rather their collective role in encouraging and teaching what is noble and important in achievements and education (IV, 7).

What exactly did Goethe himself think of the Muses' functions? Very few of the many references to the Muses that fill his works[7] address them individually. The names of six of the nine Muses occur only in the titles of the *Hermann und Dorothea* Cantos, and the rare references to the remaining three,[8] do not define any precise function or association. In these circumstances what certainty is there that Goethe ascribed any particular function to any particular Muse?

Of crucial importance here is the order of names as they appear in the titles. This is not the so-called 'canonical' order established by Hesiod and relayed through Herodotus and Diodorus Siculus, nor is it the sequence adopted by Photius or Ficino. If it is peculiar to this work alone, then it must have been established for some reason, as it is unlikely that Goethe would quite randomly rearrange an available list. The only possible explanation appears therefore to be that Goethe did indeed want to create a correspondence between at least some of the individual Muses and some of the Cantos. Since the draft of the poem was virtually complete before Goethe divided it into the nine Cantos, then, although variations in length might have made it possible to include some passages and exclude others, and although a few details could have been added, in the main the character and content of a particular Canto must have determined the choice of Muse, and not *vice versa*.

In order to evaluate the appropriateness of these dedications, it will be necessary to examine each in turn in relation to the content of each Canto, accepting, in the absence of any more precise information, the attributes of the Muses that had become established by Goethe's time, and have been accepted by the editors and commentators of *Hermann und Dorothea*.

Since Calliope presides over epic poetry, editors and commentators have usually and unarguably considered it appropriate that her name should be given to the first Canto of a work proclaimed a modern epic.

Although occasionally associated with the cithara and therefore lyrical poetry, Terpsichore was above all regarded as the Muse of the dance, and it is for this reason that an overwhelming majority of editors consider there to be absolutely no correspondence between her name and function and the content and tone of Canto II. Since, however, each Canto contains a number of different elements, it is never impossible to unearth some detail, however uncharacteristic, which might illustrate the function of any one of the Muses. For one commentator,[9] the justification for the presence here of Terpsichore is that in this Canto Hermann speaks of the fashionable social gatherings held at the rich merchant's house. This is very unsatisfactory since, firstly, these parties were completely antipathetic to the character and temperament of Hermann, whose name provides the subtitle for this Canto, and with whom it is mainly concerned; secondly, because, although singing took place there, accompanied by the piano, there is no mention of dancing; and thirdly, because the description of these gatherings extends over only 16 out of 273 lines of text (217-232), whereas 29 lines (110-138) are devoted to the account of the fire that ravaged the town, and was hardly an occasion for dancing! It has also been suggested that the reference to Terpsichore underlines the joyful bearing of Hermann when he returns from his successful mission after meeting Dorothea, and appears as *munter, lebhaft, fröhlich* and *heiter*. In support of this explanation, it could be added that, although at the end of the previous Canto Hermann was described as sluggish, timid and withdrawn, avoiding girls and dancing, the Parson, at the beginning of this Canto, is struck by the young man's changed appearance, his happy vivacity, after much appreciated human contact, now contrasting with his habitually ponderous and shy isolation. And although he is not actually now dancing, an association with this activity might perhaps be suggested by the repetition of the word *fröhlich*, previously used to describe the dancing he used to shun, and now, only eleven lines later, applied to Hermann himself. However, these details do not provide any solid justification for the association of the Muse of the dance with the general character and tone of this Canto. Hermann's changed appearance has but the briefest duration, being confined to only two lines of text, after which he immediately reverts to his usual calm and seriousness (1.10), and for the remainder of the Canto is more occupied with animated argument than with rejoicing, and expresses impatience and humiliation rather than gaiety. Still less convincing is the suggestion[10] that Terpsichore's association with harmony sets the tone for the accord which is already beginning to exist between Hermann and Dorothea. The conclusion in this matter must surely be that there is no satisfactory basis for any correspondence between Terpsichore and this Canto.[11]

As Muse of pastoral and idyllic poetry, Thalia could have presided over sections of Canto IV (e.g. ll.1-58, 77-78), but the majority of editors have underlined her more important association with comedy as justification for her appearance as dedicatee of Canto III. Its presentation, often humorous and even ironic, of the rather stereotypical middle-class views of the *Bürger* involved, the Landlord and the Chemist, indeed dominates this Canto and reveals such traits as pompous complacency, ponderous solemnity, mercenary calculation and the patronizing disparagement of women.

Although Euterpe was in later antiquity most generally considered to preside over music, being the inventress of the flute and of all wind instruments, it was also to her that some attributed the invention of tragedy. Others, however, like Horace, mentioned her in connexion with lyrical poetry and, having regard to the pre-eminence of love in such poetry, the majority of commentators and editors have found in this association the justification of Euterpe's patronage of Canto IV. Only 9 of this Canto's 252 lines are devoted specifically to the expression of Hermann's love for Dorothea, but that love is the prime mover of the events of the Canto, and indeed of the whole poem. Since, in addition, Canto IV illustrates many other forms of love, such as filial, maternal, patriotic and philanthropic, the association with Euterpe would appear, in this sense, to be well founded.

In later antiquity, Polymnia was the Muse of the sublime hymn, but was also considered to be the inventress of harmony, and was associated with eloquence, dancing, the lyre and pantomime, which in classical times could be either tragic or comic. Most commentators have found in these attributes little or no justification for the dedicatory title of Canto V. It has, however, been rather lamely suggested that the choric hymn might evoke the discussions about the future marriage of Hermann, which occupy by far the greater part of this Canto, involve several voices and do in fact finally achieve a certain harmony, although unfortunately no sublimity. According to an alternative proposal, Polymnia's association with eloquence is in accord with the Canto's subtitle: *Der Weltbürger.* It might be thought that cosmopolitanism's magnificent vision of the unity of mankind, which goes back through the eighteenth century to Zeno and the early Stoics and to Alexander, could provide ample scope for the exercise of the type of religious eloquence connected with Polymnia. If that indeed was the aim and the hope, the reality is disappointing. The aptness of the subtitle was considered to be so unclear that a number of critics have hesitated whether by the *Cosmopolitan* is meant the Magistrate or the Parson, who praises a useful labour that knows no frontiers. If, however, the Parson is excluded because this praise, apart from the fact that it extends over only four lines, is too exclusively designed to lead to the rehabilitation of Hermann in his father's estimation, then the single remaining candidate proposed for the title *Cosmopolitan* is the Magistrate who, however, appears only in the final fifth part of this dynamic and eventful Canto, and whose contention, expressed with evangelical simplicity and directness, that adversity should teach tolerance, mercy and brotherly love, occupies only 7 lines (198-204) out of the Canto's total of 244. All in all, there seems to be little justification for either the title or the subtitle of Canto V.

It is as Muse of history that Clio was mainly known, and almost all editors, even those most averse generally to recognizing correspondences between Muses and Cantos, accept in Canto VI the appropriateness of both titles, Clio's function being supported by the subtitle: *Das Zeitalter* [the age]. Against the validity of this explanation, it has been objected that the Magistrate's memories of the French Revolution occupy only a third of this Canto.[12] However, the detailed descriptions of Dorothea are motivated by her involvement and that of her first fiancé in these momentous events, and if in addition account is taken of the passages devoted to reflections on the difficulties and uncertainties of the present age, and to recollections of past, out-moded practices, it becomes clear that historical considerations fill well over two thirds of the text.

Critics have almost unanimously considered it appropriate that Erato, the Muse of love poetry should preside over Canto VII, whose subtitle *Dorothea* indicates its exclusive concern with the lovable and loved heroine, and with her relationship with Hermann.

Whilst some editors have denied any direct correspondence between Melpomene, the Muse of tragedy, and the content of Canto VIII, the latter nevertheless takes place against a threatening background of impending danger, and it has been convincingly argued that the interior struggles undergone here to conceal their true feelings by Hermann and Dorothea, whose names justifiably provide the subtitle, produce an effect of Homeric *retardatio*, and are indeed ostensibly and potentially tragic.

Disagreement among critics as to the significance of both title and subtitle of Canto IX, suggests the obscurity of Goethe's reasons for choosing Urania, the Muse of astronomy, as the patroness of this final Canto, and places in doubt the appropriateness of this choice. One explanation that Goethe thereby implied that marriages are made in heaven has been rejected on account of its unseemly mixture of sacred and profane.[13] According to other critics, Urania ensures that the great conflict of the poem will end harmoniously or, with her wider celestial outlook, will help man look for and appreciate universal values. The association of early Greek astronomy with astrological divination might of course explain the significance of Urania's presence at the beginning of a Canto which has *Aussicht* [prospect] as its subtitle, were it not for uncertainty about the nature of this prospect, and the severe restriction of the amount of text devoted to it. Does it refer to the reflections about life and its vicissitudes placed in Dorothea's mouth,[14] even though these are mainly her first fiancé's, and Dorothea's occupy only seven lines (291-296)? Or is it connected with the last six lines of Hermann's last speech about the likelihood of a courageous uprising in Germany, which might create peace?[15] Or does it just generally presage a happy future for the young lovers?[16]

Since, apart from the serious question of anachronism, the acceptability and effectiveness of the dedication of each Canto to each individual Muse must depend on a clearly established relationship between the Muse's function and the Canto's content, the foregoing examination suggests that six of the nine titles are satisfactory and that three are not. How has this situation come about? A possible explanation is that, having in front of him a list of the Muses in the 'canonical' order, Goethe, instead of following the example of Herodotus's editors, picked out first of all the names which he felt corresponded obviously to particular Cantos: Calliope for I, Thalia for III, Euterpe for IV, Clio for VI, Erato for VII and Melpomene for VIII. He then still had three slots to fill, in which he inscribed the names of the remaining Muses in exactly the order in which they were left on his list: Terpsichore for II, Polymnia for V, and Urania for IX. Any details he was able to add at this late stage were obviously insufficient to create any convincing correspondence.

On the whole, Goethe's attempt to allocate Cantos to particular Muses according to special attributes appears, for a number of reasons, to be unfortunate. Firstly, it conflicts with the classical Greek practices he has set out to imitate; and secondly, the clarity and validity of correspondences achieved in certain Cantos only underline the obscurity and invalidity of others. In addition, the rather arbitrary division of the work into categories existing in varying doses throughout is at variance with the powerful and exhilarating conception of the epic beginning to be developed at that time in Germany and, thanks largely to the influence of writers like Herder and F. A. Wolf, shared by Goethe, which stressed unity, impersonality and collectivity: the notion of the epic, this anonymous creation of the people, of nations, and of mankind itself, as the all-embracing and unifying repository of knowledge and skills where, for example, poetry and history, the comic and the tragic, religion and mythology, inspiration and science, the lyrical and the heroic, were constantly and inextricably mixed.

NOTES

1. V., e.g., L.Cholevius, *Aesthetische und historische Einleitung nebst fortlaufender Erläuterung zu Goethe's Hermann und Dorothea*, 2te Auflage (Leipzig, 1877), p. 103.
2. E.g. Josef Schmidt, Hrsg, *Johann Wolfgang Goethe: Hermann und Dorothea. Erläuterungen und Dokumente* (Stuttgart: Reclam, 1970), p. 5.
3. Bibl. municipale de Lyon, Fonds Ballanche, Ms. 1806-1810, Fossati, cahier 56.
4. *Paulys Real-Encyclopädie der classischen Altertumswissenschaft. Neue Bearbeitung, begonnen von G. Wissowa*: Halbbd. 31 (Stuttgart 1933), art. Musai, col. 684.
5. *Encyclopaedia Britannica* (London: 1963), XV, 960, art. Muses.
6. Friedrich Solmsen, *Hesiod and Aeschylus* (Ithaca, New York: Cornell U.P, 1949), pp. 38-41.
7. 140 in the *Gedenkausgabe hrsg. Ernst Beutler* (Zürich, 1949).
8. 14 in all, spread out over the 24 volumes of the *Gedenkausgabe*.
9. H. Loiseau, Goethe, *Hermann et Dorothée* (Paris: Montaigne, 1932), p. III.
10. H. Loiseau, pp. III-IV.
11. It is significant that Keith Spalding's excellent edition of the text (Macmillan, 1968) merely mentions two explanations proposed, without expressing endorsement for either.
12. L. Cholevius, p .260.
13. B. Lévy, *Hermann et Dorothée de Goethe* (Paris: Hachette, 1886), p. 96.
14. B. Lévy, p. 96.
15. L. Cholevius, p. 255.
16. K. Spalding, p. 117.

On the Unveiling of the Goddess: Some Observations on Schiller's *Das verschleierte Bild zu Sais*

Hans-Joachim Hahn (Oxford)

IN AN AGE still dominated by post-structural philosophies, it might be - in Schiller's words - 'audacious and meritorious' to revisit the intellectual milieu of Schiller's Jena. Our visit will not only attempt to examine one of Schiller's philosophical poems, but will also observe the scurrilous debates and innuendoes in the literary circles of Jena, Weimar and Berlin. Such an undertaking is intended as a light-hearted deconstruction of Schiller's moral philosophy and may contribute towards intertextual literary criticism.

Schiller's poem, in popular ballad form, relates the apparently simple tale of a young man driven by an obsessive thirst for knowledge. Truth, he believes, can be acquired only in its entirety, for to remove even a single aspect would falsify it. The hierophant, expounder of sacred mysteries, warns that such reckless desire is excessive, for the goddess has stated explicitly that 'no mortal must lift this veil', until she herself does so. He then adds paradoxically, 'whosoever lifts the veil with unconsecrated, guilty hand' will see the truth. Such equivocation, well known from riddles and fairy-tales, serves to advance the action, supplemented by a second ingredient, the desire to reveal the name of the supernatural agent, familiar from such diverse sources as *Genesis* and *Rumpelstilzchen*. Some hours later, undeterred by these edicts and entranced by the magical surrounding of an Oriental temple, our hero rejects the priest's advice. While his conscience attempts to resist his daring transgression, his natural curiosity prevails, only to unleash an awful punishment: 'Senseless and pale' he falls 'prostrate at the feet of Isis'; incapable of revealing his encounter with the statue and never regaining his former serenity, he goes to an early grave. His final words encapsulate the poem's moral: 'Woe betide him, who reaches truth through guilt! It will never bring him joy'.

It should be obvious from this résumé that this is not one of Schiller's masterpieces. Unlike his great philosophical poems, this ballad lacks the essential hymnal or elegiac tone and the uncharitable might suggest that, at the time, Schiller was rather short of suitable material for his next issue of *Die Horen*.[1] The well-known theme, reflecting an enthusiasm for ancient Egypt and Freemasonry, had been taken up by Kant, and Beethoven and popularised by Mozart's *Magic Flute*, while Schiller himself had covered the subject matter of the veiled statue at Sais on at least four previous occasions.[2] Space does not permit either a detailed comparison of Schiller's own treatment of the myth, or an account of the complicated evolution of the theme. Philologists and literary historians have traced the motif in many works, reaching back into antiquity. While such meticulous studies have proved the popularity of the subject matter, they cast little light on the position this poem held within the literary debate of Schiller's time. Furthermore, they failed to recognise the generic difference between the ballad and his essay or other literary form: Schiller's essay 'Die Sendung Moses', though sharing the same motif, was intended as an historical exercise, an anthropological study on the genesis of monotheism, which must be seen in the wider context of Lessing's *Erziehung des Menschengeschlechts*. Schiller's ballad, however, was instead concerned with a specific philosophical issue, addressing an epistemological theme which was part of the ongoing debate of the Jena circle.

The correspondence between Schiller and his contemporaries was lively and exhilarating, comparable to the media coverage of one of today's literary feuds. A first version of Schiller's ballad, now lost, reached Herder on 17th August 1795 and elicited an uncharacteristically harsh response (35/298f). Dismissing the divine decree that no mortal was to lift the veil, Herder maintained, that thirst for truth cannot be portrayed as guilt and concluded that only a cleric, not the oracle, could have conceived of such a conclusion (35/298-9). In response to his criticism, Schiller made some minor changes, which met with Herder's approval (35/375). Körner, too, exercised some critical awareness by suggesting that the subject matter was rather obscure and left him dissatisfied (35/323), but Wilhelm von Humboldt was lavish with praise and professed not to understand how Herder could have misunderstood the poem (35/316). Herder's harsh criticism testifies to his longstanding controversy with Kant, who was undoubtedly a major influence on Schiller. Herder felt a natural antipathy towards Kant's categorical divisions of nature, suggesting that Kant lacked any knowledge of living nature, that his concept of *Vernunft* stood outside nature and was part of the 'thing per se'. His attack on Kant's concept of nature, not yet fully developed in 1795, became public in his *Metakritik zur Kritik der reinen Vernunft* (1799). There he defines truth as in harmonious 'agreement with the object', suggesting that any division between subject and object will lead nowhere, will be 'a journey to the moon'.[3]

It is still generally accepted that the Sais poem relates to Kant's concept of the sublime, developed in his *Kritik der Urteilskraft* published in 1790. Schiller's reading of Kant was much influenced by Karl Leonhard Reinhold, a prominent Freemason and his colleague in Jena.[4] During his period at Jena University Reinhold published his *Briefe über die Kantische Philosophie* in Wieland's *Teutscher Merkur*[5] and also provided Schiller with the source of the Sais myth.[6] In his two essays on the sublime, published in 1793, Schiller's main interest centred on the limitations of our intellect in matters of metaphysics, as expounded in Kant's concept of the thing per se. Defining the scope of art and nature, Kant had referred to 'the well known inscription upon the Temple of Isis (Mother Nature): 'I am all that is, and that was, and that shall be, and no mortal hath raised the veil from before my face',[7] describing it as the most sublime utterance possible. No reference is made here to any sense of guilt, nor did Kant address the issue of what might lie behind this veil. In 'Die Sendung Moses' Schiller echoes Kant's view that there was nothing more sublime than the simple grandeur with which Egyptian priests referred to the Creator (17/397). In 'Vom Erhabenen', he even quotes the goddess's statement in a repetition of Kant, but adds that the mysterious and the veiled evoke 'terror' which in turn will lead to the sublime (20/191). With regard to Schiller's ballad, it is difficult to recognise this particular terror which might contribute to achieving the sublime.

However, critics are determined that the hero's few spine-tingling moments can account for the presence of the sublime in this poem. Jan Assmann even suggests that the young man's speechlessness, induced by lifting the veil, portrays the sublime in its full significance.[8] Distancing myself from this view, I would suggest that Schiller, introducing a subject matter here which *potentially* lends itself to a treatment of the sublime, then *deliberately* rejects this solution. Schiller defined the sublime as 'an object, the idea of which will restrain our sensory nature and will instead liberate our intellect, so that we lose out against it in a physical sense, but instead will gain a higher moral sense' (20/171). If applied to the poem, we recognise an initial restraint in the young man's sensory nature, but cannot find any evidence of moral superiority. In fact, the young man's utterance prior to lifting the veil suggests a stubbornly determined attitude, rather than an act of 'Vernunft': 'Whatever lies behind the veil, I'll lift it - [...] I want to see the truth.' Indeed, the young man's unrestrained action, attempting to gain access to the truth by guilty means, serves to explain Schiller's moral punishment. This then raises the question of why Schiller, so fascinated by the concept of the sublime, should have avoided the treatment of the sublime in this poem. A possible answer may lie in the gossip and innuendo of the time, traceable through Schiller's correspondence. While this was not an eighteenth century version of the *Death of a Critic*, Schiller's bitter, protracted dispute with Fichte, Reinhold's successor in Jena, goes some way in this direction. Two factors contributed to this feud between the two Jena professors: personal rivalry for Goethe's favour and an irreconcilable difference on epistemological issues.[9]

Schiller was furious about Fichte's university politics, resulting in student riots and an alleged instance of caterwauling and broken windows at Schiller's house (28/450). Meanwhile Fichte had taken flight to Oßmannstedt, and Schiller took the opportunity to ridicule Fichte's subjectivist philosophy by branding him the Oßmannstedt Ego or Oßmannstedt Majesty (35/248). The actual controversy between the two men began with Schiller's rejection, in most unflattering terms, of an article Fichte had submitted to *Die Horen*. Covering a subject matter which, in substance and style, Schiller had already addressed, he ridiculed the manner in which Fichte had illustrated his abstract philosophical arguments, calling it a 'dry, ponderous and [...] confused presentation' (27/366). Fichte's response was no less robust, accusing Schiller of an injustice and demanding an apology. Countering Schiller's stylistic criticism, Fichte retorted: 'I must first translate everything you write, before I can understand it; and others have the same problem.' (35/232).

Schiller was so incensed, that he took the trouble of copying Fichte's article and redrafting his own answer three times, consulting Goethe as to the right response, who advised moderation. Schiller also complained to his friends Humboldt, Kerner and F. Jacobi and intervened when Fichte sought to publish his works with Cotta (27/203-4).

At the heart of Schiller's irritation was Fichte's critique of his aesthetics. In the article, subsequently published in 1798,[10] Fichte had praised Goethe's power of imagination, suggesting implicitly, and with reference to Schiller's distinction between naïve and sentimental poetry, that Schiller belonged to the second rank as a writer 'who first conceives of the spirit and then searches for the lump of earth in order to breathe into it the living soul'.[11] He also took a swipe at Schiller's *Aesthetic Education*, suggesting that Schiller's concept of freedom was precious and elitist. Fichte was not out to ridicule Schiller, but he took exception to Schiller's understanding of human impulses ['Triebe']. Fichte defined the human impulse as 'uniquely independent and incapable of any outside determination', 'as the highest and sole principle of independent action', an 'epistemological force',[12] based entirely on the power of human imagination, i.e. not influenced by any outside factor. Schiller responded with his essay 'Über die notwendigen Grenzen beim Gebrauch schöner Formen', maintaining that there are instances where men have to liberate themselves 'from every sensuous influence' and must act as 'purely rational beings' in order to fulfil their duty (21/3). He clearly distinguishes between perception and sensation.

Applying these differences between Fichte and Schiller to the ballad, we notice that the hero takes Fichte's approach, focusing entirely on his epistemological impulse and attempting to appropriate the totality of wisdom. Schiller, the author, however, lurks behind the goddess's veil, from where he propels the young man into insanity and a premature death. The many reverberations of this controversy can only be alluded to here. Goethe attempted to remain impartial, intervening only indirectly to moderate Schiller's wrath. Years later he wrote a poem which may have reflected on this episode: if God revealed his ways and allowed him into the temple of truth, he would certainly remain there.[13] Novalis, apparently dissatisfied with Schiller's moralist interpretation, based both a fragmentary novel and a distich on Schiller's rendering of the Sais myth, 'deconstructing' Schiller thus: 'One man succeeded, he lifted the veil of the goddess at Sais; But what did he see? He saw, miracle upon miracle, his own self.'[14] The distich seems a direct reference to Fichte, who suggested in his article that 'the human spirit gains something belonging to itself as it were [...] and will easily recognise in the surrounding objects, as in a mirror, his own figure.'[15] Novalis later moderated his stance somewhat towards a panentheistic position, as he moved from Fichte to Schelling, suggesting that the true agent for knowledge was love, the fullest possible recognition of the Self in the Other.

NOTES

[1] Letter to Goethe of 21st August, in *Schillers Werke, Nationalausgabe* (Weimar), vol. 28, pp. 28-9, and letter from Goethe, 17th August, vol. 35, pp. 285-6. The edition will be in the text giving volume and page.

[2] 'Die Sendung Moses' (1789), *Der Geisterseher* (1789), *Der Menschenfeind* (1790), 'Vom Erhabenen' (1793).

[3] Johann Gottfried Herder, *Metakritik zur Kritik der reinen Vernunft* (Aufbau Verlag, Berlin, 1955), pp. 290-1.

[4] Cf. Christine Harrauer, '"Ich bin, was da ist", die Göttin von Sais und ihre Deutung von Plutarch bis in die Goethezeit', in *Spahiros. Wiener Studien. Zeitschrift für klassische Philologie und Patristik*, 107/08 (1994), 337-55. Norbert Klatt, '"...Des Wissens heisser Durst", Ein literaturkritischer Beitrag zu Schillers Gedicht *Das verschleierte Bild zu Sais*', *Jahrbuch der Schillergesellschaft*, 29 (1985), 98-112. Jan Assmann, *Das verschleierte Bild zu Sais. Schillers Ballade und ihre ägyptischen Hintergründe* (Stuttgart & Leipzig, 1999).

[5] *Teutscher Merkur*, Band 3, August 1786 to September 1787.

[6] Br. Decius (L. Reinhold), *Die Hebräischen Mysterien oder die älteste religiöse Freymaurerey* (Leipzig, 1788), pp. 14, 54.

[7] Immanuel Kant, *The Critique of Judgement*, transl. with Analytical Indexes by James Creed Meredith (Oxford, 1952), p. 179.

[8] Assmann, *Das verschleierte Bild*, p. 31.

[9] Both men had been appointed by Goethe, and Schiller jealously guarded the confidence and friendship which Goethe had bestowed on him only recently.

[10] 'Über Geist und Buchstab in der Philosophie in einer Reihe von Briefen', *Philosophisches Journal*, 9 (1798), 199-232 and 292-305.

[11] Günter Schulz, 'Die erste Fassung von Fichtes Abhandlung "Über Geist und Buchstab in der Philosophie in einer Reihe von Briefen" 1795', in *Neue Folge des Jahrbuchs der Goethe-Gesellschaft*, 16 (1954), 240.
[12] Ibid., p. 126.
[13] Goethe, *Großherzog Wilhelm Ernst Ausgabe*, vol. 15, p. 247. Here its original version:
Wenn ich kennte den Weg des Herrn,
Ich ging' ihn wahrhaft gar zu gern;
Führte man mich in der Wahrheit Haus,
Bei Gott! ich ging' nicht wieder heraus.
[14] Cf. H.J. Hahn, '"Einem gelang es..." – Die Grammatik der Natur in Novalis' *Die Lehrlinge zu Sais*', in *Titles, Words, Texts, Images. Papers Delivered at the CUTG Conference at Oxford University*, ed. Katrin Kohl and Ritchie Robertson (Lang: Munich, 2002), pp. 54-67.
[15] Schulz, 'Die erste Fassung...', p. 129.

Mysticism, Irrationalism, and Existentialism

J Heywood Thomas (Bangor)

MUCH INK HAS been spilt, in the name of Democracy and the tradition of European freedom, to bewail the legacy of 19th century irrationalist tendencies. It is therefore both instructive as well as interesting to consider their positive contribution, so recognizing that the modern world we know was formed by influences now hardly recognizable. Here I shall not be moving beyond the 19th century and I take for granted - what few will deny - that Kierkegaard was the father of Existentialism. Born in the Copenhagen that had barely shaken off its feudal past, a Royalist and no democrat to our way of thinking, Kierkegaard was convinced of his prophetic vocation. That was no simple matter of church reform: it was no less a task than 'introducing Christianity into Christendom'. It was indeed a protest against the hollowness of the bourgeouis existence which he saw to be masquerading as Christianity. For that reason he has been hailed not only as a Christian for the 21st century but also as a political prophet denouncing the insidious influence of populism. Whether seen as a model of Christianity for a post-Christian age or as an interpreter of modern society with greater realism than Marx, Kierkegaard must be acknowledged as a thinker with whom the 21st century is still coming to terms. Indebted as we are, then, to him, should we not remember the roots of his thinking?

To relate the story of early 19th century Danish social and intellectual history would be a lengthy business taking us far from our task; but it will suffice to say that the Copenhagen of Kierkegaard's youth enjoyed a very narrow culture and that, for all its self-esteem as a capital, it hardly boasted any throbbing native cultural development. Yet it would be wrong to read back into it a provincialism; for such would be foreign to the self-aware development that marked its social, economic and political life as much as its intellectual history. In particular, if Kierkegaard was indeed the great, if not the greatest critic of Hegel, that he has been recognized to be, that in itself shows how important the awareness of the development of German philosophy was for him and others. It is thus not surprising to discover that knowledge of and indebtedness of the course of German philosophy in the late 18th and early 19th centuries were crucial to his development. Schelling is perhaps the most obvious point of contact because of the inevitable Romantic connection. But Trendelenburg, the forgotten logician and critic of Hegel, was just as important. I leave these aside in order to fasten on two unlikely sources of inspiration - Fritz von Baader and J.G. Hamann.

Fritz von Baader was born in Munich in 1765 and studied medicine, later becoming a mining engineer. He spent four years in England (1792-6), during which time - through Boehme's influence - he became interested in mysticism. On his return to Germany he made the acquaintance of Jacobi and Schelling and became very friendly with Schelling. In 1836 he was appointed Professor of Philosophy and Theology in Munich. Completely ignored by historians of philosophy he has hardly been mentioned by Kierkegaard scholars either. Even so the contribution to the reaction against Hegel made by von Baader is as important - at least as far as understanding Kierkegaard is concerned - as the paramount contribution of Schelling. Resembling Hegel in many ways and attracted by him, von Baader nevertheless struggled against Hegel incessantly. First mentioned in the Journal entry of 13 June 1836 (*Papirer*, 1 a 174), von Baader's *Vorlesungen über Speculative Dogmatik* (Stuttgart and Tübingen, 1828) had in fact been read carefully by Kierkegaard over the two previous years. The sale catalogue of his library includes 28 single volumes by von Baader published between 1815 and 1841. Doubtless he owed his knowledge of von Baader to H. L. Martensen, his brilliant young theological teacher who later became Primate of Denmark. At this time Kierkegaard was reading and inwardly digesting most of the German philosophical tradition related to Romanticism. A Journal entry of March 1837 reveals this and his later use of von Baader. Already thinking of ideas in a true existentialist fashion as concrete realities he praises von Baader, remarking that his *Fermenta Cognitionis* has 'some good remarks about Faust'.

Reading Kierkegaard's early works we find only a few cursory references to von Baader and it is only *The Concept of Anxiety* that reveals the profound relationship between them. Here von Baader emerges as a *source* of the thinking in this seminal work. Discussing the concept of the Fall, Kierkegaard shows in that work how much he valued the thought of this extraordinary philosopher (Vide *Concept of Anxiety*, p. 29). Clearly he found von Baader's views on sin and temptation of considerable interest and importance - something which, incidentally, not even the editors of the latest edition recognize, the Cartesian idea of freedom inevitably capturing their attention. It is interesting that Kierkegaard found what Leibniz and Fichte had to say about freedom of greater interest than what he found in Descartes. As the editors remind us, Kierkegaard's reading of Leibniz, Descartes and Aristotle was followed by a study of Hegel; but the important point seems to me to be that the context in which this reading and the consequent study were undertaken was the inspiration he had found in reading von Baader. If it were not so why did he bother to acquire all those works of von Baader which were in his library? His understanding of what anxiety means was of greater and more profound humanity than the Romantic notion of a beautiful expression of mood. It was in fact an ontological break-through as well as a superb piece of phenomenological description. This, I suggest, is what he found in von Baader - a new way of looking at metaphysics because it put such a high valuation on human experience. Characteristically this underlying theme of his work is hidden by the typical wealth of philosophical allusions - to concepts as well as authors. I am well aware of his more general debt to the development of German philosophy: Trendelenburg had helped him see the basic flaw of Hegel's logic and Lessing too had contributed to the language of the argument about actual existence and logic. Yet the key to his view of anxiety is the profound grasp of the nature of finitude as something at once general and particular. Its central axiom is the principle *unum noris omnes* and the source of that is his reading of von Baader's *Vorlesungen über speculative Dogmatik* (Vide *Concept of Anxiety*, p. 59). One thing is certain: Kierkegaard's regard for von Baader remained constant into his last days (Vide *Papirer*, X^2 A 222).

There are three respects in which I suggest von Baader influenced Kierkegaard. First, he warmed to the insistence of this student of the mysticism of Eckhardt and Boehme that there should be a philosophy which unites philosophy and theology. For von Baader not to begin with God is *ipso facto* to deny him: knowledge itself is participation in divine knowledge. This must have struck Kierkegaard as a remarkable combination of humility and confidence which not only resolved the Cartesian problem of knowledge but also opened up a quite new way in metaphysical theology. Keen student of post-Kantian German philosophy as he was he knew all too well the over-weaning pride in rational knowledge which was the legacy of the Enlightenment. A clear examination of his work will reveal that in many ways he was as much an heir of the Enlightenment as any 19th century thinker. Perhaps the more important, as it is the more influential, point is that he saw the way in which these currents of thought contribute to *general* culture. The second point is a rather formal influence. One of the most encouraging things about von Baader's work for Kierkegaard must have been its unsystematic character, a more profound matter than the phrase might suggest. In 1722 in the preface to *Fermenta Cognitionis* von Baader talks of 'the very often polemical character' of this work and similarly in the first volume of his *Speculative Dogmatik* he presented his exposition of Dogmatics as polemical. Likewise in the preface to the second volume he was quite emphatic in his rejection of a *system* of doctrine, asserting confidently that this second volume would show any readers who regretted the absence of system in the first that this was in the nature of the enterprise. How eagerly must Kierkegaard have embraced this thinking. 'Polemical' was the word of criticism which had been used of him by his teacher and friend, P. M. Møller and his poignant grief at Møller's death is obvious from the Journal - and, most importantly, from the dedication of *Concept of Anxiety*. As something essentially personal Kierkegaard then grasped that it can be polemical and unsystematic. Finally, it was from von Baader that Kierkegaard first began to learn the meaning of personhood. I recall that time and again Paul Tillich used to say that for Fichte the individuality of the self is some kind of necessary imperfection. For von Baader the individuality of the creature is his truth and reality vis-à-vis God. The mysterious nature of sin, he thought, was that it destroyed this. This very statement in *Speculative Dogmatik* is the first of the excerpts that Kierkegaard copied (*Papirer*, 1 c 27). In von Baader, then, Kierkegaard found the inspiration for his critique of the anti-individual emphasis which had permeated German Idealism from the start.

If von Baader can be seen as a corrective to one strand of Romanticism's legacy there is in Kierkegaard's development a very different connection with this heritage. Walter Lowrie, the doyen of the English-speaking scholars of Kierkegaard in the mid-20th century, regarded J. G. Hamann as 'the only author by whom Søren Kierkegaard was profoundly influenced'. Regrettably, though there was at least some solid ground for such a claim, Lowrie never offered any evidence and so afforded little illumination of the nature of Kierkegaard's debt. The relation between the two thinkers had been examined as early as 1917 by H. E. Weber (*Zwei Propheten des Irrationalismus, J. G. Hamann und S. Kierkegaard als Bahnbrecher des Christenglaubens*, Leipzig). As with von Baader so with regard to Hamann we can form some idea of how much Kierkegaard valued him from the fact that the catalogue of Kierkegaard's library includes what was then the most complete edition of Hamann's writings, F. Roth, *Hamanns Schriften* (Items 536-44 of the sale-catalogue). The opening year of Kierkegaard's Journal has an entry (10 September 1836) referring to Hamann as an illustration of 'a Christian's view of paganism'. Two days later he refers to Hamann again - and once again, as before, this is a reference to Hamann's discussion of Hume. To Hume's sardonic remark that believing in Christianity was not only to believe miracles but was itself a miracle, Hamann's answer was 'Well, that's exactly the way it is'. Very obviously in this period when, as a student, Kierkegaard had already discovered his literary talent and was unhappy with his studies he found Hamann's unorthodox life and his robust faith quite fascinating. We find him thinking of Goethe's Faust, noting that Mephistopheles leads the new disciple far away from his chosen studies, denuding his academic ambitions; but immediately he is reminded of Hamann. So in his confusion about his own future and his equal confusion about the nature of a Christian existence Hamann's humour and ironic rejection of the rationalistic critiques directed towards faith must have appeared to him a paradigm. Already he had seen figures like Faust to be paradigms of a way of life. Here was something comparable but very different inasmuch as this figure was part of a cultural heritage with which he was coming to terms. He is struck by Hamann's comparison of reason with the (mosaic) law; and there is no doubt that he was sufficiently well versed in Pauline studies to have drawn the conclusion that as salvation is by grace so too spiritual understanding is something other than reason.

Hamann has been well described as 'the most obscure author of modern literature' (Unger). A remarkable opponent (and friend) of Kant, he deemed Lessing the only other worthy opponent as in his first work, *The Memorabilia of Socrates* he opposed the standpoint of faith to the rationalism of the Enlightenment. His basic criticism of these two philosophers is very significant, especially in our present context. It was not a simple opposition of pietism to the pure autonomy of reason: rather it was that they ignored or even sought to break down the natural bond between man and experience. In language that almost prefigures 20th century philosophy he argues that Kant wrongly dissociates man from ordinary speech. Experience and revelation he described as the 'indispensable wings or crutches of our reason if it is not to be lame'. Writing to Kant he insists on the primacy of our humanity - the only proper starting-point for philosophy. However, in his view, self-knowledge was not possible apart from God. Salmony, in his study of Hamann's 'Metacritical philosophy', makes the very nice point that by 'existence' Hamann means nothing more nor less than existence before God through whom alone existence is given to men. Human existence in the world suffers from an unrest and homesickness, an 'angst'. It is no surprise then to see Hamann's whole authorship and life as expressing the conviction that directness is never possible. In words eagerly fastened on and cherished by Kierkegaard Hamann had said that he would 'more often hear, with more joy, the Word of God in the mouth of a Pharisee as a witness against his will, than from an angel of light'. Significantly this is something that Kierkegaard notes in an early reference made to Hamann in the Journal; and perhaps the adjective he here uses of Hamann is equally significant - 'ironical'. Despite his proposal of a serious study of Hamann what he did was something different - he digested him, with the result that Hamann remained a potent force in his mind for the coming years. Indeed Hamann became something of an authority for him. This is most evident from the very intimate (almost confessional) entry of 13 July 1837 'made in our study at six o'clock in the afternoon' which speaks of the strange reluctance to make notes of his sporadic reflections:

'[...] I think ... that it would be good, through frequent note-writing, to let the thoughts come forth with the umbilical cord of the original mood [...] I gain [...] the advantage of what Hamann says is true in another sense that there are ideas which a man gets only once in his life' (*Papirer*, IIa 118).

What is especially significant about this is the way in which Hamann has now become a model for Kierkegaard in the process of authorship. Several undated entries in the Journal of this period take up the point just made about the *nature* of Hamann's thinking: Hamann is a humorist, 'the greatest humorist in Christianity'.

In a word, then, to read Hamann as an irrationalist was in Kierkegaard's view something far too simplistic. His had indeed been a battle fought in defence of faith; but that defence of faith was a very human matter, an appreciation of the passion and complexity of existence over against the temptations of Enlightenment rationalism. In my earliest study of what Hamann had contributed to Kierkegaard's development (*Subjectivity and Paradox*, Oxford: Blackwell, 1957, pp. 104-5) I pointed to his influence on Kierkegaard's development of the concept of Paradox. Not indeed *the* source in that Hamann did help Kierkegaard to see that philosophy after Kant needed to think in paradoxes, particularly when it deals with religious thought and practice. It could perhaps be argued that Kierkegaard's understanding of religion as always and generally a paradox owed much to what Hamann had said - in particular his comments about the nature of Christian revelation. To my mind, however, the important thing is that there is something essentially personalist about Hamann's thought which particularly resonated with Kierkegaard. The declaration in the Gilleleje entry in the Journal of 1835, 'I really need to find an idea for which I can live and die', is the clearest example of this. Like Hamann, he had rejected the notion that natural science, for all its obvious importance, was the sole or indeed the real route to a true knowledge of reality. As with Hamann so with Kierkegaard philosophy must begin with the passion of existence, the painstaking description of those moods in our life which speak to us of a destiny that is hid with the stars.

What I have tried to do is to show the way in which we are debtors to very strange bed-fellows. F. von Baader had made the thought of Boehme known to Schelling and so influenced the development of 19th century Idealism. Their influence on that forgotten but once influential figure, Martensen, unexpectedly ensured that his thought bore fruit - through Martensen's critic, Kierkegaard. Likewise Hamann will be generally known as a father of the irrationalism that is so often seen as a modern blight but hardly ever seen as a significant linguistic philosopher and critic of the Enlightenment. My point thus is quite simple. Kierkegaard was a philosophical genius with the metaphysical acuity to see the permanent value of these strange currents in the heritage of thought that he had received. In them and through them he was able to make a decisive contribution to the development of European philosophy, seen particularly in the emergence of Existentialism. Thus he gave European philosophy and culture in general a powerful reminder that it was no triviality that Shakespeare put in the mouth of Polonius - 'To thine own self be true'.

Saving the Self: Tradition and Identity in Clemens Brentano's *Rheinmärchen*

Carol Tully (Bangor)

WE ALL EXPERIENCE tradition as part of a complex system of cultural markers which help our societies function as cohesive units. The twenty-first century understanding of tradition within our Western cultures appears well-established and is inextricably linked to cultural, national, and indeed, individual identities. However, our understanding of tradition today should not be regarded as definitive but instead as part of an ongoing process which sees our notions of both tradition and identity evolve in response to developments in thought and world events. European Romanticism is a prime example of one such response, reacting to the ideals of the Enlightenment which had unsettled the established values of societies once secure in their faith, culture, and social structures. Enlightenment thought, with its emphasis on the rights of man, had taught the individual to question those beliefs which governed society, but had failed to provide a viable alternative, leaving many with a sense of cultural and social dislocation. The Romantic movement sought to challenge the perceived failings of the Enlightenment and a central theme in the work of many writers and thinkers was a renewed understanding of individuality which aimed to reunite individuals with the values and traditions from which they had become detached, thus imbuing both individual and society with a sense of self - a sense of identity.

The arguments surrounding the role of German Romantic writers in the emergence of a definable German national identity are well rehearsed. Their work marks the culmination of a process which can be traced back to the early eighteenth century and which was brought to a head by the upheaval of the French Revolution and the Napoleonic Wars. The primordialism which characterises

Romantic political and cultural notions of national identity in the German lands is essentially organicist, evolving from Enlightenment naturalism and the voluntarism of Rousseau, through Herderian historicism, towards the self-conscious belief of the Fichtean ideal. The notion of a national culture was central to this process of evolution: an identifiable common (or at least interrelated) set of practices and traditions, depicted in visual, oral, and written culture and passed down through the generations. By the time Fichte published his *Reden an die deutsche Nation* (Addresses to the German Nation) in 1808, this notion formed the basis of an ideological curriculum intended to infuse the populace of the disparate German states with a sense of national cultural pride, one which mirrored community and individual aspirations alike. If political cohesion was still a pipe dream, then cultural cohesion might at least provide the role model for future unity.

As the Romantic movement began to emerge in the German lands in the 1790s, the standing of German culture was already high. Europe had embraced the work of Goethe and Schiller, and Weimar stood alongside Paris and London as an acknowledged centre of cultural excellence. Although the notion of 'German culture' had begun to take on meaning, this still placed that culture in a universal context. The new Romantic generation, whilst expressing admiration for the achievements of their elders, set about establishing a new set of values. Modern German culture may be great, but that greatness had not emerged from a vacuum and its future did not lie in the slavish adherence to universally accepted aesthetic ideals. The Romantics sought instead to combine new developments in literature and the arts with an idealised concept of ancient German culture, what Hobsbawm terms 'a suitable historic past'. If these new Romantic values, which rejected the universality of the predominantly French Enlightenment ideal in favour of cultural pluralism, were to prevail, then a continuum with this 'historic past' must be proven. This would be achieved through the philological and literary endeavours of the Romantic school. In their work, the German Romantics were not so much inventing traditions, but rather revisiting and rediscovering those which had been forgotten, dismissed, or simply denied. Their work was in many ways an attempt to construct a new set of 'ancient' traditions from the building materials provided by the old. Hobsbawm describes the creation of such novel constructs as the exploitation of 'the well-supplied warehouses of official ritual, symbolism and moral exhortation'.[1] In similar vein, discussing the concepts which constitute our, essentially Western, notion of national identity, Anthony D. Smith identifies the interpretation of a perceived 'historical' past founded on a network of interdependent elements:

> A 'historic' land is one where terrain and people have exerted mutual, and beneficial, influence over several generations. The homeland becomes a repository of historic memories and associations, the place where 'our' sages, saints and heroes lived, worked, prayed and fought. All this makes the homeland unique. Its rivers, coasts, lakes, mountains and cities become 'sacred' - places of veneration and exaltation whose inner meanings can be fathomed only by the initiated, that is, the self-aware members of the nation.[2]

Taken in the context of such formulae, one text of the Romantic period in Germany stands out as a veritable *tour de force*. Clemens Brentano's collection of literary fairytales, *Rheinmärchen* (Tales of the Rhine), boasts a breathtaking amalgamation of location, folklore, and history, spun together into a wonderful fabric of invention and allusion. The tales, written between 1810 and 1812, with some reworking in the 1830s, were published posthumously by Guido Görres in 1846. To the modern reader, the collection of four *Märchen* is a delightful homage to Germany's landscape and culture. However, had they been available to a contemporary audience, Brentano's tales would have made a quite different impression. Written at a time when the German lands were at their lowest ebb since the Thirty Years War, many under Napoleonic occupation, the tales are a defiant celebration of all things German. The collection is loaded with cultural and political significance, carried by a set of overlapping networks which elaborate key aspects central to any national identity: topography, geography, and folklore. Brentano sets his tales along the river Rhine with specific locations such as Trier, Mainz, Koblenz, and Bingen. This has a dual significance, exploiting one of Germany's most beautiful and historical regions - seen by Brentano as his spiritual homeland - but simultaneously drawing attention to the vulnerable border with France. It is an indication of Brentano's patriotic defiance that in the tales the river is the ruling natural force and anything but vulnerable. Beyond the Rhine, the wider landscape too has a part to play. A combination of rivers, mountains, and forests interact, often through the fairytale wonder of personification, to pull the German lands together under the watchful eye of Father Rhine. These physical elements are the backdrop for a series of characters borrowed from or based on aspects of German folk culture including Loreley, the Pied Piper, and Bishop Hatto, as well as figures from a number of tales which would soon become world famous thanks to Brentano's friends, the Brothers Grimm. On a national cultural level, then, these tales represent Brentano's contribution to the Fichtean ideal. They voice an allegorical call for unity, a celebration of the German self.[3]

There is, however, a more personal aspect to these tales, one embodied by the central protagonist, the miller, Radlauf. His endeavours are in keeping with the patriotic mood and result in the defeat of evil, the restoration of natural order, and the salvation of the people of the Rhine. As the hero of the tales and ally of Father Rhine himself, Radlauf can scarcely be seen as anything less than a national ideal. One of the many characters specially created by Brentano for this wondrous world, his genetic line is clear, inheriting the charm and good fortune of the fairytale prince as well as the noble virtues of the medieval knight. He is brave, wise, and imbued with an unfailing sense of honour. His name, evoking the turning of a wheel, is itself the epitome of solid, cyclical dependability. Yet there is another side to this tenacious hero. If the tales themselves are Brentano's response to the issue of national identity, then Radlauf can be seen as the key to understanding aspects of Brentano's own, rather fragile sense of self. Following a line of enquiry left unexplored in my previous study of the *Rheinmärchen*, I would like to suggest that Radlauf is more than just a cultural construct, that he represents, in part at least, an idealisation of Brentano's great friend and co-editor of *Des Knaben Wunderhorn* (The Boy's Magic Horn, 1805-1808), Ludwig Achim von Arnim. Rereading the tales, it is certainly hard to ignore the echoes of their long and fruitful friendship, a relationship which has itself become one of the myths of German Romanticism.

The notion of identity lies at the very heart of this friendship. For Brentano, the association with Arnim was one of the defining relationships in a lifetime spent searching for a sense of self. This search involved an unusually high level of emotional and intellectual dependence on others, something of which Brentano himself was acutely aware. As early as 1801, in a letter to Friedrich Karl von Savigny, Brentano spoke of his constant need for 'ein Mittler mit der Welt' [a mediator with the world].[4] Later that same year, he met Arnim and, for the time being at least, he had found his mediator. The friendship provided Brentano with a context in relation to the world around him, a context relevant to his individual aspirations and values (something which would be repeated on a spiritual level almost two decades later as he abandoned his previous ideals to devote his life to the stigmatic Katharina Emmerich). The significance of such a context is highlighted in Holger Schwinn's study of the correspondence between Brentano and Arnim which identifies their relationship as one centred on 'Ich-Stabilisierung' [I-stabilisation].[5] This results in a highly stylised exchange which presents the relationship as an intellectual ideal. Through their letters, the two writers are consciously constructing identities for themselves which accord with contemporary ideals of friendship - often referred to as the cult of friendship - and which act as responses to the destabilising effects of social change on the individual. As such, their individual identities are effectively defined within the context of the relationship itself.

This self-contextualisation was not, however, a mere intellectual exercise. In these dangerous times, overshadowed by the perils of the Napoleonic Wars, such Utopian notions of friendship were forced to compete with other, far harsher ideals as patriotic fervour captured the Romantic imagination. Arnim, a willing combatant, inspired the otherwise politically disinterested Brentano to respond to the threat posed by the wars, and indeed the intensity of their relationship increased exponentially with the advance of the Napoleonic forces. Yet for Brentano, the primal fear was not of political occupation but rather personal dislocation. The wars represented an existential threat on two fronts: the disfigurement of his spiritual homeland, the Rheingau, so lovingly depicted in the *Rheinmärchen*, and the danger to his great friend and 'mediator', Arnim. This undermined the very foundations of the identity Brentano had created for himself. His love of the Rheingau had been awakened during a trip there with Arnim in 1802 and the resulting ideals of landscape and friendship formed an axis of physical and psychological security. The potential loss of both would be devastating. As this extract from a letter of 5 July 1813 shows, Brentano's response to this threat is self-indulgent and keeps the cornerstones of this constructed identity to the fore:

Dearest Arnim! As ever, as always, I have thought about you in all times of trouble. How jealous I was of your Home Guard company, how much I would have liked to be amongst them. The worries of the battle [of Lützen] cannot have been greater for you than they were for me. How happy your Fatherland is in its heart! You can triumph.[6]

This expression of vicarious angst provides an illustration of the nature of Brentano's relationship with Arnim. The latter becomes a channel through which Brentano is able to claim experience of war. He idolises Arnim and in so doing finds a role for himself in the action. By making a hero of Arnim in this way, Brentano is able to confront his own, essentially self-oriented fears of the war. In victory, the heroic Arnim saves not only the nation but the very core of Brentano's identity itself. The virtues displayed by the soldier Arnim parallel those accorded to Radlauf in a fusion of reality and fiction which elaborates the dual crises of identity which are central to the author's experience at this time. The depiction of Radlauf in the *Rheinmärchen* can, then, be seen as an extension of the process of 'Ich-Stabilisierung' begun in the correspondence, one which draws together issues of national and individual identity.

Comparison of Brentano's two heroes draws our attention once more to the notion of tradition. Both clearly represent the values of a bygone age, of 'a suitable historic past'. Adherence to an idealised traditional social structure is apparent in the focus on inherent nobility. Brentano, himself of second generation Italian merchant stock, clearly admires noble provenance, which is, of course, Arnim's birthright, one he shares with the fictitious Radlauf who is destined to rule with honour and takes up the challenge without hesitation. Arnim saw it as his noble duty to enlist and fight against Napoleon and Brentano viewed his friend's involvement in the war as evidence of his honour and patriotism. Both Radlauf and Arnim epitomise the ideal of the nobility as the legitimate ruling class whose positive influence ensures stability and continuity. A further parallel highlights the central role of cultural tradition. In the second tale, 'Das Märchen von dem Hause Staarenberg' (The Tale of the House of Staarenberg), Radlauf is in charge of the storytelling. He becomes the oral equivalent of the collector, assembling the parents who will each tell a tale to free their children from the waters of the Rhine. This effects a physical rather than a philological collation but the underlying intention parallels that of Arnim and Brentano's *Wunderhorn* collection: the preservation of culture for future generations. In Radlauf's case this is all the more poignant as it involves the preservation of the next generation itself, without which both culture and community would cease to exist. Through their understanding and appreciation of tradition, both Radlauf and Arnim are able to function as mediators, bringing stability and self-definition to the worlds they inhabit. Radlauf's rise to power signifies the end of upheaval and the restoration of a golden age. Arnim, for a time at least, seemed to provide Brentano with a means to understand his own world. It is perhaps no coincidence that Brentano's enthusiasm for the *Rheinmärchen* waned as his relationship with Arnim began to cool. He would later express embarrassment at the childish intensity of the tales, an attitude which itself supports the view that Radlauf's world was created in response to a time of deep insecurity, one which hindsight might consider with a degree of detachment.

The crises of identity - national and individual - which provide the impetus for the magical *Rheinmärchen* are the product of an age of change. It is in understanding and responding to such change that we find the true value of tradition, not just for Brentano and the Romantic school, but for our cultures and societies today. Tradition too is a mediator. It enables us to communicate with and understand our past. In so doing, it provides us with a context without which, our identities, national, cultural, and individual, would be meaningless.

NOTES

[1] *The Invention of Tradition*, ed. by Eric Hobsbawm & Terence Ranger (Cambridge: Canto, 1992 [1983]), p. 6.

[2] Anthony D. Smith, *National Identity* (Harmondsworth: Penguin, 1991), p. 9.

[3] For a more detailed study of the issue of national identity in the *Rheinmärchen*, see Carol Tully, *Creating a National Identity: A Comparative study of German and Spanish Romanticism with particular reference to the Märchen of Ludwig Tieck, the Brothers Grimm, and Clemens Brentano, and the costumbrismo of Blanco White, Estébanez Calderón, and López Soler*, Stuttgarter Arbeiten zur Germanistik 347 (Stuttgart: Hans-Dieter Heinz, 1997), chapter 5a.

4   *Das unsterbliche Leben. Unbekannte Briefe von Clemens Brentano*, ed. by W. Schellberg & F. Fuchs (Jena: Eugen Diederichs Verlag, 1939), p. 202. Göttingen, July 1801.
5   Holger Schwinn, *Kommunikationsmedium Freundschaft. Der Briefwechsel zwischen Ludwig Achim von Arnim und Clemens Brentano in den Jahren 1801 bis 1816* (Frankfurt/M: Lang, 1997), p. 10.
6   *Achim von Arnim und die ihm nahe standen*, ed. by Reinhold Steig, 3 vols (Stuttgart: Cotta, 1894-1913), I, 315. Letter to Arnim dated 5 July 1813.

Scott's Edward Waverley and Tolstoy's Pierre Bezukhov

W Gareth Jones (Bangor)

SIR WALTER Scott's *Waverley; or, 'Tis Sixty Years Since* had as great an impact on the development of the historical novel in Russia as in other European countries. It was published in Russian as early as 1827 at a time when a novel's translation was often the mark of the status the work had already attained amongst the literary elite who were more accustomed to read in French and German. The earliest original Russian historical novels were also heavily influenced by Scott's novels, as has been demonstrated recently by Mark Al'tshuller.[1] In 1834 with the publication of Pushkin's prose masterpiece, *The Captain's Daughter*, Scott's prestige was confirmed by Pushkin's acknowledgement of the debt he owed his Scottish contemporary. He was indebted to him for situation and plot. Pushkin mirrored Scott's story of a young English squire's confused loyalty during the Young Pretender's 1745 rebellion in an exotic Scotland, in his version of a confusion of loyalty now experienced by a Russian nobleman in alien Tatar territory in 1774 during the rebellion of the charismatic pretender, Pugachev. Crucially, Pushkin seems to have realised that it was only history that was still vivid in living memory and still had a bearing on contemporary society that should be exploited. As with Scott's *Waverley*, *The Captain's Daughter* could well have borne the subtitle, *'Tis Sixty Years Since*.

Likewise Tolstoy's *War and Peace*. Tolstoy's reliance on living memory, the recollections of his grandparents' generation, was apparent in his later failure to cope with the demands of a projected novel set in the world of Peter the Great. Despite his energetic researches, that epoch proved to be too remote from his own time. The events, and men and women of 1805, when *War and Peace* begins, were still graspable by him just sixty years later in 1865 when the first volume of his historical novel was published. Unlike Pushkin, Tolstoy paid no direct due to Sir Walter Scott. Indeed by the 1860s Scott had fallen out of fashion and the few references to him by Tolstoy are disparaging. Yet the example of the early Russian historical novels and particularly that of *The Captain's Daughter* were strong prompts for Tolstoy's choice of the recent, recoverable past for his period.

If the temporal relationship between the novelist and the age described by him is one salient feature of Scott's novel, another was the portrayal of a new kind of central character for a historical romance. Here was no passionate, committed hero. 'The "hero" of a Scott novel', maintained Lukács, 'is always a more or less mediocre, average English gentleman'.[2] It is this choice of a middling sort of 'hero' that was identified by Lukács as one of the essential features of Scott's revolutionary method. The contrast between Scott's novels and their Romantic precursors was to be found here 'in the composition of his novels - with the mediocre, prosaic hero as the central figure'.[3] The purpose of the decent, average figure, however, is not to embody a consensus in society; rather, he is designed to be able to operate in the clashing extremes within a society in crisis. Scott's inventiveness in this regard was clearly appreciated by Pushkin who presented in his Grinev, the central character of *The Captain's Daughter,* such an average Russian petty squire who provided not only a picture of a serving nobleman on an untamed frontier of the Russian Empire but also an excursion into the world of the barbaric rebel. Grinev is touched by the charisma of Pugachev just as Edward Waverley comes under the spell of the Young Pretender 'whose form and manners as well as the spirit which he displayed in this singular enterprise, answered his ideas of a hero of romance.'[4]

Pushkin's Grinev, however, is more of the average man of his class than his prototype, Edward Waverley. The latter has features that mark him out as a peculiarly eccentric character. Scott arranged for him to have a childhood open to the conflicting 'taste and opinions' (p. 11) of both his father, a conforming Hanoverian and an uncle, Sir Everard, who hankered after the old Stuart days. Confusion of political influence was accompanied by a desultory education and the indulgence of tutors who allowed him to follow his own whim in his reading. The 'evil consequences' (p. 13) of this, as Scott put it, were that the young man, despite a keen native wit, was naïve and susceptible to the impress of the range of views met on his travels. Yet, despite his willingness, he lacked the certainty to integrate himself in any particular society. He remained an outsider, and impressionable.

It is as such an outsider, with a desultory education that Pierre Bezukhov is introduced in the opening pages of *War and Peace*. And as the novel unfolds, his resemblance to the Edward Waverley prototype already long established in European literature, becomes apparent. Pierre's French name, his upbringing as an illegitimate child in France and the possession of French as his first language mark him out. As does his awkward, lumbering physique that seems to Anna Scherer to be 'too large and unsuited to the place'.[5] He is literally a misfit. Yet he strives to belong to the society in which he finds himself, making a clumsy stab in this first instance of taking part in a philosophical, political discussion in what he imagines to be an intellectual *salon* and betraying his sympathies for Napoleon and the French revolution. If Tolstoy draws upon the Waverley prototype, the Russian novelist, as was his wont, intensifies the conspicuous features of his model. Pierre is more of a misfit, more naïve and more an outsider than Edward. But essentially they share an immature unworldliness with Edward's romantic illusions seconded in Pierre's addiction to 'philosophical meditation' (p. 35), or, more accurately, to 'dreamy philosophising'.

It has been argued that Edward's continuous journeying constitute 'the central device, and one of the central metaphors of *Waverley*; they are journeys which allow Waverley to fulfil his birthright and to sway in allegiance not just between two women, but between two visions of life, two sides, two politics, two cultures, two futures.'[6] Pierre likewise is in continuous movement and prey to the dualities of the Napoleonic era. No sooner has the reader met the admirer of Napoleon in St Petersburg than Pierre is exiled to Moscow. Within a few short chapters, the reader, by following Pierre, comes to meet his two future wives, Hélène and Natasha, to contrast the artificial, dissolute Petersburg with the natural, family-centred Rostovs in Moscow, to note the conflict between the Napoleonic dreams and revolutionary fervour that have infected Pierre in Paris and the dogged, unthinking patriotism of his Russian relatives. And Pierre's wanderings are not limited to the two capitals. It is at Torzhok, a staging post on the road between them, that he has his fateful meeting with the freemason Bazdayev who causes another shift in Pierre's outlook. On a visit to his distant Ukrainian estates, he demonstrates his complete lack of understanding for the peasantry's mindset as his naïve, charitable plans for their betterment, inspired by his freemasonry, are cynically undermined by his bailiff. From Kiev via Prince Andrey's Bald Hills near Smolensk he returns to the capitals until the patriotic fervour aroused by Napoleon's invasion persuades Pierre to follow the Russian army to Mozhaisk and witness the battle of Borodino. After retreating with the army to Moscow he involves himself in the resistance, is taken prisoner and at last is obliged to come to an understanding of the Russian common people as the French retreat, taking their prisoners with them. Following his rescue, Pierre moves to Orel, a typical provincial town in the Russian heartland, a place holding no memories of his past and therefore providing neutral ground for his convalescence and spiritual renewal. Refreshed, both physically and mentally, he returns to the twin capitals to marry Natasha and settle down in Petersburg.

The restlessness with which the authors endow both Waverley and Pierre underlines the susceptibility of their minds to changing influences. Pierre's naïve optimism, apparent as he makes his rose-tinted rounds of his Ukrainian peasantry is totally different from the sober respect he develops towards folk wisdom as he mingles with the common soldiers whose imprisonment he shares. The freemasonic dreams of fraternal, universal peace garnered while he was in the depths of depression following his marital breakdown, are dissipated when he is unable to resist the communal, bellicose fervour of the Muscovite nobility threatened by Napoleon's advance. That fervour was communicated to Alexander I when he sought their support in Moscow. Pierre was among them to be impressed and converted by the Emperor's charismatic presence. Here was the encounter of the protagonist with the leader-figure which has been recognised as 'one of the canonical scenes of the genre'.[7] Scott had established the convention in his description of Waverley's audience with the Young Pretender, and Pushkin likewise ensured that his Grinev met Pugachev. Tolstoy, it is true, makes a significant variation on the convention by not arranging an unlikely face-to-face interview between Pierre and Alexander I but subsuming Pierre's personal enthusiasm in the crowd hysteria. Scott and Pushkin, by humanising the leader-figure in their meetings with an ordinary man, questioned the super-human status hitherto bestowed on the great, historical leader. Tolstoy, more intent than his predecessors on demolishing the Great Man explanation of history, also demonstrates how an ordinary mortal may have his charisma created by an aroused crowd. Kutuzov, however, is certainly humanised and demystified when he addresses a few simple words to Pierre on the battlefield at Borodino. As well as encountering the leader-figures, the protagonists also rub shoulders with the lowest, most inscrutable members of their societies and come to understand their part in the unrolling of history. In this respect, the plaid-wearing Waverley's introduction to folk culture through his acquaintance with the clansman Evan Dhu is a foretaste of the kaftan-clad Pierre's meeting with the peasant soldier Platon Karataev.

Another salient feature of the historical novels that followed *Waverley* was their account of the main character as an inexperienced outsider on the field of battle. The concept of the key-battle as a coherent, explicable historical turning point was undermined in the perspective of the confused greenhorn or civilian unable to comprehend any significance in the chaos of the happenings in which he was embroiled. Pierre's experience at Borodino unfolds in the same manner as Waverley's at Prestonpans. Initially both men view the assembling armies from a high vantage and attempt to impose a significant coherence on the military dispositions and evolutions. In *Waverley* this is conveyed in the chapter entitled 'The Eve of Battle' (pp. 219-23). In *War and Peace* on the eve of Borodino, the naïve Pierre, initially unable to distinguish between the Russian and French troops, has to ask Benningsen, a professional soldier, for an explanation of their dispositions. So clear is the elucidation that Pierre is later able to reassure Prince Andrey that, although as a civilian he is not completely appraised, 'but I understand the general position' (II, 481). In *Waverley*, the military order described in 'The Eve of Battle' is utterly overturned in the brief following chapter 'The Conflict' (pp. 223-7) where the reader is swept into the 'moment of confusion and terror' that Edward experiences in the heat of battle. The uncomprehending Pierre's own 'confusion and terror' at Borodino is detailed in three famous chapters (II, 503-17) in *War and Peace* where he stumbles into intense hand-to-hand combat.

Pierre's survival from the thick of battle is a miracle. This extraordinary luck was like that of Pushkin's Grinev in *The Captain's*

Daughter recognised by John Bayley as a feature that 'as in Shakespeare's last plays and some Greek tragedies [...] celebrates for individuals the possibility of an almost supernatural good fortune.'[8] This was certainly demonstrated in the case of Grinev's model, Edward Waverley. During a highland hunt he is saved in the nick of time by Fergus Mac-Ivor from being gored by stags who charge the hunting party; in Cairnvreckan, on his return to the lowlands, he is rescued from the wrath of a mob by Mr Morton, the local minister; shortly afterwards he is rescued by highlanders as he is being taken under armed guard to answer a charge of treason; he survives Prestonpans and later an assassination attempt by a clansman who believed that he had besmirched the honour of his clan; at Clifton it was a case of 'once or twice narrowly escaping being slain or made prisoner' (p. 279) until he is saved when a farmer's daughter mistakenly takes him to be her lover in the dark; and finally he is able to travel the length of England despite the warrants out for his arrest to get a false passport from Colonel Talbot, an erstwhile prisoner of the Jacobites whose release he had obtained in Edinburgh. Pierre's life, likewise, seems invulnerable. His escape from Borodino had been preceded by his survival against all odds in the duel fought for his wife's honour with the experienced duellist Dolokhov. He is saved from execution as an incendiary after the fall of Moscow by the one fateful look from his interrogator Marshal Davoût who recognised a fellow nobleman in Pierre's elegant French. Just as the French, as they begin their long retreat, set about shooting stragglers in the group of prisoners to which Pierre is attached, he is rescued in a daring raid by Russian officers in which Petya Rostov who would have been his future brother-in-law is killed. It is remarkable that Pierre, Grinev and Waverley are all saved in turn by both sides in the conflict in which they participate: Waverley by Jacobite and Hanoverian; Grinev by Pugachev and Catherine the Great; and Pierre by Frenchman and Russian. And the final flourish of fortune is that all three bring their travels and tribulations to a close by settling into a long and contented marriage.

NOTES
1   Mark Al'tschuller, *Epokha Val'tera Skotta v Rossii: Istoricheskii roman 1830-x godov* (Sankt-Peterburg: Akamedmicheskii proekt, 1996).

2. Georg Lukács, *The Historical Novel*, trans. by Hannah and Stanley Mitchell (London: Merlin Press, 1962), p .33.
3. Ibid. p. 34.
4. Sir Walter Scott, *Waverley; or, 'Tis Sixty Years Since*, ed. by Claire Lamont. (Oxford, New York: Oxford University Press, 1986), p. 193. Future page references to this edition will be indicated in the text.
5. Leo Tolstoy, *War and Peace*, trans. by Louise and Aylmer Maude, 3 vols (London: Oxford University Press, 1930), I, p. 10. Future page references to this edition will be indicated in the text.
6. Richard Humphrey, *Walter Scott: Waverley* (Cambridge: Cambridge University Press, 1993), p. 38.
7. Ibid., p. 40.
8. John Bayley, *Pushkin: A Comparative Commentary* (Cambridge: Cambridge University Press, 1971), pp. 346-7.

Hereditary Keeper of the Crown

Idris Parry (Bangor)

WHAT'S THE point of poetry? Rainer Maria Rilke may seem the archetypal pure poet subject only to an irresistible daemon. He confesses he understands certain parts of his own poetry 'only in isolated moments of grace'. So it must be significant when he goes out of his way to give a reason for his activity. The only purpose he ever attributes to his poetry is the preservation of tradition. This is hardly surprising in a man who sees himself as an integral part of the earth's growth. In an essay of 1913 Rilke says it must be the memory of prehistoric times which breaks out in the heart of the predestined poet.

Wherever he travels - and he is a most unquiet wanderer - Rilke always asks about the history of places, compiles facts about local families, draws up genealogies, records legendary tales, and generally gives himself as complete a picture as possible of the past in the present. Again and again in his letters (and what a mountain of these there are) he refers to the history and appearance of villages, districts, individual houses. Old things are always precious to him. He is even affected by the smell from old cupboards. And it is not only other families that interest him. He probes into his own ancestry. Fairly late in life, in September 1924, he tells a correspondent that curiosity about his own inheritance dates back to childhood; he recalls that in his eighth or ninth year this interest in his own family had become for him a passion 'without parallel'. He must have been a rather solemn child.

Rilke is by no means the first to see that modern commercial production threatens the continuance of tradition by obliterating handcraft and substituting sterile objects for things which speak of heart and mind. Nothing will come of nothing. In a letter towards the end of his life, in 1925 to his Polish translator von Hulewicz, he expresses both concern and intention. He laments that the living and experienced things are on the decline and cannot he replaced. His generation may be the last to have known such things. 'On us rests the responsibility of preserving not merely their memory [...] but their human and laric worth ("laric" in the sense of household gods).' This implies an almost religious intent. He remarks to von Hulewicz that we cannot be satisfied in the world of time, nor are we fixed in it. 'We overflow continually towards people who have lived in the past, towards our origin and to those who come after us.'

No division here. Rilke is aware of standing in the stream of history viewed as a continuum of past, present and future. The historian G. M. Trevelyan declares that 'truth is the criterion of historical study, but its impelling motive is poetic'. He echoes Carlyle, who says, when discussing the word Past, that history is the true poetry. And for Rilke poetry becomes an assessment of history, transformed into visible linguistic objects which are intended to represent life in the same way as the artefacts of vanishing crafts. To his friend Countess Sizzo he writes in 1923 that the more we are cut off from tradition 'the more important it is for us to remain open and conductive to the broadest and most intimate traditions of humanity'. He tells her he sees more and more that his *Sonnets to Orpheus* are an effort in this direction. 'We are the transmuters of the earth' he tells von Hulewicz. 'There is no other task.'

Soon after the completion of this sonnet cycle and the *Duino Elegies* in 1922 he uses a striking image to represent his feeling of personal responsibility. From this high point of poetic achievement he looks back with satisfaction at a visit to Budapest in 1895 when he was only nineteen. This was a significant year for the Hungarians: it marked a thousand years since Prince Arpád led the Magyars into Hungary. There were elaborate millennium celebrations, processions. Rilke vividly recalls his feelings when he saw the royal crown passing slowly by in its own carriage. He speaks of his excitement, of his beating heart. This crown was a symbol of the past in the present and of future promise. Just then, says Rilke, his family were pressing him to choose a profession. He goes on: 'For people like us, with our relationship to the thing [...] wouldn't there be only the *one* fully appropriate office - that of Hereditary Keeper of the Crown [Erb-Kron-Hüter]?'

What is his relationship to the thing? What indeed does he mean by 'thing'? For him as a poet the thing is an object sculpted in words. In Rilke's conception of 'thing', the influence of Rodin is profound. The two met for the first time in September 1902 at the sculptor's villa in Meudon near Paris. As they were sitting in the garden a little girl came up to them (Rilke assumed she must be Rodin's daughter); she held a tiny snail, picked up from the gravel. Rodin looked at it with interest and said to Rilke that the minute shell reminded him of the surface of Greek masterpieces. The poet never forgot this lesson in vision, how the fabulous can emerge from the fact observed without prejudice. In Rodin he notes an utter suspension of self, open commitment, patience. And a passion for work.

Writing to his wife about the impact of Rodin, Rilke must be thinking of his own earlier method or lack of it: he now says it is essential not to stop at dreams, at intentions, at waiting for the right mood, but vital 'to transpose everything into *things* with all one's strength, as Rodin has done'. The emphasis on *things* is Rilke's own, underlined in the letter. And it is to the construction of things that he now turns. Copying the sculptor, Rilke too believes he must work patiently from observed surfaces to create poems as objects, physical structures with edge and impact, as independent of each other and their creator as the separate shapes made by the sculptor. When he now talks about his work, his language takes on the vocabulary of craft.

A year after the meeting with Rodin he tells a friend he has been like a mirror turned this way and that, taking in images at random but making nothing of them. 'That's why' he says 'it is so very necessary for me to find the tools of my art, the hammer, my hammer, so that it may become master and grow above all sounds.' He goes on to say there must be work for the hands 'in this art too'. By 'this art' he of course means poetry.

We know how events which do not seem important at the time can come back to us as insistent memories. Even later, at the moment of recollection, it is sometimes difficult to understand just why *these* incidents should be selected for recall. Rilke writes in February 1924 to someone who has asked about 'influences' and, after charting 'important' events, goes on to speculate whether less obvious experiences may not have had a greater effect. He returns to his fascination with the 'made' object and traditional movements of the hands. He speaks of hours spent in Rome watching a ropemaker repeat in his craft 'one of the world's oldest gestures'; and then the potter seen in a village on the Nile: 'To stand by his wheel was so indescribably and mysteriously fruitful for me.' How fruitful we already know, because these figures appear in his statement of intent, the *Duino Elegies* (completed in February 1922). In this context Rilke uses the word 'praise' to signify acceptance and utterance; when he says 'tell' he speaks of the poet's craft; he defines the Angel of the *Elegies* elsewhere as 'the being which transcends us', a being obviously related to the Orpheus of the sonnet cycle. Access to the Angel seems easier for the craftsman than the poet. From the ninth *Elegy*:

> Praise this world to the Angel, not the untellable;
> you cannot impress him with what you've marvellously felt;
> In the cosmos, where he feels more feelingly, you are a novice.
> So show him the simple thing, formed from generation to generation, that lives as ours near at hand and in view.
> Tell him the things. He will stand more astonished as you stood by the rope maker in Rome or the potter on the Nile.

This is Rilke reminding himself of what he should do. In the *Sonnets to Orpheus* (1922) he does it as best he can. These poems are his efforts to make equivalents which can stand independently like objects made by hands. According to him, this intense cycle of sonnets was created 'in ultimate obedience'. And it is in connection with these poems that Rilke says he understands certain passages only in isolated moments of grace. But the underlying concept is the simplest of all. It is always around us - the world as an ever changing unity.

Orpheus is the perfect image for the perpetual transformation which is history, life on earth. Each poem in the cycle is an offering to Orpheus, who in legend is god as well as musician. In the *Sonnets* he has absolute powers of transformation like nature itself and, like nature, he can be seen only in one moment, the present. History is here, now. These poems are a puzzle to categorizing minds because they do not separate time from space, past from present. If the past has any existence, it can only be in the present. It is this present moment, not a pause but movement captured in passing, that the poet attempts to elevate in language. His poem becomes, he hopes, an object which will endure and carry tradition, as the old creations of manual craft accepted and continued tradition in the past.

The *Sonnets* are solid objects; you feel that if you tapped them they would ring. This cycle of poems was his 'ultimate effort', but was Rilke satisfied? Or was he working in the wrong material? As late as December 1923, nearly two years after the *Sonnets*, Rilke can still be astonished and driven close to despair by the apparent superiority of manual craft over the resources of poetry. In a letter to Countess Sizzo he describes a recent visit to the historical museum at Berne. He tells her of his admiration for early tapestries and oriental objects seen there, but what bowls him over is a display of shawls from Persia and Turkestan, old cashmere shawls of intricate design, each one (he says) 'a world in itself'. He suddenly grasps the essence of the shawl. 'But to express it? Again a fiasco.' Such essential expression can be achieved perhaps 'only in the transformations inherent in a tangible and slow manual craft'. It seems to him that the poet's language still approaches these cryptic equivalents of life 'only in a roundabout way'. He allows supremacy to the hand.

'Der Frauen Zustand ist beklagenswert': Remarks on Two Plays by von Horváth and Goethe

Dietmar Wünschmann (Gerstetten)

WALKING ALONG an avenue in Paris in June 1938, Ödön von Horváth was suddenly hit by a falling branch and killed. A few days before he had asked a soothsayer in Amsterdam about the outcome of his negotiations in Paris concerning the film version of his novel *Jugend ohne Gott*, and she had prophesied him the most important adventure of his life in that town.

In 1933 the Nazis, provoked by the author's social criticism and his attacks on nationalism and fascism, had banned Horváth's plays and declared his works of no importance whatever to the German people. Horváth, a Hungarian citizen, born in Fiume / Rijeka (Croatia) in 1901, educated in Budapest and since 1913 in Munich, wrote in German and had become a well-known intellectual in Berlin. In 1931 Carl Zuckmayer (1896-1977) praised the high quality of his plays.

After the Nazi verdict Horváth emigrated to Austria - like Keith Spalding in 1933.[1] He returned to Germany the following year trying to adjust to the political situation and hoping to make the Nazis revoke their ban; yet in vain. He returned to Austria in 1935.

Nonetheless Horváth continued writing plays in German in spite of the fact that they had no chance of being performed in Germany. Meanwhile an important change had taken place in Horváth's outlook on life, manifest in his new works as well. His experiences during the year 1933 and afterwards had made a tremendous impact on him. Moral conflicts were of considerable concern to him now and were displayed in his drama *Der jüngste Tag*, written in 1936. And so we might say Horváth definitely joined those who used their heads and were able to resist as K. H. Spalt had demanded.[2]

One kiss - and eighteen people lose their lives; from the very start the audience of *Der jüngste Tag* is confronted with the protagonists' way of coping with their guilt. In spite of doing the job of a stationmaster properly, Thomas Hudetz, married, in charge of a small railway station, is having a heated conversation with Anna, a young woman, by whom he suddenly gets kissed, though she is engaged to Ferdinand. This incident results in his failure to give the correct signal to the oncoming train in time. A few seconds later the train has run into another one.

In their row Anna and Hudetz address each other almost always in the formal way typical of formal German conversation. It is only much later that we learn that they have known each other very well for some time, even having had sexual relations. A few months after the accident and after the commission of inquiry has exonerated Hudetz, they meet secretly. On that occasion Anna makes use of the word 'erkennen' in her question (at the end of scene four) and refers by help of 'wieder' to similar events. Hudetz responds accordingly, and kisses and embraces her. German 'erkennen', 'eine Frau erkennen', meaning to have intercourse with her, 'is older than the Germanic languages as borne out by biblical usage and Latin *cognoscere feminam*. In German from OHG to 18th c., now only used when quoting from the Bible'.[3]

Despite their intimate relations Hudetz puts all blame onto Anna immediately after realising that he set the signal too late. He is not willing to admit that he neglected his duty, not even during the investigations. He resorts to a sham existence. Anna gives evidence in favour of Hudetz and even commits perjury, as Horváth shows us in the second scene. In the following two he draws attention to her deep feeling of guilt. She is convinced that her wrongdoing jeopardizes her life and demands immediate help from Hudetz. We get the impression that if both of them confessed their guilt her life could be worth living; but if she retracted her statement she would endanger him and cause an irreparable breach between the two of them, unimaginable to her. So she asks him to meet her secretly for a serious talk the following day. At first he does not want to consent, but he cannot leave her remarks 'I'm going to die' and 'Have mercy on me' (scene three) unnoticed. He agrees at last. Though saying, 'You behave as if your life were at stake', he does not take her problems seriously nor does he see the point of her remarks. The audience, on the other hand, realize that she is worried to death, and readers of the play should not be misled by the repeated stage instruction 'She smiles', and 'Anna smiles' (scenes three and four). Her smile expresses despair. Yet Hudetz is neither able to see her existential fear nor to face the fact that it should be his as well.

At their secret meeting (scene four) she draws his attention to his share of the blame for the fatal accident and wonders if he is not aware of his guilt. She even makes him think about the possibility that she might retract the false confession and the measures he would then have to take. When she asks him about the precautions he will take in that event she discovers that she has provoked in him the idea of murdering her. 'I won't kill you', he protests, but by using the decisive word himself he reveals his real thoughts and emotions, all churned up inside. Anna supports and justifies his hidden thoughts by saying 'Too bad', and 'I don't want to live any longer'. As he maintains that his conscience is clear and still lays all blame on her she is convinced that only a bigger crime will open his eyes and make him listen to reason, and tells him so. She feels that only a violent shock will make him comply with the ethical standards governing human behaviour; that is why she intends to sacrifice herself. At the same time she confesses her love: Everything and everybody have become meaningless to her except for Hudetz. When asked, Hudetz confirms that he feels the same about her. In addition to her confession she assures him of her strong belief that even in death she will belong to him, nothing can separate them. In the highly emotional scene she has created, Hudetz makes love to her and kills her.

'I know that I have murdered her', Hudetz confesses to his wife and brother-in-law shortly afterwards (scene six), thus making it clear that Anna was right. The crime he has committed has made him face reality. Although unable to recollect the details, he remembers words once spoken to him: You were exonerated, and you will have to commit a big crime to get punished. These were almost exactly Anna's words (scene four), but with a subtle difference. She had thoughtfully referred to foolish behaviour, while he clearly refers to a crime. At long last he is aware of having burdened himself with guilt.

However, Hudetz, no longer guided by Anna, is not ready to face the inevitable consequences. Instead he is going to flee. But having noticed Anna's obituary, picture, dedication and text below (scene six), he changes his mind. He refuses to take the suit of his brother-in-law, as he does no longer want to flee in disguise. He obviously wants to commit suicide. He goes to see the places of the two disasters to confront the scenes of horror. He returns to the viaduct, where he killed Anna, but does not jump to his death. He moves on to the place where the trains collided. Watching him in the seventh scene, we understand that he has not only left society, but also reality. He moves in a world of his own. In a stream of consciousness dead people become alive again, and they all converse with each other and with Hudetz. There is the engine driver who lost his life in the accident and who, of course, approves of the former station master's idea of letting himself get run over by the next train, thus avoiding any trial and punishment on earth. Hudetz seems to be convinced that 'God, if there is any, will show understanding'. But before he decides to put an end to his life, Anna becomes important in his reflections. It is she who beseeches him to stay alive. And so he does. Now he is determined to bear full responsibility and returns to reality: Immediately afterwards he surrenders to the police.

Anna, as we have seen, plays a vital role in Hudetz's life, either as a living person or in his imagination. She helps him to understand himself, his behaviour and actions, his responsibility and even his love for her. He tells Leni, the waitress, that he is 'engaged' to Anna (scene five), and also informs his wife and brother-in-law of this engagement (scene six). In doing so he tells them that Anna is of the utmost importance to him. At the same time Anna's prophecy (scene four) comes true: Even in death she belongs to him, is present and influences his actions at decisive moments.

Thanks to Anna Hudetz learns neither to exonerate himself from his guilt nor to be his own judge and escape punishment by committing suicide, a philosophy which should have appealed particularly to German theatre-goers after the end of World War II, when the play was first presented to them. Its message was deeply influenced by Ödön von Horváth's background, a fact which, according to Heimito von Doderer (1896-1966), can be generalized as well: 'Everybody gets his childhood tipped over his head like a bucket. It is only later that we find out what was in the bucket.'[4] Thanks to his sound education in schools and at the university of Munich Horváth had come into contact with classical philosophy and thus with man's never-ending reflections on life, on human conduct and behaviour towards other people.

His contact with religious thought might have shown him the endeavour of the ancients to develop moral principles by trying to be in harmony with the recorded or anticipated orders of their deities, to further their ends and particularly to win back the favour of the gods in the case of an offence by presenting offerings, even by sacrificing a human being, when they were in the most extreme plight, as told in the myth of Iphigenia, or illustrated by the sacrificial site excavated near Archanes on the Island of Crete in 1979, a place now called Anemospilia, where a young man was sacrificed in the course of a devastating earthquake about 1700 BC. Although Horváth had left the Catholic Church at the age of twenty-nine, we find the statement 'God is the truth' in his novel *Jugend ohne Gott*, written in 1937.[5] There are important allusions to Christianity in his play. The characters mention God when gossiping; the title refers to the Last Judgment, and Hudetz trusts in God's empathy with him; Hudetz registers the sound of the trumpets mentioned in the Book of Revelations; Anna resembles Eve tempting Adam; there is the biblical usage of 'erkennen' referred to by Old High German 'Adam sin wib erchande'.[6] When living in exile Horváth's, like Spalding's, 'thoughts [...] revolved around the question of religion',[7] and Spalding's assessment 'Combined with the belief in justice and freedom as the most important components of our thinking is the religious aspect, the belief in a higher power, a spirit which rules our world' can be applied to *Der jüngste Tag* as well.

Unlike Goethe's Iphigenie,[8] Anna does not allow us access to the basis and development of her thoughts. She knows the truth, feels guilty, accepts responsibility, and sacrifices herself. It is Iphigenie who discloses the train of thought in a detailed way. Being a Greek, she dislikes the life of a priestess in the foreign kingdom of Thoas, having been saved by the goddess Artemis from being sacrificed on the altar in Aulis and taken by her to Tauris. She yearns for her home country and family. Yet she finds herself incapable of dealing with her difficult situation, and it is in this context that she complains about the state of women.[9] Her problems become even more awkward, though: Thoas proposes to her; her brother Orest and his friend Pylades arrive and are captured by Thoas; her hopes for return are rekindled by their arrival; Thoas orders her to kill the two prisoners; the curse put on her family by the gods seems to be the reason for her hopeless situation; her brother's and his friend's advice to set them free, to escape with them and to commit a theft does not appear worthy of the confidence placed on her by Thoas. Iphigenie reveals her inner conflicts, her feeling of helplessness and being at the mercy of Pylades and the gods respectively. She is torn trying to tackle the problem herself. In the end she understands that it is up to her to act, and she decides to act in accord with the principles of humanity, even if she has to bear full responsibility for the consequences.[10] She tries her utmost (as Goethe's poem 'Das Göttliche' shows 'man alone can do the impossible'). Thus she has become mature. Being honest with Thoas, confronting him with the whole truth, she knows that she is now dependent on his positive or negative reaction, risking the lives of all the Greeks over whom Thoas has control (1.1936).

Iphigenie cannot be certain which of the voices within Thoas will win the battle (ll. 1979-82). Anna cannot be completely sure whether Hudetz will avoid responsibility or not. Both women put their lives at risk in defence of moral principles. They fight against inhumanity, which reminds us of the demands K. H. Spalt made. And when Thoas and Hudetz remember their partners in their later lives, their thoughts will be similar to those expressed by Shakespeare's lines, 'But if the while I think on thee, dear friend, / All losses are restor'd and sorrows end'.[11] So Iphigenie's earlier complaint about the state of women, 'der Frauen Zustand ist beklagenswert', is not justified. She herself and Anna prove their ability to take their own decisions and to act, to reconcile the individual with the fundamental moral standards of society and, as far as Iphigenie is concerned, to play her part in generating harmony between individuals and peace between peoples.

NOTES
[1] Keith Spalding, *The Long March*. (York: 1999), p. 56.
[2] Karl Heinz Spalt, *Kultur oder Vernichtung*. (Darmstadt: 3rd edition 1990), p.8.

3   Keith Spalding, *An Historical Dictionary of German Figurative Usage*. Fascicles 11-20. (Oxford: 1967), p. 677.
4   Quoted by Keith Spalding, *The Long March*, p. 67.
5   Ödön von Horváth, *Jugend ohne Gott*.(Frankfurt: 1992. st 2182), p. 148.
6   Grimm, *Deutsches Wörterbuch*, vol. iii, p. 866.
7   *The Long March*, pp. 67-8.
8   J. W. Goethe, *Iphigenie auf Tauris*. (1787). The play presents the results of Goethe's confrontation with Greek drama as well as with his own time.
9   Goethe, *Werke*. (Hamburg: 4th edition 1960), vol. v, p. 8.
10 Ibid., p. 60.
11 *Sonnet xxx*, ll. 13-14.

Pacifism and Mysticism: Aldous Huxley's Rejection of Violence and Totalitarianism

Lothar Fietz (Tübingen)

THE NINETEEN thirties were an age of polarization, persecution, commitment and conversion. Totalitarianism, chauvinism and racism joined forces both in Nazi Germany and in the Soviet Union in order to annihilate the opponents of the respective ideological systems. The political and racial purges in both systems bear witness to one and the same totalitarian strategy of eliminating those who refused to toe the line because they felt committed to inalienable human and civil rights and values such as the dignity, liberty and equality of individuals, freedom of thought, and non-violence as the prime prerequisite for a peaceful co-existence among individuals and nations. In the case of Germany in the early thirties, around the time Hitler came into power in January 1933, anti-fascism was but the lowest common political denominator shared, for a certain time, by militant communists, socialists and pacifists who, regardless of their political, social and moral aims or race, were persecuted alike as enemies by the Nazi régime. May 10th, 1933 marks a decisive stage in the process of brutalization of life: the public burning of books, defamed as 'un-German', in the presence of the Minister of Propaganda, Goebbels, at the gates of Humboldt University in Berlin. That autodafé foreshadowed the holocaust in the gas chambers of the concentration camps. In fear of their lives, writers, painters, composers, philosophers adhering to the most heterogeneous philosophies, beliefs and convictions, but united in their antagonism against fascist dictatorship, left Germany. Sanary-sur-Mer, a village on the Côte d'Azur, became the provisional refuge for many expatriate German intellectuals among whom Thomas Mann, Lion Feuchtwanger, Ernst Bloch, Bertolt Brecht and Franz Werfel already enjoyed international reputation. But the exodus also comprised younger people who felt forced to leave Germany for similar reasons: Sebastian Haffner's *Geschichte eines Deutschen: Die Erinnerungen 1914-1933*, written in 1939 and published posthumously in 2000, and Keith Spalding's autobiography *33-alles umsteigen*, published in 1992, give vivid evidence of the growing intolerance and of the fate awaiting political dissenters in Germany.

Karl Heinz Spalt, fervently committed to the ideal of non-violence, had to flee Germany in 1933 because of his pacifist creed. His *Handbook* of literary, philosophical and religious statements and confessions relating to the necessity of peace was entitled *Kultur oder Vernichtung? [Civilization or Annihilation?]*.[1] It shows a number of parallels with Aldous Huxley's 'What Are You Going to Do About It? The Case for Constructive Peace',[2] *An Encyclopaedia of Pacifism*,[3] and *Ends and Means*[4] as far as the basic pacifist convictions and intentions are concerned. But Huxley's pacifism grew out of different roots. The pacifism of those who had foreseen, witnessed and themselves endured coercion, cruelty and violence in their own country was of a more existential nature than the abstract logic of non-violence we find in Huxley's writings.

Aldous and Maria Huxley took residence at Sanary-sur-Mer in 1930. *Brave New World*, finished in August 1931, was meant as a warning of the course developments might take in the Western World. The 'gentle' coercion that the inhabitants of the New World are subjected to fails to reflect what was going on in the Soviet Union and in Germany at the time. And even when Huxley met with the German refugees at Sanary he gained little or no insight into the real situation. That was not exclusively Huxley's fault; it was also due to the pompous and detached behaviour of the *haute culture* assembled round Thomas Mann:

> The Huxleys did not take much to the German refugees. 'Rather a dismal crew,' Aldous wrote to Julian, 'already showing the disastrous effects of exile. Let us hope we shall not have to scuttle when Tom Mosley gets into power.'[5]

The 'Pyrrhonic aesthete', who had left the Savage in *Brave New World* 'only two alternatives, an insane life in Utopia, or the life of a primitive in an Indian village'[6] and had found it 'amusing', began to re-orient himself under the influence of the Rev H R L Sheppard, Vicar of St Martin's-in-the Fields, Dean of Canterbury, Canon of

St Paul's, who in 1934 had declared in public: *'We renounce war and never again, directly or indirectly, will we support or sanction another.'*[7] Huxley joined the Peace Pledge Union and on December 3rd, 1935, gave a talk at Friends' House in Euston Road, which marks a decisive turning point in his life. He spoke of a spiritual reality transcending time and personality, the experience of which would lead man to the insight that 'God [is...] present at least potentially in every human being. [...] If enough people address themselves to living up to this belief [...] then there will be peace.'[8]

The idea of a divine 'Ground', in which each individual is rooted, derives from medieval mysticism[9] and Huxley elaborated on his interpretation of 'The Nature of the Ground' in *The Perennial Philosophy* (1946). The mystical 'unitive knowledge of the divine Ground'[10] will not induce man to turn his back on temporal reality, but after re-emerging from the 'Ground' make him realize - as John Donne put it - that 'No man is an *Iland*, intire of it self',[11] but in the 'Ground' one with other individuals. This mystical belief became for Huxley the source of an ethos of love and peace and thus the basis of the pacifism he never tired of advocating from the mid-thirties onwards.

His conversion manifests itself in various ways. We come across it in the autobiographical layer of *Eyeless in Gaza* (1936).[12] Anthony Beavis undergoes a conversion similar to the one Huxley experienced at the time, i.e. passing from states of intellectual and moral 'detachment' (*EiG*, 4; 24; 87 etc.), 'lovelessness' (*EiG*, 15), 'self-emphasis' and the 'denial of others'(*EiG*, 614), to states in which he begins to transcend the 'closed universe' (*EiG*, 615) of his personality in the direction of the 'others'. In his diary Beavis begins to reflect on the possibility of a 'translation of love into terms of politics' (*EiG*, 554). The middle-class individualist - just like Huxley - expresses the conviction that

> people will behave [...] pacifically only if they have trained themselves as individuals to do so. [What is needed is the] knowledge of how to use the self and of what the self should be used for. (*EiG*, 325)

Huxley wrote those sentences under the influence of F M Alexander, who in his book *Constructive Conscious Control of the Individual* (1924) had developed techniques of the 'use of the self'. Huxley's emphasis on the rôle the individual must play in bringing about peace through an effort of 'love [...] and sympathetic awareness' (*EaM*, 125) is equally indebted to the religious mysticism of the middle-ages and to 18th century sentimentalism. However likeable and plausible that creed might still appear, it proved - tragically enough for pacifism - less than effective in subverting the power politics of the nineteen thirties and in finally preventing World War II.

Influenced by mystical and sentimentalist creeds, Huxley even went as far as advocating 'disarmament, *unilateral* if necessary' (*EaM*, 128) as part of the 'preventive ethics' (*EaM*, 16). He went even further in 'What Are You Going to Do About It? The Case For Constructive Peace' when he accused the victors of World War I of being responsible for the armaments race in the thirties:

> Italian Fascists, German National Socialists and Japanese Imperialists, despite their common doctrine of violence, have done no more to make future wars inevitable than has the American Democracy by means of the Hawley-Smoot Tariff, the war debt policy and its performance at the London Economic Conference. [...] Germany, Italy, and Japan are three countries whose position in the post-War world is fundamentally similar. All suffer from a sense of grievance - of grievance, moreover, which the existing circumstances of the world very largely justify. Germany suffered military defeat and prolonged humiliation at the hands of her conquerors. [...] The Nazis have promised to extricate Germany from this intolerable situation by force of arms, if necessary. ('What...', 396-7)

Huxley's abstract reasoning did not take into account what was really going on in Germany, Italy and Japan at the time or he would not have suggested appeasing the 'unsatisfied powers' ('What...', 398) by a 'redistribution of colonies',[13] as C Day Lewis polemically put it in his reply to Huxley's plea for peace. Huxley's translation of the mystical ethic of love into terms of politics made him blind to reality and - however pertinent and realistic the criticism of Huxley's position actually was - C Day Lewis turned a blind eye to what was actually happening in the Soviet Union when he - in opposing Huxley's fundamentalistic belief in the necessity of non-violence - deliberately ignored and even exculpated the Leninist and Stalinist use of violence:

> Violence has been used in Russia - that is enough for Mr. Huxley. The people of Russia are happier, more hopeful, better fed, better housed, better educated, in every way more civilised than under the Czarist régime - but all that, for Mr. Huxley, is irrelevant. He is only interested in Absolute Happiness, Absolute Justice. (*CDL*, 18)

The controversy between Aldous Huxley and C Day Lewis is symptomatic of the polarization of attitudes and the general aporia concerning the problem of non-violence and pacifism in the nineteen thirties.

Huxley took great pains to validate his ethic of love and non-violence, deriving from the mystical assumption of a divine 'Ground' common to all individuals. In *Ends and Means: An Enquiry into the Nature of Ideals and into the Methods Employed for their Realization* he undertook a book-length effort to underpin his religiously motivated pacifism by a logical and philosophical argument:

> Good ends, as I have frequently pointed out, can be achieved only by the employment of appropriate means. The end cannot justify the means, for the simple and obvious reason that the means employed determine the nature of the ends produced. [...] Wars do not end war; in most cases they result in an unjust peace that makes inevitable the outbreak of a war of revenge. (*EaM*, 9; 112)

Huxley's plea for 'constructive peace', disqualified by C Day Lewis as 'nothing more solid than a great big, beautiful idealist bubble - lovely to look at, no doubt; charming to live in, perhaps: but with little reference to the real facts and [an] inadequate protection against a four-engined bomber' (*CDL*, 3), converged with the appeasement policy towards Nazi Germany, a policy that failed, however, to prevent World War II.

Far from the madding war that raged in Europe Huxley went on cultivating his mystical and pacifist ideas while on the other side of the Atlantic Ocean pacifists, convinced of the necessity of peace, felt forced to stand up, and even to take up arms, against the fascist aggression.

In *Island* - his last novel, which appeared a year before he died in 1963 - Huxley mapped out a Utopian society in which the mystical awareness of every individual soul being rooted in a common divine 'Ground' results in the establishment of a social order resting on the pillars of love and peace. In the end, Pala, the 'best of all the worlds',[14] falls victim to the power politics of the world around it. In spite of his disenchantment Huxley, the irrepressible idealist, let his novel end on an optimistic note: 'Disregarded in the darkness, the fact of enlightenment remained.' (*Island*, 286).

NOTES

[1] (Heide in Holstein: 1933; Darmstadt: 3rd ed. 1990).
[2] (London: 1936). Reprinted. in: *Stories, Essays and Poems* (London: 1937) pp. 380-406 - Hereafter referred to as 'What...'
[3] (London: 1937).
[4] (London: 1937; Collected Edition, 1957). Hereafter referred to as EaM.
[5] Sybille Bedford, *Aldous Huxley: A Biography*. Vol. One (London: 1973; London/Glasgow: 1987), pp. 275-6.
[6] *Brave New World* (London: 1960) - Foreword [1946], pp. vii-viii.
[7] Quoted after Sybille Bedford, op.cit., p.309. - Cf. Sybil Morrison, *I Renounce War: The Story of the Peace Pledge Union*. Sheppard Press Ltd., 1962.
[8] Quoted after Sybille Bedford, op.cit., p.312. - Cf. Lothar Fietz, 'Huxleys Rückwendung zur Mystik' In: *Menschenbild und Romanstruktur in Aldous Huxleys Ideenromanen* (Tübingen: 1969), pp.117-38.
[9] Cf. H. Kunisch, *Das Wort 'Grund' in der Sprache der deutschen Mystik des 14. und 15. Jahrhunderts*. (Osnabrück: 1929).
[10] *The Perennial Philosophy* (London, 1945; [6]1957), p. 29.
[11] John Donne, *Devotions Upon Emergent Occasions* (Montreal: 1975) - Meditation 17.
[12] *Eyeless in Gaza* (London: 1936; Collected Edition, 1955). Hereafter referred to as EiG.
[13] Cf. C Day Lewis, *We're not Going To Do Nothing: A Reply to Mr. Aldous Huxley's Pamphlet, 'What Are You Going to Do About It?'* (London: 1936) p. 23. Hereafter referred to as CDL.
[14] Cf. *Island* (London: 1962), p.129.

Engaging Discovery: Inspirational Reading in Dark Times

Hinrich Siefken (Bangor / Nottingham)

ON 26 MAY 1940 Helmuth James von Moltke, the central figure of the Kreisau circle, which looked beyond the Third Reich to a federal Germany of peace with justice and a Europe of cooperation between states and nations, wrote to his wife Freya. He did not want 'to float here, in Berlin; for that I find the other people to disgusting', but hoped to spend 'time gained' profitably. He 'might learn Spanish', but would 'prefer to work at something that required more concentration'. 'The trouble is, however', he added, 'that everything one does, even if it's historical or philosophical, whether it is Tolstoy or the Bible, seems so uncannily topical'. In the attempt 'to master the chaos here', 'to escape intellectual isolation', to retain a sense of purpose and direction, he discovered, perhaps initially to his surprise, the potential of tradition to turn topical in personal discovery.[1] That was, and still is, a common experience in the fight against the 'Ungeist' of ideological prejudice. In its search for a fundamental renewal,[2] the Kreisau circle emphasized the responsibility of the individual for the well-being of society. Texts from the past read by chance can acquire topical significance in the search for the affirmation of human values in the present. The students of the *Weiße Rose* put this discovery to use in their leaflets, hoping that readers would realise a new significance in specific allusions to Schiller and Goethe, Lycurgus and Solon, Lao-tse and Cicero, St Augustine and Aristotle, to the Bible, Novalis and Theodor Körner.[3] The network of the Kreisau circle included Pater Alfred Delp, in charge of the church at München-Bogenhausen. On 1 August 1943 Moltke recorded details of a visit to Munich, where he attended mass at St Michael's and met Delp. 'We didn't go out to Delp's', he wrote. His wife knew that the rectory in Bogenhausen had been a meeting place before.[4]

One of Delp's parishioners was Theodor Haecker who knew him well.[5] Haecker had lectured on *The Chaos of Our Time* in the Auditorium Maximum of the University in November 1932. In April 1933, after the *Machtergreifung*, the lecture was published in Carl Muth's *Hochland*. Reworked that year, it became part of Haecker's book *What is Man?* According to his diagnosis, the chaos of the 1930s was the result of human perversion of the true order. Human hubris, trying to act like God, now assumed that power alone was the raison d'être of politics. To illustrate the perversion, he referred to Virgil whose work, although still pagan, had become an inspiration to him. In the figure of *pius* Aeneas Virgil had celebrated justice and peace based on love as the true base of the body politic.[6] For Haecker Virgil became the father of Western civilisation, the 'Vater des Abendlandes'. On 6 August 1943 he gave a copy of *What is Man?* to a friend, inscribing it with the motto of his book on Virgil of 1931: 'In times like these, my friends, let us reflect early on what we should take with us as we escape from abominable devastation'. It was a Kierkegaardian gesture. Shipwrecked, humankind had to hang on in the *naufragium* to the essentials, which might keep it afloat and alive. Haecker meant the Cross of Christ. Reflecting publicly in similar vein on the true *imperium*, he had provoked a dangerous clash with the National Socialist regime.[7] However, his discovery of the contemporaneity of Virgil went back to the turmoil of the early Weimar Republic. It had begun before 1920 with the translation of the Fourth, Messianic, Eclogue, traditionally read as a vision of the peaceful kingdom of Christ.[8] For Haecker, there were two other writers of even greater relevance, Sören Kierkegaard and John Henry Cardinal Newman. His edition of Kierkegaard's diaries of 1923 was, topically, re-printed in 1941. The new preface, first drafted in his secret diary, showed how much he identified with the Dane, 'that melancholy figure, on patrol duty in the no-man's land of the spirit'. Newman had become even more significant. Haecker had started translating Newman's work in the autumn of 1920. It literally changed his life. On 5 April 1921 the devout Protestant had become a Catholic.[9] But now, between 1933 and 1945, Haecker's translations of Kierkegaard and Newman acquired a new relevance for many readers. When the author could no longer publish his own work in the Third Reich, he became a translator of Newman's sermons, publishing personal selections chosen with great care.[10]

Young soldiers, like Heinrich Böll and Christoph Probst, read them.[11] The painter Richard Seewald, a close friend then living in Switzerland, writing of the 'uncanny topicality' of Augustine's sermons, recognised immediately this hidden dimension in some of Newman's sermons chosen by Haecker for translation.[12] In the epilogue to the second volume of sermons Haecker urged his Christian readers to use their heads to understand what they believe, and what faith demands of them.[13] It could be read as an invitation to discover the continued relevance of tradition. In March / April 1931 a new weekly *Der Staat seid Ihr*, Carl Muth and Thomas Mann amongst its editors, had published both Mann's essay *The Rebirth of Decency* and Haecker's *The Political Murders*. Two Munich writers, who had despised or ignored each other's work, shared a platform, defending a common tradition.

Mann would read Haecker's *What is Man?* in 1933 and be impressed. By that stage Mann was *de facto* where Haecker felt himself to be metaphorically: in exile.[14] Mann's lecture on Wagner of 10 February 1933, given in the Auditorium Maximum of the University to the same Munich Goethe Society which Haecker had addressed in May 1932 with '*What is Man?*', had forced him into exile. Mann challenged the terrible simplifications of Wagnerian worship. If Wagner's music was indeed representative of German art, he had said, it was also its 'histrionic staging' to 'the extremes of the grotesque, of parody', a 'nationalism imbued with European artistic sophistication'.[15] Munich objected. In the Goethe centenary year of 1932, Mann had in Berlin and Weimar celebrated a European and cosmopolitan Goethe who transcended national boundaries. That Goethe was the true model for Germany, the permanent Goethe. On all three occasions Mann had responded to official invitations triggered by major anniversaries, but re-discovered at some cost the potential topicality of the subject of these anniversary celebrations for 'the day and the hour'. Mann had struggled throughout the years of the Weimar Republic with a contemporary image of Goethe. In exile, he completed the novel *Lotte in Weimar*, and produced an anthology *The Permanent Goethe*. The essence of Goethe's significance was contained in a quotation from a love poem that the very meaning of life is love, and spirit is the essence of life: 'Denn das Leben ist die Liebe, und des Lebens Leben Geist.'[16] Haecker adored Goethe, and treasured Carl Muth's book *Schöpfer und Magier*, publicly dedicated to him.[17] He would not have disagreed with Mann's emphasis. Thomas Mann did in fact see his own life as a writer as one great *imitatio* of Goethe, walking in the footsteps of a master, and knew that this was *Hochstapelei*, a game he had to play.

By 1943 Dietrich Bonhoeffer, the Protestant pastor of the Confessing Church, was in prison in heavily-bombed Berlin, awaiting trial. He too found himself 'in the midst of chaos'. 'The only things that one can do here [are] reading and writing'. He knew, as his letters show, 'what it means to possess a past and spiritual inheritance independent of changes of time and circumstances'. He felt 'borne up by a spiritual tradition that goes back for centuries'. It gave him 'a feeling of confidence and security in the face of all passing strains and stresses'.[18] Reading he discovered the work of Adalbert Stifter and was engaged with it 'almost every day. The intimate life of his characters [...] makes one think of the things that really matter in life'. He was impressed by Stifter's 'refusal to force his way into man's inner life', the 'respect for reticence', and 'his willingness to observe people more or less cautiously from the outside'. 'There is something more at stake then self-knowledge' or 'psychology'.[19] One of the pertinent discoveries of the months in prison was Stifter's novel *Witiko*. On 29/30 January 1944 he wrote about it to his close friend Eberhard Bethge, a pastor conscripted and with the German army in Italy, where he saw the Allied fleet through his binoculars. In 'the present situation', Bonhoeffer said,

> the man who allows himself to be torn into fragments by events and by questions has not passed the test for the present and the future. In the story of the young Witiko we read that he set out into the world *'um das Ganze zu tun'*. [...] Witiko 'does the whole thing' by trying to adapt himself to the realities of life, by always listening to the advice of experienced people - i.e. by showing he is one of those who are 'whole'. We can never achieve this 'wholeness' simply by ourselves, but only together with others.

He explained that this is the 'wholeness' of which Matthew wrote: 'You, therefore, must be perfect (complete), as your heavenly Father is perfect' (Matt. 5. 48), and he contrasted it 'to the double-minded man of James 1.8'. Reading Stifter reaffirmed his own position, grounded in theological conviction.[20] A fortnight later he wrote that Stifter helped him 'see the difference between simpleness and simplicity'. 'Simpleness is an "innate gift", analogous to purity.' Once lost it can only 'be given back to us in faith'. Stifter, however, knows what is still achievable: simplicity, analogous to moderation. That was an essential clarification. Simplicity is worth striving for, 'once we have lost our purity - and we have all lost it'. In ourselves, 'as living and developing persons,' Bonhoeffer wrote, 'we can no longer be "pure" but only "moderate", and that is a possible and necessary aim of education and culture.'

Moltke, Haecker, Mann and Bonhoeffer, keenly aware of the relevance of their discoveries, were driven by a desire to share them. Moltke's time went preparing the meetings of the Kreisau circle, in an endeavour to facilitate a sharing of the best ideas for a rebuilding of Germany, so that the expertise of Protestants, Socialists, Catholics, industrialists and legal experts, of the young and the old, of Germans and their friends abroad, would fuse.[21] Thomas Mann expended much time and energy trying to make his fellow citizens see the immediate significance of great writers like Goethe and Lessing, Novalis and Sigmund Freud. The letters Haecker received from his readers, particularly from the younger generation, the generation of the *Weiße Rose* and of his own children, show how desperate they were for the guidance of his writing, which in turn was fed by discoveries made reading. Forbidden to publish, he risked - with Reinhold Schneider and Gertrud von le Fort, and others - illegality. He travelled to Colmar where Rossé at his Alsatia press would gather the most poignant Haecker passages in a slim volume, easy to send by post, under the title *Über den abendländischen Menschen*. On 19 October 1944 a young soldier, who in Oslo had seen the copy of Haecker's son Johannes, wrote for a copy to be sent to Breslau. It touched on matters which had troubled him for a long time.[22] By then Haecker had, at considerable risk, shared his views with the students of the *Weiße Rose* in two secret readings in Munich, and after their arrest and execution Freisler had tried, unsuccessfully, to convict him too of involvement in high treason. To his great sadness Dietrich Bonhoeffer learned in prison that many of the young pastors he had trained for the Confessing Church had lost their lives. His work with them had grown into the book on the Sermon on the Mount, *The Cost of Discipleship*, still in print today. After the arrest of members of the *Weiße Rose* on 18 February 1943 Moltke had ensured that the text of one of their leaflets reached England, by taking it personally to Oslo. It later returned to Germany as a leaflet dropped by the RAF.[23] Reinhard, the youngest of Haecker's three children, seventeen at the time, recorded in a letter to his father his reaction to Alfred Delp's execution on 2 February 1945: 'The death of Delp has affected me deeply, because it's always the best who cop it'. Delp died for his alleged involvement in the plot to assassinate Hitler. Bonhoeffer would be executed for the same reason on 9 April 1945. By coincidence that was also the day Haecker died in Ustersbach, deprived of insulin in his refuge from the heavy bombing of Munich.

Stifter's 'almost feverish desire to improve human beings and make them more understanding' drove him to pursue education. In one of his favourite passages Stifter speaks of the 'invisible way he was able to communicate with other individuals sharing human feeling and gifts of the spirit'.[24] While we were planning this volume, one of Keith Spalding's friends wrote to me that more than fifty years ago he became a 'guide, inspiration & friend. He introduced me to ,"edel sei der Mensch, hilfreich und gut"'.[25] Famous lines from Goethe's poem 'Das Göttliche'.

NOTES

These reflections relate to publications on Thomas Mann (Munich: 1981), Theodor Haecker (Marbach: 1989; Esslingen: 1995; Rottenburg-Stuttgart: 2001) and the *Weiße Rose* (Manchester: 1994) not explicitly quoted here. Malcolm Jones and Angela Smallwood were helpfully critical readers of this paper.

1. Helmuth James von Moltke, *Letters to Freya 1939-1945*. Ed. and translated by Beate Ruhm von Oppen. (New York; Vintage Books, 1995), pp. 71, 123, 131.
2. Ger van Roon, *Widerstand im Dritten Reich*. (Munich: Beck, 1979), pp. 165 and 170 stresses this as the common concern of all the representatives of the many different groups, which Moltke brought into contact with each other.
3. For further details see the paper on the influence of Dostoievski, Berdiaiev and Russia in *GLL*, NS 47 (1994).
4. *Letters to Freya*, p. 327. Next day he wrote: 'My love, chaos is coming now'. Ibid. p. 328.
5. The evidence is contained in Haecker's letters and those of his youngest son.

6   Theodor Haecker, *Das Chaos der Zeit*, in Hochland 30, (1932/33), vol. 2, April 1933, 1-23. The book *Was ist der Mensch?* was published by Hegner: Leipzig 1933. In 1932 Haecker had toured Germany and Austria with public lectures on these topics.
7   *Betrachtungen über Vergil, Vater des Abendlandes*, Der Brenner, 13 (autumn 1932), 3-31 contained a sharp attack on the swastika as the symbol of political dishonesty. Arrested on 20 May 1933, but released the following day, he narrowly escaped 'Schutzhaft'. As the Third Reich began to collapse, Haecker, thanks to Delp in temporary shelter after the destruction of the house in which he lived, received a letter from Peter Schifferli in Zurich (27 December 1944, unpubl.) who hoped to rescue the book on Virgil and others for posterity in his new publishing house *Die Arche*: 'zur Bergung jener wesentlich abendländischen Geistesgüter'.
8   In *Der Brenner*, 6, 6 (August 1920), 401-3.
9   Erik Peterson, then a close Protestant friend, had offered to read the proofs, but returned them unfinished fearing they might change his life too. He later became a prominent Catholic.
10 *Die Kirche und die Welt. Predigten.* (Leipzig: Hegner, 1938 and 1940). *Der Traum des Gerontius.* (Freiburg: Herder, 1939). *Das Mysterium der Dreieinigkeit und der Menschwerdung Gottes.* (Leipzig: Hegner, 1940). Comparing the contents with Newman's *Sermons bearing on Subjects of the Day* [S.D.] and the eight volumes of *Parochial and Plain Sermons* [P.S.] establishes that Haecker chose nine from S.D. and 6 from volumes i and ii of P.S. for the first, and twelve from volumes i, ii, iii, iv and vi for the second volume.
11 Cf. Heinrich Böll, *Briefe aus dem Krieg*. 2 vols.(Cologne: Kiepenheuer & Witsch, 2001), pp. 231, 816, 824. Böll was given 'das dicke Tagebuch' by his brother in the summer of 1941. He returned to it in the summer of 1943. Christoph Probst read the diaries in the summer of 1942 (unpublished letter of 4 July 1942).
12 Unpublished letter to Haecker of 11 October 1943: 'Predigten, des H. Augustinus [...] Von einer unheimlichen Aktualität', 'Predigten Newmans [...] die nicht weniger aktuell sind in einigen Stücken'.
13 *Das Mysterium der Dreieinigkeit*. pp. 190-1.
14 See Mann's diaries of 20th November 1933 and 23rd August 1934. Details in *Thomas-Mann-Studien*, vol. 7, (Berne: Francke, 1987), pp. 246-72. Haecker desribed himself in letters as 'exul in partibus infidelium' (24 August 1933, to R Seewald), and 'in meinem eigenen Vaterlande [...] zum Staatsfeind ernannt' (5 February 1936, to A Dru).
15 Thomas Mann, *Gesammelte Werke in 13 Bänden*. (Frankfurt: S. Fischer, 1974), vol.ix, pp.422-423.

16 The quotation is used in 1931 in the speech *Die Wiedergeburt der Anständigkeit* (XII, 674) as it was in 1930 in *Die Bäume im Garten* (XI, 869), Mann's plea for common European ideals. It is taken from *'Nimmer will ich dich verlieren!'* in the *Buch Suleika* of *Westöstlicher Divan* (*Goethes Werke*, Hamburger Ausgabe. Vol. 2, p. 75. (Hamburg: Wegner, 1960)). It was written in October 1815, the period central to Mann's perception.

17 Leipzig: Hegner, 1935 'Theodor Haecker zu eigen' (on Klopstock, Goethe and George).

18 *Letters and Papers from Prison*. Ed. Eberhard Bethge. (London: SCM, 1999), pp .153, 113, 133, 165.

19 Ibid., pp. 50, 158, 162. Gotthelf and Fontane were less significant favourites for the same reason.

20 Ibid., pp. 200 and 212.

21 All of them had considerable knowledge of foreign countries, and strong, and often personal, links with Britain.

22 Unpublished letter.

23 Attempts to establish contact between the Kreisau circle and the *Weiße Rose* had not succeeded in time. Cf. Ger van Roon, *Widerstand im Dritten Reich*, p.168.

24 Cf. Keith Spalding, *Alles umsteigen*. (Lübeck: Edition outline, 1992), p. 210, and his *Selections from Stifter*. (London: Macmillan, 1952), p. vi.

25 Unpublished letter by David W M James of September 2002.

Some Uses of Tradition: Heinrich Böll and John Henry Newman

J H Reid (Nottingham)

HEINRICH BÖLL'S impetuosity in public affairs is notorious: best known is his explosion of rage over a headline in *Bild-Zeitung* at the end of 1971, which led to the article published in *Der Spiegel* in January 1972 in which he proposed that the urban terrorist Ulrike Meinhof might be offered 'safe conduct' on condition she surrendered; the ensuing massive right-wing campaign of hatred and defamation rumbled on to the end of the decade. In an interview with Saarland Radio he was asked whether the expression of his views had not been 'somewhat literary' and therefore confusing. He replied: 'That's not my problem. I'm a writer, and when I articulate a response to something it may well be literary, but then I assume that anyone who comments on it responsibly will know other texts of mine and will not take such an utterance in isolation.'[1]

Some years before, in a letter to the editor of the *Frankfurter Allgemeine Zeitung* published on 28 April 1964, Böll had had occasion to defend in similar terms a letter which had been printed a fortnight earlier. The occasion this time was the newspaper's publication of a paper by Bernhard Hanssler, spiritual director of the Central Committee of German Catholics, on the Second Vatican Council, the meaning of ecumenism and the implications of the Council for a Catholic conception of literature. Postwar German literature, said Hanssler, had hitherto been just that: defined by the 'German catastrophe', unable to free itself from the personal experiences of its authors, it was 'in a frightening if understandable sense literature of the crippled (*Versehrtenliteratur*)'. Now, however, it was time to leave this 'abnormal condition' behind. The Council had looked forward; it was time for literature to do so too.[2]

Böll reacted indignantly; just back from visiting Verdun, he found Hanssler's condescension towards the victims of two World Wars disgraceful. And was not in any case Christianity a religion of the crippled? After all, Paul Gerhardt's hymn 'O Haupt voll Blut und Wunden' was sung in all the churches during Lent.[3] Hanssler was promptly defended in another letter to the *Frankfurter Allgemeine Zeitung*: Böll's irony was 'insupportable', the language of his letter not conducive to any fruitful dialogue.[4] Böll defended himself in a further letter:

> That as well as my attribute as contributor of income tax to the Catholic Church I am also an author, as an author, incidentally, also a satirist, and as a writer of letters I remain an author, sometimes becoming a satirist - that is something which anyone may take up with me who would accuse the trees of turning green in spring. One expresses oneself as well as one can, and, after all, the western world has produced two satirists, one of whom was called Jonathan Swift, Dean of St Patrick's, the other John Henry Cardinal Newman: so there are Christian models to stand godfather for a satirist beside the heathens Aristophanes and Juvenal.[5]

The unspoken context of the dispute was the previous year's series of attacks on the role of the Catholic Church in the 'German catastrophe' from Rolf Hochhuth (*The Representative*), Carl Amery (*The Capitulation*) and Böll's own *Clown*;[6] that Böll should react allergically to criticism of a 'literature of wounds' might have been expected, as his 1951 literary credo 'In defence of the literature of ruins' had insisted that the 'wounds' inflicted by war and National Socialism would not easily be healed. Böll was always good at turning the tables on his critics by appealing to tradition: in that same essay he had defended post-war writers, accused of depicting only war, the returning soldier and the ruins he encountered at home, by referring to Homer, who had done just that. Now he was appealing to Christian models. Swift was an obvious authority; in an interview of 1956 Böll claimed to have read his complete works in the 1930s several times over,[7] and he alludes to him frequently elsewhere. As far as I am aware, however, this is the only occasion on which Newman is mentioned in Böll's writings.

Whether the name of Newman occurred to Böll in connection with the Vatican Council is not clear, although it has been suggested that the Council fulfilled many of Newman's ideas.[8] Werner

Becker reports that in Böll's Cologne in October 1945 the centenary of Newman's conversion was celebrated amidst the ruins of that city by a 'university week', with lectures by various theologians who described themselves as 'united in their devotion to Newman'.[9] One of the speakers was Robert Grosche, whose informal seminars in the 1930s had been attended by Böll and who may have introduced him to the ideas of Newman then. Becker links the Catholic Renewal in Germany from 1920 onwards to a 'Newman renaissance'.[10] The pioneering spirit behind this renaissance was a man much admired by Böll, the critic and translator Theodor Haecker, who translated numerous texts by Newman into German, including the *Grammar of Assent*, and published essays on Newman. As a subscriber to the journal *Hochland* Böll would certainly have encountered some of Haecker's translations there.[11]

When Böll describes Newman as a 'satirist', however, he was almost certainly thinking of the novel *Loss and Gain: The Story of a Convert*.[12] Written by Newman shortly after his conversion to Catholicism, it appeared in 1848, was translated into German as early as 1861 and came out in several editions in the 1920s. There is evidence to suggest that Böll read it in 1936, before he had turned twenty, and there is a copy in his library.

Loss and Gain is in some ways a very German kind of novel. It is a novel of ideas, ideas which have largely to do with theological questions - the extent to which faith is rational or received, the unity of the Church, the relative authority of Scripture, the Prayer Book and the Thirty-Nine Articles, celibacy and the priesthood - but it also contains general discussions of an intellectual nature: on parliamentary democracy, on the press and on music. It is also a kind of *Entwicklungsroman*. After an uneventful education at Eton Charles Reding goes to Oxford to study theology with a view to following his father into the Anglican priesthood. Initially he is happy to compromise, his favourite maxim being 'that it was a duty to be pleased with every one' (p. 34). The Oxford he finds, however, is a hothouse of conflicting theological ideas. It is the time of Tractarianism, of debates on Anglo-Catholicism, of rumours of yet another defection to the Roman Church. Reding encounters a variety of individuals and ideas: his friend Sheffield is a brilliant intellectual, for whom, however, religion is 'but a secondary matter' (p. 230) and who refuses to contemplate the logical consequences of his insights; Bateman is an aesthete, who wishes to restore the outward trappings of the Old Church without recognising their implications for liturgical and theological content; there is in particular the example of Willis, who becomes a Catholic, and when Reding attempts to persuade him to return to the fold it is Reding who ends up 'unsettled' (p. 114). Reding wishes for clarity in theological matters; but the lectures he hears on the Thirty-Nine Articles produce greater uncertainty than before and he realises that at the end of his course he will have to sign them even although they are ambiguous and everyone disagrees on them. A turning point comes when he is refused further residence at the University on suspicion of apostasy, although at that moment he himself is still convinced that he will remain within the Anglican Church. He increasingly feels that he is 'a stranger in the Church of England' (p. 254), 'loses' the cosy assumptions and compromises of Anglicanism and finally 'gains' a new home in the Roman church.

While the form of the novel would thus have been familiar to a German reader in the 1930s, it is not otherwise obvious why the young Böll should have been interested in Newman's novel nor why it should have come back to him in 1964. Like G. K. Chesterton's novels, which Böll devoured in the 1930s, *Loss and Gain* must have appeared exceedingly exotic to a German schoolboy. Largely set in the academic milieu of Oxford University with its eccentric assembly of dons, masters, fellows, tutors, proctors and scouts, its 'schools' and its academic gowns, it shows nothing of the actual social conflicts of the England of its time. The characters are exclusively well-to-do, female characters almost entirely stereotyped. While at one point Reding attacks some of the dons for their worldliness: 'the notion of evangelical poverty, the danger of riches, the giving up all for Christ, all those ideas which are first principles in Scripture, as I read it, don't seem to enter into their idea of religion' (p. 258), this is a side issue. For social realism Böll read Dickens and Dostoevsky.

There will have been biographical reasons for Böll's interest. In the mid-1930s the young Böll was himself going through a religious crisis, and Newman's novel may well have strengthened his faith. The theological discussions reproduced in the novel must have touched on questions which concerned Böll and his friends too. The list of Catholic converts whose books Böll and his family read in the 1930s is in any case a long one: Chesterton, Evelyn Waugh, Werner Bergengruen, Gertrud von le Fort, Theodor

Haecker, Paul Claudel, Francis Jammes. There was a family myth that their ancestors had emigrated from England to escape religious persecution under Henry VIII - Newman's spectacular 'return' to the Church of Rome was evidence of the righteousness of their cause. Moreover, the injustices meted out to Catholics in the England of the 1840s had their parallels in the conflict between the Protestant Prussian state and the Catholic Church in the 1890s in Germany, the so-called 'Kulturkampf'. By 1936 renewed pressures on the Church from the National Socialists had given this analogy another dimension.

Beyond this, however, there are a number of points of contact between the ideas of Newman's novel and those which were dear to Böll - both then and later. Figures like Bateman, who are preoccupied by aesthetics at the expense of content, recur frequently in Böll's works. Böll too was to attack compromise, what Sheffield early in the novel calls 'fudge and humbug' (p. 22) and which Reding is initially prepared to accept. In *Loss and Gain* Anglicanism appears as a wishy-washy compromise, a bundle of contradictions which nobody is prepared to question: thus one of Reding's lecturers tells him it is well 'to avoid both curious questions and subtle answers' (p. 127). While Anglicanism was, of course, hardly a real issue for the young Böll, the compromisers, those whom, after the words of Revelation, he calls 'the lukewarm', are repeatedly attacked in his early texts; their opposite are 'those who burn', as in the title of a story of 1936/37.[13] But there is a phrase which occurs repeatedly in the novel and which foreshadows another of Böll's much later addresses for which he found himself under attack. When Reding begins to ask questions his tutor warns him: 'some of your remarks and questions at lecture were like a person pushing things *too far*, and wishing to form a *system*.' He goes on: 'Clever men say true things, Mr. Reding, true in their substance, but [...] they go *too far*.' (p. 81; italics in original). In 1966, in his address on the opening of the new theatre at Wuppertal, Böll was to state categorically: Art must always go 'too far'.[14]

This is not the place to speculate on the possible influence of Newman's theology on Heinrich Böll. *Loss and Gain* is a satirical novel, and it contains numerous comic incidents, mainly at the expense of the anti-Catholic establishment, whether it be the porter convinced he has seen the Pope in Oxford, recognising him 'by his slouching hat and his long beard' (p. 116), or the representatives of a series of obscure sects who descend on Reding at the end of the novel, attempting to convert him to their particular cause. The novel by Böll which comes closest to it is *The Clown*. There are numerous differences, of course: in Böll we find no real theological arguments; nor do any of his protagonists pass through the kind of inner conflict suffered by Charles Reding. Conversely, there is no love story in *Loss and Gain*: even before his final break with Anglicanism Reding is attracted by the notion of celibacy, while for the young Böll it was precisely the celibacy of the Catholic priesthood which deterred him from embarking on a university course in theology.[15] But it is surely no accident that the name of Newman was mentioned by Böll just a year after his *Clown* appeared: 'Views of a Clown' is a more accurate rendering of the original title, and early on in Newman's novel there is a discussion of 'views' and 'viewy people' (p. 16).

NOTES

[1] Quoted from *Heinrich Böll: Freies Geleit für Ulrike Meinhof. Ein Artikel und seine Folgen*, edited by Frank Grützmacher (Cologne: Kiepenheuer & Witsch, 1972), p. 96.

[2] A substantial part of Hanssler's paper is reprinted in volume 14 of *Heinrich Böll Werke: Kölner Ausgabe*, ed. J. Schubert (Cologne: Kiepenheuer & Witsch, 2002), pp. 538-41.

[3] 'Unversehrter Prometheus', ibid., pp. 124-5.

[4] Quoted ibid., pp. 550-1.

[5] 'Unbefangenheit und Noblesse', ibid., p. 133.

[6] For an account of the controversy see my *Heinrich Böll: A German for his Time* (Oxford: Berg, 1988), pp. 135-6.

[7] *Le Figaro littéraire*, 4.2.1956, p. 3.

[8] B. C. Butler, 'Newman and the Second Vatican Council', in: *The Rediscovery of Newman: An Oxford Symposium*, ed. J. Coulson and A. M. Allchin (London & Melbourne: Sheed and Ward, 1967), pp. 234-46; Werner Becker 'Newman's influence in Germany', ibid., pp. 174-89, here p. 189.

[9] Ibid., p. 182.

[10] Loc. cit. (note 8), p. 179.

[11] 'Der Glaube und die Welt' (1937/38); 'Die Religion des Tages' (1938/39); 'Die Universität Athen' (1939/40). On Haecker and Newman see also Curt Hohoff, 'Theodor Haecker: Eine Erinnerung', reprinted in: *Theodor Haecker: Leben und Werk. Texte, Briefe,*

Erinnerungen, Würdigungen, ed. B. Hanssler and H. Siefken (Esslinger Studien, vol. 15), pp. 145-60, esp. pp. 153-6.
12 Page references in the following are to the 16th impression of the 6th edition (1874), London: Longmans, Green & Co, 1906.
13 See *Revelation* 3:15-16 and Böll's essay 'Gegen die Ahnungslosen' *Heinrich Böll Werke: Kölner Ausgabe*, vol. 2, ed. J. H. Reid (Cologne: Kiepenheuer & Witsch, 2002), p. 145. 'Die Brennenden' was published posthumously in Heinrich Böll: *Der blasse Hund. Erzählungen*, ed. V. Böll and K. H. Busse (Cologne: Kiepenheuer & Witsch, 1995), pp. 9-36.
14 Heinrich Böll, *Werke. Essayistische Schriften und Reden*, vol. 2, ed. B. Balzer (Cologne: Kiepenheuer & Witsch, 1978), p. 228.
15 *Was soll aus dem Jungen bloß werden? Oder: Irgendwas mit Büchern* (Munich: dtv, 1983), p. 66.

Antikes Erbe in neuem Gewand: Johannes Bobrowski 'Der Soldat an der Birke'

Peter Jentzsch (Metzingen)

MOTIVE DER Weltliteratur gehen auf ihrer Zeitreise zuweilen seltsame Wege. Besonders überlebensfähig erscheint ein antiker Motivkomplex, den Bobrowski, ein Dichter mit humanistischer Bildung, in seiner Kurzgeschichte 'Der Soldat an der Birke'[1] aufnimmt. Der Text zeigt ein reizvolles Spannungsverhältnis von 'tradition', 'adaption' und 'actualisation' - Kernbegriffe der Überlegungen zur Würdigung Keith Spaldings -, das bislang, soweit ich sehe, von Forschung und Fachdidaktik nicht wahrgenommen wurde.[2] Doch zunächst eine Kostprobe des Textes und eine kurze Inhaltsangabe:

> Es ist Herbst und gegen Abend zu kalt auf den Feldern vor der Stadt Lüneburg. Ein Sandweg kommt da aus einer flachen Senke herauf mit vielen Räderspuren, vertreutem Gerät und Fetzen von Wagenstroh. Hier und dort ist die Asche eines ausgebrannten Feuers zu finden.
> Aus einem niedrigen Haus, auf das ein fauliges Schilfdach herabsinkt - darüber wird das Gestänge des Giebelgerüsts sichtbar und ein wenig Rauch kräuselt umher - tönt seit Stunden ein dünnes, immer gleich bleibendes Jammern. Der Soldat, der ein Stück vom Hause fort an der Straße steht, hört es und wartet, dass es endlich erstürbe [...] Er steht und wartet, aber er hat noch anderes zu tun.
> Vom unteren Ast der kümmerlichen Birke, gegen deren ausgeblichenen Stamm er sich jetzt lehnt - erst mit der Hand sich daran stützend, als lausche er noch einmal in den windigen Abend hinaus - baumelt ein Erhängter. Ein Soldat, wie man sieht, von irgend einem Regiment; denn es ist schon lange her, dass man sie an Uniformstücken erkennen konnte. Der Erhängte ist sehr lang und dünn, er hat einen wüsten roten Bart,

und der Soldat ist hier aufgestellt, damit keiner den Rotbärtigen herabnehme und verscharre. Er soll hängen, denn er hat dem Obristen ins Gesicht geschrien, dass er nach Hause ginge und dass es übergenug sei. Nach Lübeck hinauf wollte er gehen, denkt der Soldat, und aus dem Haus an der Straße, wo der Rauch im Dachgebälk umherirrt, tönt unausgesetzt das Jammern herüber.

In diesem düsteren Ambiente beginnt ein Kabinettstück deutscher Nachkriegsliteratur, thematisch angesiedelt auf jenem spannungsvollen Problemfeld, auf das sich auch Keith Spaldings Erstling, *Kultur oder Vernichtung?*, begab. Bobrowski führt uns in eine Welt des Krieges, gezeichnet von gnadenlosem Durchhalte-Fanatismus und Tod; selbst Landschaft und Natur sind auf düstere Töne gestimmt. Er evoziert anfangs eine Endzeitstimmung, doch im Fortgang der Erzählung keimt zaghafte Hoffnung auf, Signal einer humaneren Kultur, die sich in Form und Inhalt des Textes wie im Umgang mit der Motivtradition zeigt.

Doch zunächst der weitere Inhalt: Angelockt von der jammernden Stimme und getrieben vom Wunsch nach Wärme, verlässt der Soldat seinen kalten Posten; er geht zu dem baufälligen Haus und wird unvermittelt von einer (nicht mehr weinenden) Frau an das wärmende Herdfeuer eines rauchgeschwärzten Raumes gezogen. Ein wortkarger Dialog enthüllt, dass 'sie' (vielleicht marodierende Soldaten) ihren Mann erschlagen haben. Seine Leiche liegt in der Kammer nebenan. Nach einer langen Anwärmphase kommt man sich näher; sie tragen die Leiche aus der Kammer und finden sich gemeinsam im Totenbett wieder. Details übergeht der Erzähler diskret, indem er mit wenigen Sätzen einen zweiten Erzählstrang einfügt: Im Schutze der Nacht nehmen zwei offenbar desertierte Kameraden den Hingerichteten von der Birke und erweisen ihm - ein Antigone-Motiv - mit dem Begräbnis die letzte Ehre. Selbstloser Wagemut trotzt der Vernichtungsmaschinerie einer inhumanen Militärjustiz. - 'Im Haus ist das Feuer erloschen.' So schließt der Erzähler (mehrdeutig?) die Nebenhandlung ab. Als der Soldat am Morgen die Folgen seines Wachvergehens sieht, will auch er desertieren und fordert die Frau zur gemeinsamen Flucht auf; das Ende bleibt offen.

Es wäre nicht ganz abwegig, hier an 'Erinnerungsliteratur' zu denken und die erzählten Ereignisse mit der Endphase des II. Weltkrieges und dem Untergang des 'III. Reiches' in Verbindung zu bringen,[3] einer Zeit, die von vernichtender Henkerjustiz und gnadenlosem 'Standrecht' geprägt war. Bobrowskis Leben (1917-65) stand im unheilvollen Bannkreis dieses Krieges, als Soldat (1938-45) und Gefangener (im Donezbecken bis 1949). Lokal- und Zeitkolorit jedoch - auch das wurde bislang übersehen - verweisen eher auf frühere Epochen, z. B. das 'nackte Gestänge des Giebelgerüsts' (anstelle von Balken), das Schilfdach oder der vom offenen Herdfeuer rauchgeschwärzte düstere Innenraum. Archaismen, etwa das Attribut 'Stadt' vor dem Ortsnamen, vor allem aber die Rangbezeichnung 'Obrist' sowie die indefiniten 'Uniformstücke' und schäbigen 'Monturen', sprechen eher für einen historisch älteren Kontext, den auch der ursprüngliche Eingangssatz bestätigt: 'Wir schreiben das Jahr 1645.'[4] Ob er gestrichen wurde, um zeitübergreifende Allgemeingültigkeit zu suggerieren, kann nur vermutet werden.

Das Problemfeld 'Kultur oder Vernichtung' lässt sich unter verschiedenen Aspekten in dieser Kurzgeschichte aufspüren: Inhaltlich führt der Autor seine Figuren aus der anfänglichen Endzeitstimmung von Chaos und Tod zu Überlebenshoffnungen [1]. 'Kultur' manifestiert sich aber auch in der Gestaltungsform, z.B. in der überraschenden Variation tradierter Erzählmotive [2] und in der Neubewertung des ethischen Konfliktpotenzials [3], in der für Bobrowski typischen Erzähltechnik [4] und schließlich in einer Prosa, hinter der die poetische Bildkraft des Lyrikers aufscheint [5].

[1] Das Handlungsgerüst wird von einer kontrastiven Personenkonstellation getragen: Der Soldat verlässt seinen Posten und tröstet die trauernde Witwe, nachdem beide den toten Gatten entfernt haben. Mit dem Wachvergehen und der allzu raschen Neuorientierung brechen die Hauptfiguren herkömmliche Normen. Diametral entgegengesetzt agieren die beiden Deserteure: Sie wagen unter Lebensgefahr einen Rechtsbruch militärischer Normen, um die ethische und religiöse Pflicht der Totenehrung zu erfüllen. Ihr kurzer Auftritt wird mit wörtlicher Rede szenisch vergegenwärtigt und damit erzählerisch aufgewertet; ihr hingerichteter Kamerad trägt als einzige Figur im Text einen Eigennamen: sicherlich Signale der Sympathie für die 'underdogs'. So prallen in antithetischer Personenkonstellation Schein und Sein in nahezu barocker Dichotomie aufeinander: Die vordergründig Rechtschaffenen, Witwe und Wachsoldat, verletzen um des eige-

nen Überlebens willen militärische, soziale und ethische Normen; die Deserteure hingegen, 'outcasts', erfüllen unter Gefahr für Leib und Leben ethische und religiöse Pflichten. Diese chiastische Motivkomposition könnte man im Blick auf die Konfliktpotenziale in einer Skizze, grob vereinfacht, darstellen.

Personenentwicklung und Komposition der Erzählmotive

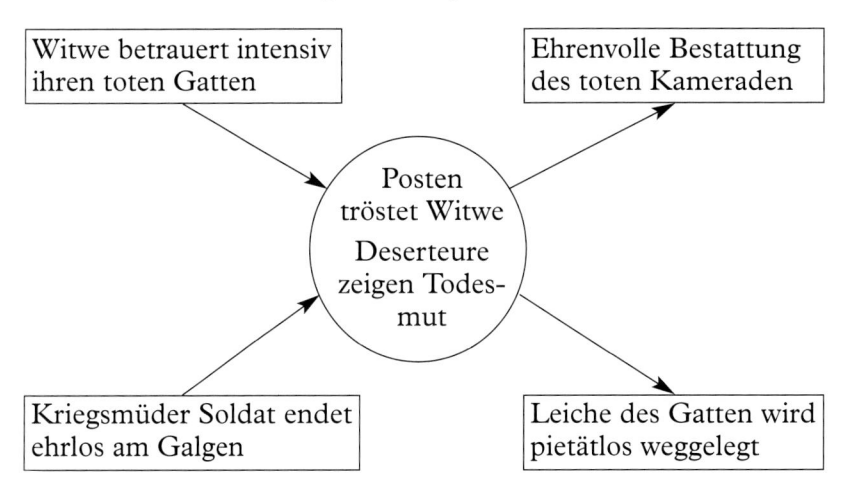

Witwe betrauert intensiv ihren toten Gatten		Ehrenvolle Bestattung des toten Kameraden
	Posten tröstet Witwe / Deserteure zeigen Todesmut	
Kriegsmüder Soldat endet ehrlos am Galgen		Leiche des Gatten wird pietätlos weggelegt

[2] Die hier skizzierten Erzählmotive einer außerordentlichen Begebenheit sind in der Form weder reale Erfahrung noch individuelle Fiktion Bobrowskis. Sie entstammen vielmehr einer fast zweitausendjährigen Stofftradition,[5] deren Zusammenstellung[6] jedoch ergänzungsbedürftig ist. Es ist die Geschichte der *Witwe von Ephesus* aus dem *Satyricon*[7] des Petronius, jenes , 'beißende Märchen, [...] die unstreitig bitterste Satire, die jemals gegen den weiblichen Leichtsinn gemacht' (wurde),[8] so Lessing, dessen Dramatisierung (*Die Matrone von Ephesus*) Fragment blieb. Mehr Erfolg hatte z.B. Christopher Fry mit dem Versdrama *A Phoenix Too Frequent* (1946), dessen Heldin Dynamene den 'ekstatischen Triumph des Willens zum Leben über die Instinkte der Selbstzerstörung'[9] stellt. Zwischen Fry und Petronius bearbeitete mehr als ein halbes Hundert Autoren - in jeweils zeitgeschichtlich getöntem Ambiente - das Thema, teils mit Verständnis für die Witwe, teils mit heftiger Kritik. Auf einen kunstvollen Puppentrickfilm aus der Prager Filmhochschule und einige didaktisch ergiebige Texte habe ich bereits früher hingewiesen.[10]

Bobrowskis verständnisvoll sensible Bearbeitung des Themas gewinnt ihr Eigenleben noch intensiver vor der Folie der petronischen Satire: 'In Ephesus lebte eine Dame, deren Keuschheit in so hohem Ansehen stand, daß auch die Frauen aus den Nachbarstädten kamen, um sie zu bewundern. Als sie ihren Gatten zu Grabe tragen mußte, war sie nicht damit zufrieden, nach der landläufigen Sitte dem Trauerzug mit gelösten Haaren zu folgen [...], sondern sie begleitete den Abgeschiedenen bis in seine Gruft [...] und begann bei ihm Wache zu halten und ihn Tag und Nacht zu beweinen.' - Vergeblich versuchen Verwandte, Magistrat und Magd, sie von ihrer exzessiv selbstzerstörerischen Trauer abzubringen. Dieses Trauertreiben beobachtet ein Soldat, der bei drei Gekreuzigten Wache hält, damit sie nicht heimlich bestattet würden. Neugierig geworden, verlässt er seinen Posten und bringt der von tagelangem Fasten geschwächten Witwe Nahrung und Wein. Unterstützt von der Magd, die es mit Versen von Vergil versucht ('gegen besseres Wissen / bekämpfst du die Liebe') bewegt er sie zur Rückkehr ins Leben. Der Erzähler resümiert augenzwinkernd: 'Was soll ich euch weiter aufhalten? Die Frau fastete auch hier nicht länger, und der unüberwindliche Soldat hatte sie in beiden Fällen besiegt.'

Die Kernmotive werden in der Gegenhandlung weitergeführt: Während Witwe und Wachsoldat drei Tage und Nächte in der Grabkammer verweilen, nehmen Verwandte - in einer gerafft erzählten Nebenhandlung - einen der Hingerichteten vom Kreuz (das Antigone-Motiv). Als der Soldat die Folgen seines Wachvergehens bemerkt, sieht er nur noch den Selbstmord als Ausweg, den ihm die Witwe energisch ausredet: 'Lieber will ich den Toten ans Kreuz hängen, als daß ich auch noch den Lebenden verliere.' Die schwungvolle Antithese leitet das Ende ein; sie befiehlt, den 'Leichnam ihres Mannes aus dem Sarge zu heben und an das leere Kreuz zu schlagen', was bald von einer verwunderten Öffentlichkeit spottend bemerkt wird. - Zwei kontrastive Kommentare schließen die Erzählung ab: verschämtes Verständnis neben schärfster Ablehnung.

Personenkonstellation und Konfliktpotenzial sind also schon bei Petronius in chiastischer Konfrontation vorgegeben und ließen sich wie bei Bobrowski skizzieren: Die Witwe ehrt den toten Gatten durch exzessive Trauer, die aber - durch die Liebe zum (desertierten) Wachposten - in Leichenschändung umschlägt.

Auch hier ist die Nebenhandlung diametral gegenläufig: Ein Gekreuzigter, zum Ehrverlust verurteilt, wird durch (hier allerdings) zivilen Ungehorsam (Antigone-Motiv) heimlich bestattet und findet seine Totenehrung. Auch hier das chiastische Wechselspiel von Schein und Sein. Der Meister feiner Sitten (*arbiter elegantiarum*) und des gepflegten Stils zur Zeit Neros stellt die brüchige Moral von Oberschicht (Witwe) und Militär dem couragierten Ethos der 'underdogs' gegenüber, allerdings im Gewand der Satire. Ob Petronius, Zeitgenosse des Apostels Paulus, mit der Kreuzabnahme neben antikem Ethos auch die christliche *pietas* (hier der gesellschaftlich Ohnmächtigen) im Auge hatte, kann nur vermutet werden.

[3] Bobrowski übernimmt zwar wesentliche Elemente der Vorlage, z.B. die diametral antithetische Personenkonstellation in Haupt- und Nebenhandlung, das Antigone-Motiv und die Zuwendung der Frau zu einem neuen Partner. Aber er hat einige neue Akzente gesetzt: Nicht die Witwe, sondern 'der Soldat an der Birke' wird zur Titelfigur; grammatikalisch kann damit der Wachtposten ebenso gemeint sein wie der Gehenkte, der Mittäter und das Opfer der Militärjustiz, Männer, die bis vor kurzem Kameraden waren. Während der antike Vorgänger stürmisch um die Frau wirbt, erscheint Bobrowskis Soldat weniger aktiv, was wiederum der Witwe keinen so augenfälligen Sinneswandel abverlangt. Die exzessive Trauer wird reduziert, die Standesunterschiede (in Ephesos eine angesehene Dame, bei Lüneburg eine arme Kätnerin) sind bei Bobrowski geringer; auch wird die Leiche des Gatten schonender behandelt: ihm bleibt die Rolle als Ersatzmann am Galgen erspart. Dies alles mindert die ethisch-moralische Fallhöhe der Witwe und zieht der Satire die Zähne. Bobrowski hat überdies die Szenerie zeitgemäß geändert: Sein Hintergrund ist nicht die scheinbar geordnete Welt einer saturierten Stadtgesellschaft, sondern das von Krieg, Chaos und Vernichtung gezeichnete Umfeld kleiner Leute, eine Endzeitstimmung, in der traditionelle Moralvorstellungen obsolet geworden sind. Bobrowski stellt nicht bloß, er wirbt um Verständnis, Toleranz und Humanität, wenn er, wohl aus seiner christlichen Grundposition, kontrastive Lebensentwürfe skizziert: materiellen Überlebensdrang (Wärme, Zuwendung, Sexualität, Eros?) neben couragiertem, religiös begründetem Ethos, der das eigene Leben für eine Totenehrung aufs Spiel setzt.

[4] Bobrowskis versteht seine Erzählweise als individuelles 'Hausrecht' des Autors,[11] einer Verbindung der auktorialen Perspektive mit der 'Erzählrede';[12] das ist ein bewusst mündlicher Erzählstil, wie er ihn z. B. bei Sterne und Gogol, Leskow und Jean Paul schätzte. Der Erzähler redet, als habe er die Zuhörer direkt vor sich, spricht im Präsens, nicht im epischen Präteritum und nutzt z. B. demonstrative Signale ('da herauf') oder subjektive Empfindungen ('zu kalt'), den Gedankenmonolog ('Er soll hängen') und die szenische Vergegenwärtigung in kurzen Dialogen, um damit Authentizität und unmittelbare Nähe zum Erzählten zu suggerieren. Die Kurzgeschichte ließe sich, von den lyrischen Bildern abgesehen, gut verfilmen: Landschaftstotale am Anfang, Schwenk und Zoom zur Birke, Nahaufnahme des Soldaten und Details des Gehenkten. Fahrt zum Haus. Halbnah und Naheinstellungen: Innenraum, Herd, Soldat und Frau mit Gestik und im Dialog (Schuss-Gegenschuss) usw. Der Text bietet keinen Anlass, indiskret zu werden. Vor dem Allzumenschlichen im Zusammenspiel der Figuren bleibt der Erzähler stets in respektvoller Distanz, trotz der zupackenden Erzählrede.

[5] Besondere atmosphärische Dichte prägt Bobrowskis Sprache innerhalb der Erzählrede. Wortfeldverbindungen, lyrische Stimmungsimpulse und Dialoge werden, z. T. leitmotivisch, zu einer komplexen Prosatextur verknüpft. Wort- und Bildklammern rahmen die unwirtliche Herbstkälte ('Asche eines ausgebrannten Feuers' - 'kalt') ein; antithetisch dazu signalisiert das Wortfeld Feuer / Herd / Glut die bescheidene Geborgenheit im Hause und begleitet die Annäherung von Frau und Soldat leitmotivisch. Olfaktorische und visuelle Sinnesbereiche werden angesprochen ('der Geruch des Herdfeuers') und Bilder belebt, wenn 'ein fauliges Schilfdach herabsinkt' oder sich der Wind 'in das Dachgebälk drüben verirrt'. Von ähnlicher dynamischer Bildkraft sind auch die Personifikationen: 'Die Nachtkälte sitzt ihm überall in den Gliedern' und 'Qualm fährt ihm entgegen'. Selbst die wortkargen Dialogansätze gewinnen strukturierende Bedeutung: Mit einem lakonischen 'Komm' der Frau beginnt die Begegnung im Haus; 'Komm!' ist das letzte Wort der Geschichte, mit dem der Soldat die Frau zur Flucht auffordert und eine gemeinsame Zukunft andeutet.

Kurz, unter der Oberflächenschicht handlungsbezogenen Erzählens liegt eine von Wortkorrespondenzen durchwobene Textur, hinter der man die am Barock geschulte Musikalität des

Klavier- und Orgelspielers Bobrowski zu hören glaubt: Zu den düsteren Tönen von Krieg und Tod am Anfang der Erzählung gesellen sich, stärker als bei Petronius vorgeprägt, nahezu kontrapunktisch zwei hellere Gegenstimmen: einerseits der vitale Überlebensdrang des fluchtbereiten Paares, andererseits die couragierte Treue der Kameraden über den Tod hinaus. Die Welt der Vernichtung wird in Bobrowskis Umgang mit der Tradition jedoch nicht nur in seiner unverwechselbaren Sprachkomposition überwunden, auch aus der Variation von Inhalt und Erzählmotiven spricht eine Kulturvorstellung, die von einer verständnisvoll christlichen, zutiefst humanitären Grundhaltung geprägt wird.

NOTES

1. Johannes Bobrowski. *Gesammelte Werke in sechs Bänden*. Hrsg. E. Haufe. (Stuttgart: DVA, 1988), Bd. 4.
2. R. Könecke, *Interpretationshilfen. Deutsche Kurzgeschichten 1945-1968*. (Stuttgart: Klett, 1995), S. 84-94.
3. Könecke, S.91.
4. H. Gehle, in Johannes Bobrowski, *Gesammelte Werke. Bd.6 Erläuterungen* (1999), S 438, Anm. 1.
5. E. Grisebach, *Die Wanderung der Novelle der treulosen Witwe durch die Weltliteratur*. (Berlin: 1889). G. Huber, *Das Motiv der 'Witwe von Ephesus' in lateinischen Texten der Antike und des Mittelalters*. Mannheimer Beiträge zur Sprach- und Literaturwissenschaft, 18. (Tübingen: Narr, 1990). (Eine äußerst intensive, anregende und lesenswerte Analyse.)
6. E. Frenzel, *Motive der Weltliteratur*. (Stuttgart:1998).
7. Petronius Arbiter, *Satyrikon*. (Darmstadt: WBG 1966), S. 134ff.
8. G E Lessing, *Hamburgische Dramaturgie*. 36. Stück.
9. Zitat: *Kindlers Neues Literaturlexikon*. Hrsg. W. Jens. Bd. 5, S. 885.
10. P. Jentzsch, 'Textlektüre, Hörspielproduktion und Filmanalyse im themenzentrierten Literaturunterricht. Die erschröckliche Geschichte eines gar leichtfertigen Frauenzimmers [...]'. *Information und Beispiel*. Landesbildstelle Karlsruhe 1987/88, S. 53-73, 102-110. (Film: *Vidova z Efesu*. Prag 1971.)
11. Zuletzt E. Haufe, '*Zu Leben und Werke Bobrowskis*' in: *Gesammelte Werke*, Bd. 1, S. lxxiii, Anm. 1.
12. B. Leistner, '*Johannes Bobrowski. Studien und Interpretationen.*' *Neue Beiträge zur Literaturwissenschaft* 42. (1981), 109-22. E. Ribbat, 'Erzählte Mündlichkeit. Aspekte der Sprache im Prosawerk Johannes Bobrowskis', in A. Kelletat, hrsg., *Samartische Zeit. Erinnerung und Zukunft*, Neue Folge, 69 (1989), S.43-56.

The Break with Tradition in Literary Criticism and in Literature Today

G A Wells (St Albans)

Motto: 'Leider läßt sich der größte Teil der Menschen immer noch durch Phrasen einnebeln.' [Sadly, most people still let themselves be befogged by empty talk].

THE TYPE OF literary criticism that has established itself over the past half century shows that these words of Keith Spalding are as true today as when he wrote them, in quite another connection, in 1933. Wimsatt and Brooks, in their well-known *Literary Criticism: A Short History*, first published in 1957, exemplify the phenomenon both in their own opinions and in those of the critics they discuss. Thus, referring to the views of Jung, they say: 'a poem is organic' - a safe statement, since it does not admit of any kind of test - and 'is filled with implicit meaning'. But nearly all meaning is implicit, in that words can only imply meaning, can convey meaning only if properly interpreted. The suggestion here, however, is that a poem characteristically means something more than appears, to an extent that is not true of other speech.

This is also advocated by Wellek and Warren in chapter 12 of their *Theory of Literature* (1949). But first let us note their complaint that in the past too much attention was given to what they call 'the setting' of a work, and too little to study of it as something in its own right, so that 'the task of actually analysing and evaluating' it was woefully neglected. But the 'setting' surely includes previous literature of the same type, and as an author usually aims at modifying the techniques of predecessors in certain respects, we shall have to know the setting in order to 'evaluate' his work. We cannot consider a poem in itself, without reference to others; for this would mean banishing from one's mind all thought of any conventions of verse, language, metrical form and poetical manner, and so divesting oneself of all criteria of judgement.

Wellek and Warren not only suggest that the poem is an independent entity with which we must deal directly, but they also hold that its 'aesthetic effect does not reside in what is commonly called its content', for 'there are few works of art which are not ridiculous or meaningless in synopsis'. It is of course true that we are not impressed if told that *Faust* is about a professor who seduces a girl, or *Hamlet* about delay in killing an uncle. Such a 'synopsis' omits the most important elements of the content, namely the ideas and emotions of the characters. In many plays these may be aesthetically effective even independently of the way they are arranged into a plot - otherwise we could not derive the pleasure we do from reading some speeches in isolation from their context, even in ignorance of it. Wellek and Warren are not merely claiming that the effect of a poem depends largely on the way the individual words are put together, for that is true of the effect of any coherent writing or speech. What they are advocating is the doctrine of the 'new critics', endorsed by Elizabeth Wilkinson in a 1951 article in *German Life and Letters* (and in her numerous later publications), where she says that these critics pursue the 'internal relationships' of a work of art 'in the knowledge that its *explicit* theme or content is the mere vehicle of a meaning which can only be grasped through apprehension of its formal structure and function' (italics original). And so the critic's task is to search for verbal analogies between the supposed gist of the poem and the arrangement of the words and sentences. Such criticism degrades a work into an elaborate cryptogram, full of secret references from one part to another, and carrying beneath its surface meaning all kinds of messages for the 'perceptive' reader to divine.

In this connection, great play is made with 'ambiguity'. 'The machinations of ambiguity', says Empson at the beginning of his *Seven Types of Ambiguity* (1930), 'are among the very roots of poetry'. The more uncertain the meaning of a poem, the more scope the critic has in interpreting it. Empson believed that it is the number and variety of associations of the words of a poem that count. But most words are apt to excite in the hearer's mind a variety of thoughts and memories if time is allowed for their revival, and a word or phrase does not have more associations when it occurs in verse rather than in prose. It may be that, when we come across the word 'golden' in a poem, we shall not expect to find the precious element referred to, as we should if we found the word in a jeweller's catalogue. But this difference can only be due to the fact that, when reading poetry, we adapt ourselves to its conventions, insofar as they are known to us. The associations are in our minds, and may or may not be evoked. Admittedly, in poetry and literature, where the author's purpose is not to elucidate the properties of the universe, the range of suggestiveness can be greater than in chemistry or physics. But we may profitably distinguish between those associations likely to be common between poet and readers - such there must be, otherwise there would be no common language - and those which are peculiar to one reader, and may well result only from protracted reflexion. Empson is typical of the modern critic who, by a process reminiscent of that of psychoanalysts, explores such of his own associations and then says that they are in the poem. He picks out a number of words from, for instance, a Shakespeare sonnet or a speech of Macbeth, searches - sometimes by resort to his dictionary - for alternative meanings, and pretends that these are somehow present in the listener's mind when the words are spoken, so that the poetical effect is produced, or at least enhanced, by 'a sort of ambiguity in not knowing which of them to hold most clearly in mind'. This theory makes it easy for the critic to find beauties in almost any kind of verse which, for whatever reason, he wishes to admire.

If we now look at the position of the student, we find - taking as our example today's English-speaking student of German literature - that he or she no longer has recourse to excellent editions of the eighteenth- and nineteenth-century classics, with copious notes for readers whose native language is not German, such as the Pitt Press Series edited by Kart Breul. The market for such editions dwindled once schools began to concentrate on twentieth-century literature, and sales to university students were insufficient to give publishers an adequate return. As a result, today's students commonly work from a plain Reclam text. That they do not properly understand it is evidenced by complaints from training colleges for teachers that the modern language graduates passed on to them might well be capable of ingenious textual exegesis, but have a poor grasp of the language they will be teaching.

In a *Times Literary Supplement* article of 27 March, 1969, Douglas Hewitt noted that the professional lives of today's critics are often so arranged that they never have to deal with normal persons, but only with fellow practitioners and with student trainees. They live in what he calls 'a large self-contained empire which does not need to export its wares to common readers'. In other words, they form a kind of mutual admiration society, advertising one another's books and recommending them to their students, who are rewarded for learning and applying the relevant jargon and doctrines. As the students of today will be the professors of tomorrow, the system is self-perpetuating, especially as the same fraternity acts as readers to publishers. Hewitt notes that, since most of what can be sensibly said about literary classics has been stated by previous generations of commentators, today's critics pretend that any work which they discuss 'is radically different in kind from what readers have always thought it to be', and 'achieves its proper dignity' only as a result of their 'critical meditation'; and this latter - in order that they may show that their 'discipline' requires as much sophistication as is commanded by their colleagues in well-developed sciences - operates with considerable 'stylistic complexity', in terms of 'myths, archetypes, semantics, structuralism', and so forth.

There is a parallel development - towards meaningless originality - among the artists themselves. Although originality has often been admired in the arts, maximum effectiveness is achieved when it is tempered by a certain conformity to traditional rules; for although an artist who slavishly follows tradition will bore us, one who breaks with it completely will be merely bewildering. But the combination of originality and convention becomes, over the centuries, more and more difficult. As the conventions are relaxed and modified again and again, the stage must eventually be reached when they are all annihilated and originality attained by every kind of freakish novelty. Over a century ago, the Austrian dramatist Franz Grillparzer felt that to be novel without being artificial ('gekünstelt') was becoming increasingly difficult. He knew too that there is such a thing as original nonsense, and that originality is all too easy if no relation to reality is required. Rilke advised a young poet not to write love poems, since it is hard to be effective in a field where so many have already worked so well, whereas if what one writes is novel, it cannot be compared and contrasted with any standard model. It is hardly surprising that, as a result, so many writers (including sometimes the later Rilke himself) have taken to writing about nobody quite knows what.

But, alas, near meaningless statements are found not only in literature and literary criticism, but have come to be almost ubiquitous. Religion provides many examples. The sociologist Steve Bruce, surveying the overall scene in his *Religion in Modern Britain* (1995), sees 'an increasingly secular people gradually losing faith in the specific teachings of the Christian tradition, but retaining a fondness for vague religious affirmations'. Quite generally, freedom of ideas and of expression is all too often degraded into licence to talk at random and to make what Spalding, in my motto above, called empty talk. In the concrete branches of science, words and phrases are kept in constant touch with real things, so that nonsense is excluded or easily detected. But in the humanities what is propounded frequently has no contact with reality except to be verbally repeated in various combinations.

Arnold Schoenberg and Radical Guardianship

Robert Pascall (Bangor)

SCHOENBERG'S LIFE was one of aspiration and striving.[1] That his religious and artistic quests were intertwined has long been accepted, particularly by commentators on his biblically-based works. Such intertwining provides lessons not only in artistic creativity but also in the essence of humanity itself; and the power of these lessons is that they can never be exhausted, remaining as beacon and challenge for our own individual journeys. An arguably important source in tracing Schoenberg's quest(s) - one not yet taken up by the literature on him - is the 'Introductory Note' to *Moses und Aron* by his pupil and fellow composer, Egon Wellesz: 'Born in an age of religious indifference, in his formative years Schoenberg was more attracted by the psychological subtlety of Strindberg's plays than by the mysticism and quest for justice of Dostoevski, who was Mahler's favourite novelist. It may well be that Mahler's second symphony gave an impulse to Schoenberg's already changing outlook. It was at this time that religious ideas began to attract him until at last they took complete hold of his personality. I remember a rehearsal which Mahler conducted in Vienna in November 1907 with the Philharmonic Orchestra after he had resigned his post as Director of the Vienna State Opera. After the *Urlicht*, he addressed the orchestra in an unusually solemn way and said that the symphony symbolized the struggle of Jacob with the angel: "I will not let thee go, except thou bless me". It is possible that Mahler had discussed this interpretation of the symphony with Schoenberg who, at the beginning of 1915, began to write the text of his oratorio *Jacob's Ladder*'.[2]

Before then, however, Mahler had died and Schoenberg had already written his two essays on the composer (the second polished many years later). Schoenberg began the first, 'Gustav Mahler: in Memoriam' (1912) with the one-sentence paragraph

'Gustav Mahler was a saint' and towards the end we read: 'To Gustav Mahler's work! Into its pure air! Here is the faith that raises us on high. Here is someone believing in his immortal works, in an eternal soul. I do not know whether our soul is immortal, but I believe it. What I do know, though, is that men, the highest men, such as Beethoven and Mahler, will believe in an immortal soul until the power of this belief has endowed humanity with one.'[3] Towards the close of the second essay 'Gustav Mahler' (1912, 1948) Schoenberg wrote: 'The genius is our future. So shall we too be one day, when we have fought our way through [...]. The genius lights the way, and we strive to follow. Do we really strive enough?'.[4]

Sadly, Schoenberg wrote no essay on Beethoven, though in the compositional aspect of his quest, Beethoven was arguably an equally if not in some respects more important figure for him to 'strive to follow'. He included Beethoven (and not Mahler) in the list of his five teachers in the essay 'National Music (2)' of 1931: 'My teachers were primarily Bach and Mozart, and secondarily Beethoven, Brahms, and Wagner [...]. From *Beethoven* [I learned]: 1. The art of developing themes and movements. 2. The art of variation and of varying. 3. The multifariousness of the ways in which long movements can be built. 4. The art of being shamelessly long, or heartlessly brief, as the situation demands. 5. Rhythm: the displacement of figures on to other beats of the bar.'[5] It may be that Beethoven grew in significance in the lively environment of Schoenberg's creativity after his emigration to the United States; what is certain is the pre-eminent position Beethoven took in his compositional teaching there. In each of his two textbooks specifically on composition the clear majority of examples from the music of other composers given, analysed and commented upon is by Beethoven, and Schoenberg's own especially composed demonstrations are in pastiche Beethovenian style.[6] In addition Dika Newlin's diaries of her study with Schoenberg testify to the important role Beethoven's piano sonatas, string quartets and symphonies played in the sessions.[7]

Schoenberg remained convinced that the best way to become a composer was to understand how masters of the 17th to the 19th centuries had composed. When, in a first flush of enthusiasm, he extolled his evolution of the 12-note serial method to his pupil Josef Rufer 'I have made a discovery thanks to which the supremacy of

German music is ensured for the next hundred years'[8] he was assessing not only the new method but also the German (read Germano-Austrian) tradition itself, together with the relationship he perceived between the two. His first pieces harnessing the new method, the *Klavierstücke* op.23, the *Serenade* op.24, and the *Suite for Piano* op. 25 drew on historical genres and forms - notably baroque binary form and classical sonata form - in a creative move which explored and tested both the method's viability and emergent possibilities for renewing the expressive vitality of traditional modes of structural thought. Indeed when he explained the new method to a group of pupils in 1923 he concluded with the telling statement 'You use the row and compose as you had done it previously'.[9] Schoenberg's traditional formalist leanings proved a stumbling block for Boulez and Adorno,[10] though neither gave weight to the need for strong thematic and structural profiling which lies at the heart of the 12-note system - for it is only thus that row initiations and manipulations can be articulated, valorised and endowed with meaning.

Schoenberg held that the opening of a piece presented a problem, or postulated 'unrest', which was then worked through and resolved during its course - in contrapuntal music the form of the opening was the basic combination, to be transformed by the compositional principle of unravelling, in homophonic music it was the motive, to be transformed by developing variation. The ideals which composition served were 'unity, relationship, coherence, logic, comprehensibility and fluency.'[11] Schoenberg's holistic stance is thus clear, embracing at once musical connectedness as compositional ideal, with perceptual salience as its outcome.

He wrote his fourth and last String Quartet in the summer of 1936; it is arguably his most Beethovenian work.[12] He wrote a brief introduction to it in the essay 'Analysis, (in the Form of Program Notes) on the Four String Quartets' around Christmas 1949, a good ten years after the music had appeared in print.[13] In this he hints that the first movement uses sonata form and that it also consists of 'continuous variations'. A close reading of the movement in the light of Schoenberg's pedagogy concerning sonata form reveals that the correspondences between precept and practice are impressively fine-grained at the architectural level, amply demonstrating also points 1-4 of those techniques he considered he had learnt from Beethoven (see above).[14] Richard Kurth has charted the rhythmic displacements and manipulations in the opening period of this movement and thus exemplified in addition the fifth of the points.[15]

The musicologist Peter Gradenwitz promotes especially the last quartets of Beethoven as a significant source of Schoenberg's inspiration, drawing particular attention to the four-note motive which underlies them, and to the special importance the C# minor Quartet op.131 had as a direct influence on Schoenberg's Fourth Quartet.[16] Silvina Milstein, in her work on the third movement of Schoenberg's Quartet maintains: 'aspects of detail and large-scale processes invite a comparison with the third movement of the First *Rasumovsky* Quartet, which, analysis suggests, may have served as an archetypal model.'[17] If I may add my own remarks, the structural parallels between the first movements of Beethoven's A minor Quartet op.132 and Schoenberg's 4th are particularly striking in the developmental treatment of the recapitulation and the recapitulatory treatment of the coda; the musical materials of the two development sections have similar use of march-like dotted figures, and the extreme rhythmic variety and vitality omnipresent in Schoenberg's movement also emphasize the work's specifically Beethovenian heritage. Furthermore, the combination of lyricism and dance in Schoenberg's extended second movement reminds one forcibly of the second movement of Beethoven's op.132.

Arnold Whittall has put forward an alternative and (in light of the argument here) also a complementary reading: 'it is useful to place Schoenberg's [first] movement in the context of the Mahlerian symphonic march. This model comes especially close to the surface in a passage like that beginning in bar 111 [...] and we can easily begin to hear Schoenberg's entire discourse within the framework of Mahlerian march patterns, and to sense that those patterns underpin the basic contrast in the movement embodied by the expressive terms used by Schoenberg in his score - 'energico' and 'impetuoso' on the one hand, and 'dolce' on the other. [...] as far as Schoenberg's march-like quartet movement is concerned, it might seem not only to mock what the march once was, but also to hint at what the genre might - positively - be again.'[18]

In 1947 Schoenberg composed perhaps his most Mahlerian work *A Survivor from Warsaw*, op.46, a scenic cantata, which he nevertheless characterised as an 'orchestral piece with a speaker and male choir' - in terms therefore reminiscent of Mahler's designation of the orchestral song-cycle *Das Lied von der Erde* as a symphony. The work responds to the unimaginable horror of the holocaust by setting, dramatising and immortalising an actual event - in universalised terms - from the Warsaw ghetto. The work begins with a trumpet reveille, at the very outset therefore presenting a form of creative 'unrest' directly invoking Mahlerian precedent. The story is vividly narrated by an anonymous survivor, who tells of a brutal arrest carried out by the sergeant, the Feldwebel and a soldier, of how he survived after being hit over the head and taken for dead, and how, after the roll-calls and an overwhelming orchestral climax, he hears (as we do) the victims singing 'Sh'ma Yisroel' as they are taken off to the gas chamber - their song of courage, defiance and spiritual affirmation. Vividness is accentuated by switches into direct speech, present tense and appropriate languages (German and Hebrew) for the story's characters. Schoenberg's musically astonishing, indeed terrifying setting of his own (English) text combines pointillist orchestral and motivic techniques of his expressionist period, serial constructive means used throughout (also therefore for his original cantilena setting of the Jewish hymn of faith), and all the depictive dramatic power he had learnt from composing *Gurrelieder* and *Moses und Aron*. Schoenberg thus here continued Mahler's line of setting texts of death in war, of combining song and symphony, of using a large orchestra in chamber-like ways, of drawing stylistic plurality into compelling unity, and of giving artistic expression to fundamental values of the human spirit.

Schoenberg ended the essay 'National Music (2)' with the following self-assessment: 'For if I saw something I did not leave it at that; I acquired it, in order to possess it; I worked on it and extended it, and it led me to something new. I am convinced that eventually people will recognize how immediately this "something new" is linked to the loftiest models that have been granted us. I venture to credit myself with having written truly new music which, being based on tradition, is destined to become tradition.'[19] Thus Schoenberg's aspiration and striving founded themselves on his having lived and interiorised his past, having listened closely to what his great predecessors had to tell him and having let this listening open creative paths for him. In spite of its constructive intricacy and density his music is never just pattern: this is aspirational music with an ethical dimension. Let us recall and, at this juncture, complete the quotation from the end of 'Gustav Mahler: in Memoriam': 'men, the highest men, such as Beethoven and Mahler, will believe in an immortal soul until the power of this belief has endowed humanity with one. Meanwhile, we have immortal works. And we shall know how to guard them.'[20] His hard-won creative responses expressed his own form of radical guardianship.[21]

NOTES

1. I am most grateful to Philip Weller and Arnold Whittall for their comments on a draft of this study.
2. The 'Introductory Note' appears in the programme-book (pages unnumbered) for the first British performances of Schoenberg's Opera, given at the Royal Opera House Covent Garden on 28 June, 1, 7, 10, 13, and 16 July 1965.
3. Arnold Schoenberg, *Style and Idea*. (London [2]1975), pp. 447-8.
4. *Style and Idea*, p.471. Peter Franklin described this essay as 'a most valuable document in the case-study of Schoenberg's own creative quest for an art of mystical revelation' in: *The Idea of Music: Schoenberg and others*. (Basingstoke and London: 1985), p. 87.
5. *Style and Idea*, pp. 173-4.
6. *Models for Beginners in Composition*, Los Angeles ([1]1942; New York: [2]1943; Los Angeles: [3]1972, revised by Leonard Stein). *Fundamentals of Musical Composition* (written 1937-1948) published posthumously: London: 1967, edited by Gerald Strang with the collaboration of Leonard Stein.
7. Dika Newlin, *Schoenberg Remembered: Diaries and Recollections (1938-76)*. (New York: 1980), passim.
8. Willi Reich, *Schoenberg: a critical biography* trans. Leo Black. (London: 1971), p. 130.
9. *Style and Idea*, p. 213.
10. Pierre Boulez, 'Schoenberg is Dead' in: *Stocktakings from an Apprenticeship*. (Oxford: 1991), pp .209-14. Theodor Wiesengrund Adorno 'Zum Verständnis Schönbergs' in: *Gesammelte Schriften 18 (= Musikalische Schriften V*; Frankfurt a/M: 1997), pp. 428-45; here p. 444; and *Philosophie der neuen Musik (= Gesammelte Schriften 12*; Frankfurt a/M: 1997), pp .93-6.
11. Arnold Schoenberg, *Fundamentals of Musical Composition*. (London: 1965), p. 8. This formulation is specifically a description of the power of the motive in homophonic music but draws in terms applied more generally to all music elsewhere in his writings.

12 Stravinsky named it as one of Schoenberg's 'best works' in: Igor Stravinsky and Robert Craft *Dialogues and a Diary.* (London: 1968), p. 108.
13 The manuscript of 'Analysis, (in the Form of Program Notes) on the Four String Quartets' is dated December 29 1949 and the folder-cover title 30 December 1949. The working notes, manuscript and typescript are housed in the Archive of the Arnold Schönberg Center, Vienna under call-mark T70.02. The essay was written for concerts by the Juilliard String Quartet.
14 Robert Pascall, 'Theory and Practice: Schönberg's American Pedagogical Writings and the First Movement of the Fourth String Quartet, op.37', *Journal of the Arnold Schönberg Center 4/2002: 'Arnold Schoenberg in America'* (Vienna: 2002), pp. 229-44.
15 Richard Kurth: 'The Art of Cadence in Schönberg's Fourth String Quartet', ibid. pp. 245-70.
16 Peter Gradenwitz, *Arnold Schönberg. Streichquartett Nr.4, op.37.* (München, 1986), pp. 7, 22.
17 Silvina Milstein, *Arnold Schoenberg: notes, sets, forms.* (Cambridge, 1992), p. 99. Timothy Jackson considerably adds to debate on the relationship between the two movements in his review of Milstein's book, in the *Journal of Musicological Research*, 15 (1995), pp. 285-311.
18 Arnold Whittall, 'Fulfilment or betrayal?' in: *Musical Times*, 40, no.1869 (Winter 1999), 11-21; here 18-9.
19 *Style and Idea*, p. 174.
20 *Style and Idea*, pp. 447-8.

Hans Erich Nossack: New Beginnings

Peter Prochnik (London)

UNFORESEEN EVENTS can often have such explosive consequences that the fragility of routine existence is easily disrupted, but occasionally their destructive power is of such fundamental force that the reverberations and symbolic meanings go far beyond the account of an immediate incident. In July 1943, aged 42, Hans Erich Nossack experienced such a catastrophic event that not only marked the destruction of his previous literary existence, but also determined the course of his future life. *Der Untergang*, Nossack's account of these events, can be seen as a metaphor of the central experience of his life in that the authorial, first person narrator is described in a concrete, historical situation.

Nossack was born in Hamburg in 1901 into a bourgeois family with its traditional values typical of this Hansa city. He studied at Jena University, but financial difficulties forced him to give up his studies. Rejecting his family's bourgeois values and background, he cut his ties to his family who had objected to his wanting to become a writer and tried his hand at a number of jobs including that of factory worker. Basically, however, he led an impoverished existence. He joined the communist party, but eventually, to avoid trouble with the Nazis, Nossack felt forced to return to his family working in father's coffee importing business, writing clandestinely. It was not until after the Second World War that Nossack came to the attention of the German reading public with a collection of poetry entitled *Gedichte* (1947), and *Nekyia. Bericht eines Überlebenden* (1947) which describes a catastrophe set in a mythical location. Nossack followed these works with a collection of short pieces *Interview mit dem Tode* (1948) which contained *Der Untergang* which had been written earlier in 1943. *Der Untergang* caused an immediate stir and even came to the notice of Jean Paul Sartre, editor of *Les Temps Modernes*, who published it in the journal in translation in 1949. Nossack continued to publish a considerable number of prose works and essays until his death in 1977. However, despite the numerous literary awards he received over the years, confirming his stature, he has remained a relatively unknown writer to the public at large.

The genesis of *Der Untergang* with its combination of sober realism and mythical, fairy tale elements which have always attracted Nossack, is the result of the bombing of Hamburg and what he experienced between July 24 and August 15, 1943. It had been the first time in five years that Nossack had left the city for a short break in the country south of Hamburg in the tiny village of Horst near Maschen. He and his wife had difficulty finding accommodation, but settled into an uncomfortable weekend cottage and began to forget the war, although in retrospect certain incidents of a threatening nature proved to be ominous auguries: a sinister large black dog, a ceaselessly lowing cow, a goat of frightening prehistoric proportions and two pine trees resembling wolves leaping at the crescent moon with slavering mouths. Already an atmosphere of the mythical and of unreality permeates the scene emphasising the timelessness of the heath. The idyll, the acceptable face of the abyss, has revealed its darker, threatening side.

On July 24, three days after the couple's arrival in Horst, Operation Gomorrah was launched by the allies, during which Hamburg was almost totally destroyed by the bombing. For four nights Nossack stood outside his cottage watching the city burn until even the heath was set alight. Nossack lost his home and possessions, and, almost more importantly for him, all his manuscripts and diaries, which he had maintained since the age of 15, were burnt in the conflagration. However, despite this grievous personal loss, the fate of the city on another level was welcomed by him as a release from the fetters of old traditions. He felt himself 'charged to render an account' and to record the destruction 'which had made one speechless'.

Der Untergang was Nossack's first attempt at writing after the catastrophe. Written for 'therapeutic reasons' in prose of clear restraint, Nossack produced a dispassionate inventory of what had been lost. He later explained to his friend the novelist, Hermann Kasack, that this work could be called a 'confession' as well as an 'intimate account' of a walk through a dead city. 'I believe I had indicated in *Untergang* the feeling of awakening or release that overcame me with the destruction of the city.'[1] The experience had confirmed for him the frailty, uncertainty and vulnerability of a life to which he could never return. The old, traditional structures and values were changed and now worthless, and no human construct could provide security.

Nossack felt himself inextricably connected with the fate of the city, a fact that he often reiterated. 'I can do no other than to view the destruction of the city in a closely bound relationship with my own fate.'[2] He felt that the individual had now been released into a void and was forced to be self-reliant in rediscovering himself. This, however, is a precarious enterprise, for the individual is faced not only with the solitude of the freedom he has now acquired, but also with a feeling of abandonment. Nossack tries to make sense of his world through his writing and, as Kasack pertinently remarks, Nossack has now been 'freed inwardly'. 'The feeling of standing at a turning point or indeed of having taken a few steps beyond it, dominates me and I am careful not to miss the opportunity.'[3]

Nossack as a survivor is also an outsider, a figure he returns to in all his works. The dominant themes of his subsequent works are distinguished by a sense of loss which is the first step in self-release and the 'crossing of boundaries' consistent with stepping out of time, of needing to journey into undefined regions. These 'expeditions' as he calls them are the start of the search for an alternative system or reality, a reality truer than the facade of the false reality by which we live. Nossack comments in his diaries that it is difficult to live without a past, but nonetheless 'if I have freed myself for other things, then much has been achieved.'[4] The zero starting point is the events of *Der Untergang* whose themes and images Nossack develops in later works which are characterised by his rejection of the past.

Having witnessed the destruction of Hamburg as a spectator, Nossack feels the urge to return to the city despite its horrors. On his arrival nothing is familiar any longer and the survivors he encounters are in a state of disorientation. The world has changed, but so too has Nossack. This act of transformation is typical for Nossack who is always very much concerned with extending borders. In *Der Neugierige* (1955) a fish finds that its usual element of water is too constricting and endeavours to save itself in a new existence, in an alien element. *Spätestens im November* (1955) is an account rendered from the grave. In *Spirale* (1956) a boy tries to swim to another forbidden riverbank, while in *Nach dem Letzten Aufstand* (1961) there is a report from an individual who has already escaped. In *Der Fall D'Arthez* (1968), however, a new figure, that of the 'partisan' appears.

The 'partisan' is a figure that accepts his isolation voluntarily as the condition for his existence, for only by becoming a 'partisan' does one protect oneself from the dehumanisation of society, a society that no longer serves the needs of man. Loneliness is the unavoidable consequence of individuation and the sphere in which the 'partisan' or outsider exists is called 'exterritorial' which becomes a metaphor for the individual's apartness. The reality of the 'partisan' is totally different from that of others, 'as I see it at present there can only be a voluntary retreat into a partisan existence; for the struggle is no longer about a principle, but about the existence of mankind'.[5] Nossack's characters tend to defy the present, always driving onwards into the unknown, into landscapes of estrangement as in the short story *Das Mal* in order to reject the aridity of frozen and worthless traditions. The characters represent possibilities of identity, a theme which has preoccupied Nossack who wondered how many forms an artist has to adopt in the search for the true self.

Nossack writes with persuasive force how to combat challenging circumstances. For him it was always a matter of intellectual resistance, never a physical one: he was concerned with an inner biography:

> I have never made a secret of the fact that the destruction of Hamburg in July 1943 signified a turning point in my life. It confirmed that which until then I had never dared to utter clearly, namely that we had to acknowledge the task forced upon our generation i.e. to live a life in a void without any support.[6]

'Heimat' means nothing to him, which patently accounts for the outsider in his works inhabiting a reality that fails to correspond to our real world.

> One day, however, one notices that one no longer belongs and is standing outside one's usual environment. Everything that we had been led to believe, including the social rules of others, seems to be wrong [...]. One has no support.[7]

All the eternal and absolute values fail and are only an outmoded facade. Nossack believes that one must live 'outside' history and lead a 'partisan' life. One's origins and background are meaningless yardsticks with which to determine one's next steps. He adds 'The notion of tradition needs a new definition [...] it is nothing other than the wish to cling to a nest that for a long time has not been home.'[8] The last few decades have forced people to lead a problematic existence, clinging to an invalid past that Nossack wished to reject.

The ideas implicit in Nossack's works become more explicit in his essays which elucidate his search for a private truth. His works define his way of life despite his belief that he was the best-camouflaged writer. Nossack wrote for self-expression rather than communication and although his works commence from the same point of departure and he uses first person narrators, there is always a multiplicity of perspectives in his struggle to find identity. The boundaries between life and death, dream and reality disappear, hence Nossack's view that the negation of old values is a precondition for the search for new values or an individual truth that might only be imagined or dreamt at this stage.

In many respects, as an unconventional writer, it is difficult to fit Nossack's works into clearly defined categories of novel or stories. However, what does emerge is his great integrity, as a writer who did not shrink from exploring difficult territory. Nossack's characters are solitary individuals, standing apart from society and threatening the established norms, searching for a way out of uncertainty. He uses language not to convey information, but to articulate the self, as a means of self-assertion against society's increasing mechanisation and uniformity and social programming. Critics have often complained that Nossack steps outside society rather than becoming involved with it. However, he has turned political and social issues into intellectual problems of morality in his determination to arrive at his own reality. 'Is not the fact that we talk to ourselves proof that we cannot exist without even an imaginary sphere before us?'[9]

NOTES
1 *Hans Erich Nossack. Die Tagebücher 1943-1977.* Vol. 1. Ed. G. Söhling. (Frankfurt/Main: 1977), p. 451.

2   Letter to Hermann Kasack 8/12/43. In: *Hans Erich Nossack. Geben Sie bald wieder ein Lebenszeichen. Briefwechsel 1943-1956.* Vol. 1. *Briefe.* Ed. G. Söhling.(Frankfurt/Main: 2001), p. 19.
3   Letter to Hermann Kasack 12/12/43. Ibid., p. 23.
4   *Op.cit.*, p. 20.
5   *Jahr und Jahrgang 1901.*(Hamburg: 1966), p. 57.
6   Ibid., p. 86.
7   Ibid., pp. 55-6.
8   Ibid., p. 59.
9   *Nachmittägliche Zwischenbemerkung.* In: *Hans Erich Nossack. Pseudoautographische Glossen.* (edition suhrkamp).(Frankfurt/Main: 1971), p. 166.

The Poet Between War and Peace: Marie Luise Kaschnitz's Essays *Menschen und Dinge 1945*

Anthony Bushell (Bangor)

THE BRIEF period that existed between the collapse of the totalitarian National Socialist state and the full imposition of Allied control following Germany's unconditional surrender offered little space or opportunity to hear individual German voices reflecting upon the state of the nation and its citizens in the wake of the immeasurable physical destruction and mental anguish which war and defeat had brought to Germany. Subsequently cold war politics and a remarkable economic revival, which saw West Germany industry recover to achieve by 1950 production levels of 1936-37, provided little incentive to dwell on such intangible matters as the psychological and spiritual well-being of Germany, especially of its young people, whilst the desire to achieve material security naturally claimed its citizens' attention and considerable individual and collective energy.

It is for this reason that Marie Luise Kaschnitz's collection of twelve essays printed almost immediately after the war under the intentionally elementary title *Menschen und Dinge 1945* has a particular value. The essays yield insight into the state of mind of an intensely reflective and sensitive German as the country stood between war and peace and into those values that could still be espoused when so much that Germany had stood for had been exposed as barbaric. These essays, however, did more than take stock of those moral and ethical values which had either survived or perished. They gave a first indication of the nature of the language and the very rhetoric that would be employed to give tentative initial expression to a nation emerging from a state of trauma and entering upon an uncertain future.

The essays were published as a collection in 1946 by the Heidelberg publisher Lambert Schneider under American licence.[1] They formed part of a special number of *Die Wandlung*, edited by Dolf Sternberger, and this special series had a distinguished editorial board consisting of the philosopher Karl Japers, the Romance language scholar Werner Krauss and the sociologist Alfred Weber. Three of the essays had appeared even earlier, including the opening essay, 'Vom Ich', in the first edition of the journal *Die Wandlung* (Heft 1 1945/46) and the eleventh essay, 'Von der Schuld', in the second number of the journal. It is clear from the content and the tenses of verbs used that certain of the twelve essays had been composed during the last stages of the war and others in the immediate aftermath of capitulation.

Although Kaschnitz became a much respected and fêted writer in the Federal Republic of the 1950s, receiving the prestigious *Büchner-Preis* in 1955, she had in 1945 yet to produce much of that work, especially poetry, upon which her subsequent reputation rested. In the *laudatio* delivered by Kasimir Edschmid in 1955 she had been presented as the voice that had spoken for a whole generation, a voice both of opposition and affirmation: 'Ihr Gedicht war der Ausdruck der Epoche und gleichzeitig die Überwindung dessen, was in dieser Zeit satanisch war. Ihre Aussage war im Kern Opposition *und* Bekenntnis'.[2] But in 1945 she was not yet a figure of national standing. Born in 1901, she belonged neither to the older generation of writers whose reputation had been firmly established before 1933 nor to the younger generation to emerge immediately after the war and associated with, for instance, the Gruppe 47.

Kaschnitz was highly critical of her own passive role during the years of National Socialism. Whilst meeting in secret with writers and academics opposed to Hitler, she had not made public statements denouncing the Nazis nor had she taken on herself the isolation of exile, both acts of resolution she admired in other writers and would have acknowledged in the life of fellow Germans such as the young Keith Spalding. Nor was she willing to inflate her mental reservation and loathing of National Socialism with the title of inner emigration or internal resistance. This personal acknowledgement of her failings was an immediate hallmark of the essays. (She carried too the burden of a strong sense of guilt over the way she had requested from the publisher Bruno Cassirer, shortly before the outbreak of war, the return of the manuscript of a book she had written, convinced that there was little hope of a Jewish publisher being allowed to continue producing books in Germany.)[3]

The encouragement to write the essays and to see them published in those difficult post-war days was largely due to the influence of Dolf Sternberger, a family friend from before the war. He had been the cultural editor of the *Frankfurter Zeitung* until his liberal views had incurred the displeasure of Goebbels, resulting in Sternberger being forced from his post. As one married to a half-Jewish wife the war years had been particularly difficult for Sternberger but a strong bond had developed with his near neighbour Marie Luise Kaschnitz and in the light of his opposition to the Nazis the Americans swiftly granted him a licence in post-war Germany when he became the founding editor of a journal with the programmatic title *Die Wandlung*. It began to appear as early as November 1945 with an initial circulation of 35,000.[4] (The journal was one of the few internal literary endeavours that won the admiration of Thomas Mann, who was to contribute to the journal and who from his exile had had generally a very low opinion of much that was being produced in Germany by those who had remained there throughout the war years.) Sternberger sought Kaschnitz's collaboration from the very inception of *Die Wandlung*. When he received the manuscript of her essay on guilt he wrote to her in November 1945 to tell her it was the most profound statement he as an editor had received on this theme. Kaschnitz herself was taken aback by the intensity of the response the essays were to receive from readers.[5]

The twelve, terse titles of the essays, opening with the simplest of expressions, 'Vom Ich', through to such fundamental concepts as 'Von der Natur', 'Von den Dingen, 'Von der Gotteserfahrung', 'Von unseren Kindern', 'Vom Hunger', 'Von der Schuld' and 'Von der Verwandlung', already mark the terrain Kaschnitz intended to evoke and explore; they are at once intensely physical in a time of extreme deprivation but also open to a spiritual regeneration: her fourth essay bore the title 'Vom Wiedererwecken'.

Her first essay, 'Vom Ich', a title echoing Jaspers' concern with the self and its position in the new order (and which he went on to explore in works such as *Wohin treibt die Bundesrepublik?*), took the simplest element left to those that had survived the war. Kaschnitz does not offer facile optimism but insists, however, on the presence of 'Mut'and 'Hoffnung', for she claims that these are the gifts of the eternally recurring regeneration ['Wiedergeburt'] that accompany all life. Regeneration does not lead us back to our beginnings for to have lived is to have experienced and experience brings with it transformation. Just as the mature adult cannot return to childhood, no age can return to an earlier innocence. Even if the present time has been one of tremendous oppression and cruelty, Kaschnitz argues that we must not cease trying to rediscover ourselves and our central place in the created order. Each individual must once more become fully conscious of himself or herself, ['zu sich selbst erwacht', p. 10], a term Kaschnitz's readers would surely have sensed was in diametric opposition to the collective and numbing call of 'Deutschland erwache!' which had plunged them into their present misery.

Kaschnitz acknowledges that what has been lost has been more than the bricks and mortar of the physical world. Certainty and dreams have been destroyed: the certainty, for instance, that boyhood would naturally lead to manhood or the security of familiar sights and smells. Trust, too, has been lost and Kaschnitz pleads that it is in finding qualities such as courage and the freedom to do good in ourselves that we will be ready to look for those qualities in others, and that ultimately our belief in our fellow men is rooted in our belief in God. Yet Kaschnitz's voice is far from being otherworldly. The self is bound up with the immediate, with hunger, despair, self-destruction and restlessness. Yet reflected in this chaos is also light. She and her fellow Germans presently inhabit two worlds; despair walks side by side with reverence for, and a sense of, the divine. The experience of the night is answered by a Goethean optimism as she concludes her first essay: 'Aber die Welt, die vor unsern Blicken liegt, ist jung wie am ersten Tag' (p. 14).

In her second essay, 'Von der Natur', Kaschnitz explores the power exerted by nature. At first sight nature appears callous and indifferent to the fate of men and women: 'Durch die Verwesung der Schlachtfelder führt mit enger Unbekümmertheit der Bach seine melodische Flut' (p. 15). Yet this indifference is contradicted by the joy evoked by the sight of a young tree, or blades rising from a field or the appearance of flowers in spring. The dichotomy -

'Naturnähe und Naturferne' - can only be overcome by accepting all the manifestations of the cosmos in their entirety. Only when the non-material world, the world of 'Geist', is accepted and embraced will human suffering be reduced. At present men are uncertain, their longing for God's kingdom is in the form of a pained question; it has yet to become a surrendering to the whole of his being.

Her third essay, 'Von den Dingen', shows that Kaschnitz does not wish to deny the material world: 'Verleugnen wir die Dinge nicht. Sie haben uns gehalten. Und sie haben uns erhöht' (p. 25). Our memories are populated by objects and herein resides their potency: they evoke past times. But at the moment there is no choice: the material world has been destroyed and we have only ourselves left. The two auxiliary verbs, 'to be' and 'to have', have acquired the most profound significance and, of the two, it is the verb 'to be' that is now the dominant.

Memory concerns Kaschnitz in her fourth essay, 'Vom Wiedererwecken'. Evoking the past is a task left now for the elderly. Those struggling in the midst of life have little space for the past, yet the present offers faint prospect of creative or fulfilling work; so much creative time has been lost crouching in cellars, hiding from danger. The present generation may not have much to evoke from its past, but Kaschnitz encourages her readers to engage with the past for it is the way in which we learn to respect the present and develop a faith in the unseen future.

Germany is at the temple of Janus, standing between war and peace. Some will not survive to know and experience that peace, Kaschnitz argues in her eighth essay, 'Von der Stille', and their life's work will remain uncompleted and later generations will be the poorer for this. As peace now approaches it is hard to discern if the sound that can be dimly heard is the music of creative life and of work returning or the anguished scream of a nation humiliated and about to take revenge upon itself. The climax of the war may have been reached, but the catharsis has yet to begin. Kaschnitz issues a cry of yearning for at least one moment of stillness.

Kaschnitz's reputation as a writer of short stories that examine the world from the perspective of children was well-established in several anthologies in post-war Germany. Her interest in children was profound and she had a strong sense of the damage that the experience of war had caused them. In her ninth essay, 'Von unseren Kindern', she reflects on the nature of that damage. Again her perspective is different to many others; she acknowledges the obvious suffering children have experienced, some have been forced into bearing arms in the dying moments of the war, but she goes on to argue that, as strange as it might sound, fighting and dying in a group has been easier for this generation of children than being alone for a single hour: 'Und die Begegnung mit dem Feind war ein wirkliches Kinderspiel gemessen an der Begegnung mit Gott' (p. 74). This generation has been deprived not only of the physical manifestations of civilisation but also stripped of wisdom and an ability to yearn.

The eleventh essay on guilt, the one which so impressed the editor of *Die Wandlung*, begins with a question that is simultaneously an accusation; 'Und was tatest Du?' Kaschnitz acknowledges that many will bridle at this when it is asked not on the Day of Judgement but by fellow men. There is a natural instinct to defy those that raise their finger in accusation, but Kaschnitz asks her reader to accept that they have failed to act. Many acts of evil had been committed in their name. Individual responsibility had yielded to the collective will ['Wille der Allgemeinheit'] and thus it is possible to speak of collective responsibility ['Massenverantwortung']. The individual has been paralysed and unable to oppose evil because of the sheer magnitude of that evil; Kaschnitz even speaks of a sense of awe in the face of evil (p. 92). All have fallen victim to its power. Yet Kaschnitz claims it will not require the strictures of their victors to make them aware of this: 'Denn sie können uns nicht lehren, was wir nicht selber wüßten' (p. 93). She is aware that the outside world harbours a deep sense of bitterness towards Germans on account of their passivity but she asks those that stand in judgement to first understand that power which was responsible for tearing their souls apart.

In her final essay, 'Von der Verwandlung', Kaschnitz asserts that no amount of destruction can overshadow the miracle of continued existence and the recurrence that takes place in nature: in plants and in animals. But what of the author and her readers? Kaschnitz offers the image of migrants waiting at the quay-side for a ship whose name and destination are as yet unknown to them. Only here does Kaschnitz's prose engage exceptionally and directly with a precise historical context:

[...] wäre es doch an der Zeit, etwas anderes zu erstreben als den alten Kampf um die Macht, der sich unter der erhabenen Ägide der Wissenschaft und in dem reichen Kleide bürgerlicher Kultur so lange schweigend vollzieht, um dann plötzlich seine ganze Brutalität an den Tag zu kehren. Es wäre an der Zeit, die Bahnen zu verlassen, die der unvergängliche deutsche Idealismus eingeschlagen hat und die für ein der Harmonie und Heiterkeit entbehrendes Volk so gefährliche waren. (p. 101)

These twelve essays have not claimed much attention in subsequent Kaschnitz scholarship. At the time of their writing there is evidence of unease amongst the editorial board. Whilst Sternberger was hugely impressed by the essays his fellow editor Werner Krauss, a Marxist imprisoned by the Nazis and who in 1948 was to move to the Soviet zone to take up a post at the university of Leipzig, found them too detached, reproaching them for their 'Unverbindlichkeit'.[6] Changes in Kaschnitz's prose style and her move to a far more sober tone of writing place these essays clearly in an earlier phase of her work, and in their choice of imagery, often ecstatic, the essays were untypical of that work upon which her later reputation rested, yet these facts do not detract from their importance as a sustained first attempt in the most difficult of circumstances to survey those areas of life that had been assailed for all Germans. They predated Allied attempts at re-education amongst Germans and were motivated from within rather than from without. Their lack of precision was not the result of a reluctance or inability to handle history. A degree of circumspection was unavoidable for essays that had been begun whilst the author was still living under National Socialism. But Kaschnitz's concern was not only with the here and now but with the very essence of all human life: its dignity, its responsibilities and its joys, values affirmed by both Kaschnitz and by the man commemorated in this volume.

NOTES

[1] Quotations are from this edition. The essays were later reprinted in volume seven of the *Gesammelte Werke*, published by Insel Verlag in 1989.

2 Kasimir Edschmid, 'Huldigung für Marie Luise Kaschnitz', in *Deutsche Akademie für Sprache und Dichtung: Jahrbuch 1955* (Heidelberg-Darmstadt: Lambert Schneider, 1956), p. 76.
3 Dagmar von Gersdorff, *Marie Luise Kaschnitz: Eine Biographie.* (Frankfurt am Main: Insel, 1997), p. 105.
4 Janet K. King, *Literarische Zeitschriften 1945-1970.* (Stuttgart: Metzler, 1974), pp. 19-20.
5 Gersdorff, op. cit., p. 174.
6 Gersdorrf, op.cit., p.174 and p. 181.

On Revering the Old and Espousing the New: Friedrich Christian Delius *Die Birnen von Ribbeck*

G L Jones (Aberystwyth)

DELIUS'S SHORT story *Die Birnen von Ribbeck* (1991) is set in the village of Ribbeck, situated some thirty kilometres west of Berlin, and immortalised in Theodor Fontane's poem, *Herr von Ribbeck auf Ribbeck im Havelland* (1889). On a March day in 1990 a large group of West Berliners arrive in the village intent on celebrating the centenary of Fontane's poem and the imminent unification of the two German states. The planting of the West German pear-tree in the East German village is symbolic of the annexation of the GDR by the Federal Republic. The action of the story is virtually completed by the end of the opening paragraph - in it the anonymous narrator recalls in militaristic terms the 'advance' of the West Berliners from the east, their 'occupation' of the village, their profferment of gifts to the natives, the planting of the new pear-tree, the celebratory dance around the pear-tree, the acquiescence of the local mayor, the recording on video of the planting, the visitors' sense of triumph - as if they had 'placed their flag in conquered territory' - and their embracing of the local inhabitants. By the end of this first paragraph they are passing around drinks and addressing the locals in familiar terms as 'ihr' and 'du'. At the end of the narrative the visitors 'withdraw', leaving the narrator, now in an advanced state of inebriation, to offer a final, somewhat incoherent comment on the 'blessings' which have been bestowed on the village during the day's celebrations. For the remaining 189 paragraphs the narrator recounts the history of the village over the previous two to three hundred years, but focuses particularly on the fate of the ordinary people of the village during the twentieth century, during the feudal era, the Nazi period and the forty years of socialist rule.

The story is written in the form of a monologue, delivered ostensibly by a local tractor-driver who has spent the whole of his sixty-odd years in the village. Although the narrative is divided into paragraphs of varying length, it consists of only one lengthy sentence, punctuated mainly with commas and containing only one full-stop at the end of the final paragraph. The reader is borne along by the narrative tempo which reflects both the author's awareness of the speed with which changes were taking place in the GDR and the narrator's delight in his new-found freedom of speech. 'I'm not going to be told to shut up,' he declares, 'for forty years I have shut up and am I now to stand there like the cows [...] and chew over what I swallowed all those years' (BR, 53). In part Delius's narrator is based on his first informant in Ribbeck, a man whom he met in January 1990 beside the church near the famous pear-tree and who could hardly stop, once he had started speaking (VW, 60). Delius was attracted to Ribbeck, so he tells us (VW, 60-1), so that he might become 'the medium for people who had been liberated from forty-plus twelve years of silence'. The word he uses is 'Sprachlosigkeit' - literally, 'speechlessness'. The experience of speaking freely is so alien to the narrator that he is afraid to stop in case he will be told 'to shut up' (BR, 27). From his own experience in the GDR he knows that even after joining the Party in order to be able to voice his opinion, he was expected to 'shut up' and conform (BR, 67-8). He fears that his new-found freedom of speech will be curtailed in the new Germany if he dares to express dissatisfaction with the market economy; he will be silenced in 'the new old way' (BR, 27).

In some ways the monologue is effusive, it is an outpouring, but paradoxically, it is also delivered in a cautious and circumspect manner. Here is a man who has had to learn how to express his own opinions, how to use the first person singular 'I' in place of the socialist collective, 'We' (BR, 14). He needs to learn a new vocabulary, to rid himself of old-fashioned political terms like 'Junker' (BR, 48); he needs, like his creator,[1] to overcome his diffidence, his stuttering: 'Language came again and with language stuttering' (BR, 10). The division of the text into paragraphs also exerts a retarding effect on the narrator's effusiveness. The narrator himself is aware that his thoughts are being expressed too precipitately (BR, 70), that his sentences are 'mutilated' (BR, 78), that his listeners - in so far as they are listening at all - will soon tire of him (BR, 27), that they will need to recover 'from all these strenuous words' (BR, 28). At the same time he reminds them that if listening to him is trying for them, speaking is even more strenuous for him. The monologue is indicative of the speaker's isolation; he has no interlocutors amongst the West Berliners. As the monologue proceeds, he expresses his increasing impatience with the visitors who are not really listening to what he has to say. The familiar forms of address, noted at the end of the opening paragraph, are not reciprocated by the narrator. As the celebrations come to an end, he muses on the West Berliners' assertion that they are all now in the same boat; 'we cannot', he declares, 'climb so quickly into your boats and slip into your skins, neither can you slip into our skins, we supply the pears and you fuck the pears, sorry, I won't use such filthy words as "you" and "we" again ...'(BR, 76). It emerges that the narrator has as much difficulty in using the 'We' of a new collective German identity, as he experienced in moving from the socialist collective 'We' to the 'I' of individual utterance. The narrator's only 'listener' is, in fact, a creation of his own inebriated imagination - the Old Master of Ribbeck who is resurrected from his grave towards the end of the narrative.

If Delius had been satisfied to suppress his own opinions on unification and simply to act as a medium for and chronicler to the inhabitants of Ribbeck, his narrative would not have differed basically from the many documentary accounts of the experiences and opinions of the citizens of the GDR which were published in the 1990s - e.g. Helga Königsdorf's *Adieu DDR* (1990).[2] It would have imparted knowledge to the reader, but not have engaged him or her actively in the issues it raises. Paradoxically, Delius's text, which only contains two question marks, is, above all, interrogative in mode. These question marks occur in the third paragraph when the narrator is commenting on the fact that the visitors from West Berlin 'even brought journalists with them who kept asking: What do you think of all this? and if we didn't immediately utter a sentence they could use, they asked: Don't you think it's great? so that we could only say: Yes, and avoid them because they were so similar to our journalists who never wanted to hear No and only wanted to hear answers they already knew' (BR, 8-9). Such questions are not really questions at all; those who pose them, only seek confirmation of their own actions and opinions. Delius's text constantly poses the question which the natives of Ribbeck expect to hear from their visitors at the end of the first paragraph, namely: What do they, the people of Ribbeck, really think of the new pear-tree? The visitors themselves never pose the question; they are confident that they know all the answers.

The text engages the reader in several ways: unlike the declarative text it does not proceed in a linear, chronological manner. It constantly moves within the same paragraph from one main theme to another, from one era to another. At times the reader is not entirely certain which period is being commented on. In this way Delius suggests parallels between the treatment of the workers during the feudal age and during the forty years of socialist rule. The reader's puzzlement parallels that of the author himself when he first listened to his initial informant's account of the history of Ribbeck: 'What he narrated, fascinated me just as much as the manner in which he narrated it, i.e. "jumbled": you could never tell whether what he was narrating, had occurred three months or three years or three decades ago.'[3] Or again: 'What he narrated, was in no way ordered, certainly not chronologically, but all the stories [...] and the commentaries on them, were narrated in a jumbled, associative manner' (VW, 60). By emulating his first informant's manner of speech, Delius retards the narrative tempo and in so doing, stimulates his readers to reflect on the issues being raised. In conversation with Keith Bullivant Delius expressed his criticism of the speed with which German unification was being discussed: 'People were talking everywhere incessantly and in an ever more abstract - and loquacious manner'.[4] In these 'heady' times, he declared, he needed to stop, to pause. What drove him to Ribbeck, was 'repugnance at all the empty talk about German unity, even the highly intelligent talk in the better newspapers and television channels' (VW, 62). Ribbeck and its pear-trees provided Delius with a concrete example of the problematic nature of the proposed union of the two Germanies. Within the narrative itself the narrator comments continually on the speed of the changes that are taking place and the pressures on the East Germans to accelerate so that they might catch up with their Western compatriots. For Delius literature itself eschews the alacrity which characterises contemporary capitalist society. In *Die Verlockungen der Wörter* he writes of literature: 'It probably gains more by not pandering to impatience, by refusing to be fast, and by not being immediately intelligible [...]. It entices with the luxury of slowness, pausing, stopping, questioning' (VW, 96-7).

It is clear that the narrator of *Die Birnen von Ribbeck* is not based solely on Delius's first or even his subsequent informants in Ribbeck, although he does acknowledge his indebtedness to them at the outset of the text (BR, 14). The narrator's knowledge is by no means limited to agricultural and local matters, but encompasses a great deal of social, political and literary history. Durrani is right to stress that 'a plurality of voices can and indeed must be discerned'[5] in Delius's narrator. In spite of the range of his knowledge the narrator is not depicted as omniscient. Delius's concern is not so much with imparting knowledge about the history of Ribbeck as with inviting reflection on the interpretation of past events. Thus, for example, the narrator offers various, conflicting accounts of the arrest and death of the last Master of Ribbeck at the hands of the Nazis (BR, 43-5). The interpretation of the past, the exploration of the village's literary heritage, determines the manner in which Fontane's poem is presented in the text. Although the text presupposes a detailed knowledge of the poem, it is never quoted in its entirety. Instead, individual lines are interpolated throughout the text in a way which defamiliarises them and subverts their original meaning; in this way the legendary munificence of the Old Master of Ribbeck is exposed as a figment of the poetic imagination. Delius is not implying that the poem should be consigned unthinkingly to oblivion. He is critical of the manner in which the last Master of Ribbeck neglected the family's heritage and dismissed Fontane as a 'fraud' ('Schwindler', BR, 29) whilst at the same time displaying cynical opportunism in his own dealings with the Nazis. He certainly does not approve of the suppression of the poem in the schools of the GDR; the Party, he comments caustically, was continually talking about its heritage, and the name of Fontane was even used in Ribbeck as a designation for 'repair-shops, collective farms and pleasure-steamers' (BR, 15), but it proscribed the poem which celebrated the benign feudal Master of Ribbeck and which might have provoked unfavourable comparisons between his legendary munificence and its own parsimonious treatment of the people of Ribbeck. Neither does the narrator approve of the ignorance of the visitors from West Berlin; they are ostensibly celebrating the centenary of Fontane's poem, but not once do they quote from it. In fact, they are simply indulging their nostalgia for the good old times which never existed in reality (BR, 17). Delius's text prompts us, his readers, to turn back to the poem and consider whether it has any value for us. After all, he reminds us, the poem, although based on a myth, has 'outlasted all the rigid curricula' (BR, 56) and still attracts visitors to Ribbeck.

As the day draws to its end, the narrator invites the Old Master of Ribbeck to join him for a last drink in the local inn in order to celebrate his resurrection. On their arrival at the inn they discover that it is closed - as was so often the case in the GDR. From memory the narrator quotes in a slightly inaccurate form some lines from Fontane's novel *Der Stechlin* which still hang inside the inn 'in ornate script, like a Biblical verse' (BR, 73): 'Alles Alte, soweit es Anspruch darauf hat, sollten wir lieben, aber das Neue recht eigentlich leben.' [We should love everything old in so far as it merits our love, but really live for the new]. The first part of the quotation is unproblematic and calls for no further comment from the narrator; but the second part worries him. 'Explain to me,' he says to the Old Master, 'what does "really" mean?' (BR, 73). In the remaining paragraphs he returns twice to this question. How can he, a tractor driver in his sixties who is about to be made redundant, face the future with confidence and 'really live for the new'? In the last three paragraphs a final act of cultural and political colonisation is described - Stalinstrasse is about to be renamed Fontanestrasse so that the visitors might find their way more quickly to the numerous pear-trees which will flourish in Ribbeck and thus, indulge their 'wishes for pious rule, friendly customers and fertile quotations' (BR, 79). The most fertile of these quotations, the concluding couplet in Fontane's poem: 'So spendet Segen noch immer die Hand / Des von Ribbeck auf Ribbeck im Havelland' [Thus, the hand of von Ribbeck auf Ribbeck in the Havelland still bestows blessings] inspires little confidence in the narrator as he contemplates in a somewhat befuddled manner yet another new beginning. In Fontane's poem the concluding couplet contains a confident affirmation of the eternal benevolence of the Old Master of Ribbeck; in Delius's narrative the fragmentation of the couplet is indicative of the narrator's apprehension regarding the future of Ribbeck and of the GDR in a united Germany. It emerges that neither the old nor the new, in both a literary and political sense, can be revered and espoused unthinkingly.

NOTES

Quotations from Delius's work are translated from the following editions: *Die Birnen von Ribbeck* (Reinbek: Rowohlt, 1991); = BR. *Die Verlockungen der Wörter*. (Berlin: Transit, 1996); = VW.

1. In *Der Sonntag, an dem ich Weltmeister wurde* (1994) Delius describes his own struggle to overcome his stutter and liberate himself from the authoritarian religious language used by his father and mother.
2. Karoline von Oppen discusses Delius's narrative as an example of documentary ethnography in her article '"Wer jetzt schwarzweiss malt, hat keine Ahnung": Friedrich Christian Delius's *Die Birnen von Ribbeck* and the Predicament of "Wendeliteratur"', *German Life and Letters*, 54 (2001), 352-65.
3. Keith Bullivant, ' "Das könnte dein Schreiben sein". Gespräch mit Friedrich Delius' in Durzak / Steinecke, eds., *F C Delius. Studien über sein literarisches Werk* (Tübingen: Stauffenburg, 1997), p. 231.
4. Ibid.
5. Osman Durrani, 'From Monologue to Dialogue: The case of Friedrich Christian Delius's *Die Birnen von Ribbeck*', in Williams, Parkes, Preece (eds.), *'Whose story?' Continuities in contemporary German-language literature*. (Berne: Peter Lang, 1998), p. 170.

Ludvik Kundera: A Question of Understanding

Ian Hilton (Chipping Campden)

> And the poets?
> What do the poets perform
> For the weeping world?
> (Jaroslav Seifert, *Raindrops*)

EVEN AS KEITH Spalding was undertaking his doctoral researches in exile in England, Ludvík Kundera's own studies were perforce terminated with the closing of Czech universities following the German Occupation. Born in 1920 in Brno, Kundera was in his third semester. But an interest in literature and the theatre was already aroused and his first verse appeared in *Mladá kultura* before the war. He had also embarked upon what was to be a lifelong *affaire de coeur* with the art of translation - his first venture, a schoolboy attempt to produce a Czech version of poems from Heine's *Buch der Lieder*. Both Czech and German were spoken in the home (his father was Czech, his mother half-Austrian, half-Hungarian) and the house was well stocked with books. The beginnings of linguistic and cultural interaction were in place.

The assassination of the Reich Protector Heydrich in Prague in May 1942 unleashed savage reprisals. The following year, Kundera was sent to a forced-labour camp in Berlin-Spandau to work in armaments, but diphtheria left him so seriously ill that he was allowed to return in 1944 to Brno. During and after convalescence, he still continued his translations from the German, pursuing his quest for linguistic/cultural affinities in the literature of the current oppressors in tandem with his own writing through the war, despite ever-tighter censorship, of Resistance poetry (by definition, against the German occupiers). For Kundera and indeed the Czech people, František Halas, in the van of intellectual resistance, proved a hugely significant inspiration.[1] Halas would remain friend and mentor to the young writer up to his own premature death in 1949. For his part, Kundera has acknowledged that friendship and the importance of Halas in twentieth-century Czech literature ever since, in editing Halas' works in five volumes (1968-1988) as well as in his own numerous writings, including the first ever biography in Czech.[2]

In 1946, before Eastern Europeans began to encounter travel restrictions to the West, Kundera went to Paris. He was seeking possible new books for a Czech publishing house. There a chance meeting with Hans Arp led to an association lasting two decades to the latter's death. Already back in 1944 Kundera had become interested in Dada (and hence in Arp) and Surrealism, a strong tendency in Prague before the war. Better known as painter, graphic artist and sculptor, Arp was also a poet, and how the bilingual Alsatian approached language and what he did with words particularly intrigued the Moravian. If Halas proved a rich seam of Czech myth and history, generating a national context for Kundera's own writing, Arp was the first living writer/artist Kundera met to provide an international dimension. Arp would remain his favourite poet.[3] What especially attracted Kundera was the sense of lyric humour that Arp instilled in his verse as well as a penchant for striking imagery and word associations that disregarded grammatical connections and bordered on the absurd - immediately exemplified in *Weißt du schwarzt du* (1930), a copy of which Kundera received. Arp's intentions for a poetry that was 'Ohne-Sinn', whereby the alogical becomes the normal, leading to a new consciousness of life, clearly struck a chord with Kundera, first in those final dark years of Nazi occupation. That Dada tradition of revolt would resonate further during the communist regime in Kundera's sustained interest in the poetry of Arp, Schwitters, Huelsenbeck, Ball and others with its aesthetic and political orientation.

The immediate post-war years held much promise. Kundera's interest in Dadaism and Surrealism led him to become a founding member of the neo-surrealist group Ra (1945-49), linking up with the artists Lacina, Istler, Tikal and Zykmund. On the literary front, his 1947 Czech version of the Expressionist Alfred Kubin's *Die andere Seite* was actually the first of several translations then beginning to appear in different languages of that 'fantastic novel' (seen by critics as a forerunner to Kafka's tales) which enjoyed a remarkable revival following its original publication in 1908.[4] He undertook the editing of small magazines and journals such as *Blok* and *Rovnost* and by 1948 had seen published three volumes of verse and two prose collections.

But Kundera and fellow Czechs were also facing the realization that a further readjustment in their thinking was inevitable as the communist thrust gathered momentum in the post-war era. And whilst some writers had faithfully recorded the new dawning, others became disillusioned. Halas, criticised now for his poetry and anti-Stalinist stance, died embittered in 1949, Biebl committed suicide in 1951, their last gloomy verses containing coded messages. Writers fell into disfavour, were censored, some, like Zahradníček and Novomeský, imprisoned in the Fifties when the purges got under way. Kundera's own Party membership and occasional writing of conventional verse (eg. *Treptow Park*) was never sufficient to make the authorities overlook his Dada/Surrealist predilections so clearly distant from the demands of social realism. Their interference 'from above' ensured that his contact with Arp in these years remained intermittent, with some correspondence disappearing altogether. Nevertheless he did edit *Host do domu*, the monthly journal of the Brno Branch of the Czech Writers Union, in the mid-Fifties and a temporary thaw in cultural-political relations following the death of Stalin enabled Kundera to benefit from a two-month visit in 1954 to East Germany. A meeting with Brecht in East-Berlin and their subsequent association for the next two years to Brecht's death proved of great and extended significance. Armed with the German dramatist's written authorization, Kundera started translating Brecht's plays in the late-Fifties.[5] His versions - in collaboration with Rudolf Vápeník - of, for example, *Baal, Coriolanus, The Good Person of Sezuan, The Caucasian Chalk Circle, The Threepenny Opera, Mother Courage, Galileo, Arturo Ui*, would all be used for Czech stagings of Brecht's plays. Indeed the staging of Evzen Sokolovsky's production of *Arturo Ui* (the choice of play with its theme of fascism and war is relevant here!) at the State Theatre, Brno in 1959 achieved a breakthrough in the reception of Brecht in Czechoslovakia.

Through that cultural thaw and his interest in German literature, Kundera got to know many East German writers in those years, not least Peter Huchel, now accepted as a truly authentic poetic voice in twentieth-century German letters. But as editor of the prestigious journal *Sinn und Form* (to which Kundera contributed), Huchel himself had experienced difficulties with the authorities in the Fifties for not sufficiently toeing the party line and been grateful certainly on one occasion for Brecht's supportive intervention. In the early Sixties, he was forced to resign from the editorship and forbidden to publish. Kundera's poetic rapport with Huchel had already resulted in the publication of his Czech versions of the first two collections of the latter's verse.[6] His own first major play *Total Cock-Crow* (*Totální kuropění*) (1961),[7] an 'Occupation' play based on life in a wartime labour-camp outside Berlin (therefore redolent of his own experiences) was dedicated to Huchel, 'without whose encouragement and urging this play would not have come into being'. It was Kundera's visit and week-long stay in 1963 at Huchel's 'exile' retreat in Wilhelmshorst, with the Stasi car parked outside, that accentuated the solidarity involved, inducing Huchel to write warmly of the Czech as 'the only friend in difficult years'.[8] This conscious act of friendship in turn unsurprisingly brought Kundera to the uncomfortable attentions of the Czech cultural functionaries in Prague. Moreover, his monograph of Huchel, commissioned by the Academy of Arts in East Berlin to mark Huchel's 60th birthday and already well advanced, was abruptly dropped. Yet Kundera's action at the time was not a solitary act of defiance. The current struggle by Czechs to get the anxiety-ridden, largely surrealist tales of Prague-born Kafka published in Czech had become a rallying cry for intellectuals in their demand for more freedom of expression. A conference on Kafka held in 1963 near Prague, and attended by delegates from most of the socialist states of Eastern Europe, marked a turning-point.

The Prague Spring merely delayed the hard-line response. Kundera, in common with other Czech writers and artists, enjoyed the brief surge of creative freedom.[9] He was able, in 1966, to undertake trips to Austria, West Germany, Italy and Yugoslavia; was co-founder of the surrealist group Q (1967-70); and spent the years 1968-70 as dramaturg at Brno, working in the theatre with the director Milos Hynst. But the ruthless suppression that followed Dubček's short-lived political experiment brought Kundera's expulsion from the Party in 1970 and barring from publishing. The Seventies and early Eighties proved hard times for Ludvík Kundera professionally (he chose to stay rather than go into exile like his cousin Milan) and for his family. In 1976 they left Brno for the Moravian countryside and the village of Kunštát, where Kundera had first met Halas and where the latter lies buried. The mood of pessimism yet also defiant resolve of those years underlies such poems, with their irony and reflection and use of the first-person singular, as *I hope* and *They say: it's a shame that*, and *I have decided*:

I HAVE DECIDED

- today, the 25 November 1979 -
no longer to call trees trees,
but to address them by name:
correct ones, fabricated ones, nicknames,
never a term of abuse:

Hullo, mountain ash in front of the window,
Are you waiting to see the fieldfares again this year?
Ciao, cat's apple tree in the backyard!
Do you dream, pear tree, of future carved incisions?
The spruces are called
Nicholas, Henry, Rene.
The snowberry bush cries out
To be corrupted,
Even the word can be trampled underfoot.
Elms, bear up.

That Brecht's plays ceased to be performed in the Seventies in Czech theatres was due to the cultural functionaries' unwillingness for the translations of Kundera and Vápeník to be used. Official attempts were even made - but in the event, unavailingly - to persuade Brecht's daughter to withdraw her father's original authorization. It was then too, when Kundera was effectively *persona non grata* in his own land, that his East-German writer-friends displayed their solidarity towards him, not least Franz Fühmann. He made possible the publication of Kundera's selection of the Czech poet Vítězlav Nezval's work in 1978 in the Reclam Verlag, Leipzig. Similarly, Fühmann was the inspiration in 1974 behind Kundera's editorship of the two-volumed *Die Sonnenuhr*. The most comprehensive anthology of Czech lyric poetry over eleven centuries in German translation to-date, it was eventually published 1986-87, again by the Reclam Verlag, Leipzig. A new up-dated edition appeared in 1993.

Furthermore in the Seventies, Kundera drew on the experience gained during the Nazi Occupation of the tradition of writing and printing clandestinely in times of oppression, in a series of *zamisdat* publications. A dozen of these small-run bibliophile editions (each little volume comprising half graphic art, half verse from various hands) were printed before he was subjected to harassment by the secret police. Occasional pieces of his appeared too under the name of friends who were able to publish and prepared to 'lend' their name' (*pokryva*). But essentially his own plays and verse, which Huchel, a decade earlier, had encouraged Kundera to spend more time on, as against translating activities, had to stay in the bottom-drawer. Indeed it was to the tradition of translation that Kundera turned for his basic spiritual - and financial - survival. Translating has been a marked feature of Czech literary life - the classic attempt of a smaller nation to gain access to a wider cultural world in its desire to communicate, to reach out for communion of mind and spirit, a means of dialogue. For obvious historical reasons, the German language long provided for Czechs the way into that larger arena in the first instance. Hence the irony of Kundera's conscious decision to continue translating from the German during the war, rather than refuse to use that language. Hence, after the war, the establishing of the (for Kundera) understandable and politically feasible link with East Germany.

The Velvet Revolution brought Ludvík Kundera's name - quite literally – before the eyes of a wider international public, when TV news programmes flashed on screens worldwide the scene of Czech citizens retrieving and saving individual case files which the state secret police were trying even then to incinerate in those heady, confused days at the end of 1989. By way of illustration, one such case file - charred at the edges, but the name of the targeted person still legible - was held before the camera. It was that of Ludvík Kundera. Finally free of all creating restrictions, he now opened the bottom drawer. An edition of his works in seventeen volumes started appearing in 1994 under the imprint of Atlantis, Brno, including the substantial corpus of his translations.[10] And in the year that the German Government raised the question of financial compensation for the expulsion of Germans from the Sudetenland after the Second World War as a bargaining-chip regarding the

Czech application to join the EU, there is a measure of poetic justice in Kundera being awarded in October, 2002 the Adalbert Stifter Prize for German-Czech Understanding. Politics and art are rarely far separated.

NOTES

1. Halas's *Torso of Hope* (1938) poetically responded to the Czech people's need for hope. By 1940, it had reached its fifth edition. That same year his verse collection *Our Lady Božena Němcová* was printed and soon reached its fourth edition. Kundera too captured the mood of the day in his poem *Audible Fall 1938*: 'Calm. Leaves are falling./ Rustling in the grey orchard./ Beneath a thousand elytra/ invisible columns are on the march./ Towards morning the demarcation line/ looms large./ Whoever speaks/ is the enemy.' In 1942, Kundera's *Rhoztrhane panenky* was printed (but predated 1937).
2. Kundera's own monograph *František Halas* appeared in 1999.
3. Arp sent several books to Kundera, who also wrote to Huchel (16.6.1957) asking for books by Arp. Kundera has worked throughout on Dadaism and Expressionism, and his volume on Dadaism is now ready for publication. His immediate tribute on Arp's death is contained in *Hans Arp, d. 7 June 1966*, a poem that fittingly captures the Arpian essence.
4. The English translation of Kubin' novel by Denver Lindley was published by Gollancz only in 1969 under the title *The Other Side*.
5. Eight volumes of the German dramatist and poet's writings translated into Czech were to appear over an extended period (1959-89). Kundera's own monograph *Brecht* was published in 1998.
6. Under the titles *Dvanáct nocí* (1958) and *Silnice, Silnice* (1964).
7. Kundera's experiences in Berlin-Spandau are also reflected in his poem *A Girl of Very Bad Repute* and in the story *Berlin*.
8. Unpublished letter of 7 November, 1963. Huchel also dedicated the poem *Mist* to Kundera.
9. Kundera's own published writings in the Sixties included three volumes of verse, a book of poetry/prose, a book of prose, and three plays. The *staccato* final paragraph of Kundera's letter to Huchel (16.August, 1966), in which he outlines his current work and future plans, encapsulates the Czech's enthusiastic vitality (Peter Huchel, *Briefe 1925-1977*, Suhrkamp, 2000, pp. 416-7).
10. Besides the enormous number of translations of German (East and West) writers, Kundera has also translated from French, Slovakian, Serbian, Bulgarian and Russian literature.

'The most painful poetry I know': Uwe Saeger and Georg Trakl's 'Grodek'

Owen Evans (Bangor)

PUBLISHED IN 1991, Uwe Saeger's *Die Nacht danach und der Morgen* [*The Night After and the Morning*] represents one of the earliest reflections on the legacy of East Germany following unification and is a veritably diverse text.[1] The author carefully avoids any specific genre designation, which on one hand is easily explained for it comprises a dazzling array of different types of document such as essay, prose, poetry, diary entries and a film screenplay. Nevertheless, the impression abides that Saeger has produced an essentially autobiographical analysis of his experiences of GDR life, with particular emphasis not only on his role as a writer, but also on the psychological impact of his eighteen months' national service in the National People's Army (NVA). Biographical sketches of Saeger's life reveal that during this time in the NVA, he spent a year as a border guard at the Berlin Wall, which suggests that the descriptions of military service in Berlin at the outset of *The Night After and the Morning* do indeed correspond to the author's own experiences. Thus, even allowing for any fictional adaptation of this material, the personal nature of such reflections is underpinned by the text's apparent adherence to Philippe Lejeune's autobiographical pact, which is based on the synonymity of narrator, protagonist and author.[2] In *The Night After and the Morning*, all three can be identified unequivocally as Uwe Saeger.

The subjective nature of the text is further reinforced by the author / narrator's exploitation of intertextuality at certain key moments when he is unable adequately to explain or interpret his actions himself. The choice of quotations and extracts bespeaks a very private concern, as these documents appear to spring to Saeger's mind readily in a manner which suggests they have often been used to help him come to terms with his perceived failings. It becomes apparent from the outset that his deployment at the Wall - where he would naturally have had to shoot possible fugitives or suffer the consequences - remains the source of great personal shame: 'This year was a rupture in my life' (5). When contemplating his ineffectual response to duty at the Wall, for example, Saeger compares himself unfavourably with Willy Brandt, whose own reaction as reigning mayor of West Berlin to the events of August 1961 he cites at length. Where 'Private Saeger' (192) sought to evade any contemplation of his posting 'eye to eye with the so-called class enemy' (5) by drinking heavily, he quotes in stark contrast Brandt's dignified, but firm, refusal to accept the division as in any way permanent or insurmountable. Although this and quotations by other figures such as Thomas Mann shed light on Saeger's dismay both at his own perceived impotence and the inability to express this meaningfully himself, the best cipher for the author's sense of guilt, and the psychological ramifications of this experience, is the reference to Georg Trakl and his haunted poem 'Grodek'.

Trakl's last poem, 'Grodek' was named after the battle on the Eastern front in September 1914 during which the poet was left in charge of a barn full of severely wounded soldiers. This harrowing experience clearly underpins the poem, which was sent together with another poem - 'Lament' ('Klage') - to Trakl's friend Ludwig von Ficker. In the accompanying letter, Trakl gave a clear indication of his state of mind when writing the poem, signalling the apparent inevitability of his subsequent death from a cocaine overdose: 'I feel as if I have already passed beyond this world'.[3] Whilst the precise circumstances of the poet's death are still shrouded in uncertainty - it is generally believed that he committed suicide, having earlier tried to shoot himself on his way back from the front - the poem reinforces the sense that Trakl had long since lost any hope, not just for himself but also for future generations:

Grodek[4]
At nightfall the autumn woods ring to the sound
Of deadly weapons, the golden plains
And blue pools, above them the sun rolls darker still;
    the night enfolds
Dying soldiers and the wild lament
Of their broken mouths.

Yet quietly amidst the willows red clouds gather
Wherein lives an angry god, the spilt blood,
And the coolness of the moon;
All roads lead to dark decay.
Beneath golden branches of the night and stars
The sister's shadow sways through the silent grove,
To greet the ghosts of the heroes with their heads bleeding;
And in the reeds the dark flutes of autumn softly sound.
O sorrow more proud! You altars of bronze
Today the spirit's burning flame feeds a powerful pain,
The grandchildren yet unborn.

The poem has aptly been described as a 'product of personal despair' with its deeply melancholic imagery, and especially the concluding lament for the innocents who will never be born.[5] The reference to evening and the use of autumnal motifs, such as dark colours, are typical of Trakl's work, but it is the apocalyptic foreboding at the very heart of the poem - 'All roads lead to dark decay' - which resonates so strongly in view of Trakl's subsequent fate. There is a clear sense that there is no way to evade the decay, both physical and spiritual, which faces mankind.

Even though the poem appears in many ways to have been written from a detached perspective, one cannot but feel the profoundly personal dimension therein. The reference to the figure of the sister hints unmistakably at Trakl's very close relationship with his sister, Grete. Yet it is the title more than anything which underlines this aspect of the text. So many of his poems have such general titles, such as 'Lament', 'The Evening' or 'The Night', that the specificity of 'Grodek' immediately tightens the focus. It provides an unequivocally autobiographical coordinate in the poem, shedding light on the gap that exists between the controlled, almost indifferent, depiction of carnage therein and the poet's own traumatic experience of being unable to alleviate the suffering of those wounded soldiers in his charge. It looks as if Trakl has tried to suppress his own intense grief so that the only cries of despair in the poem come from the dying soldiers. But their mouths are broken, and their complaints barely disturb the poem's inherent, chilling serenity, reflected in the soft autumn flutes and the red clouds gathering quietly amidst the willows. Whilst this is clearly the menacing calm before the storm, more significantly still the tranquillity of 'Grodek' does make it possible to hear the poet's own cries of despair after all.

Uwe Saeger describes 'Grodek' as 'seventeen lines of the most painful poetry I know' (192), but in view of how much use he makes of quotation elsewhere in the text it is interesting that he does not quote directly from the poem. He does however cite a letter Trakl wrote to von Ficker shortly after the battle, in which the traumatic effects of the experience and the reason for his subsequent hospitalisation for the monitoring of his mental health are laid bare: '"It seems that they are preparing for another big battle. Let Heaven be merciful to us this time"' (192).[6] In this way, Saeger seems particularly drawn to what the poem represents, namely the articulation of Trakl's inner turmoil at having participated in such a terrible skirmish. His citation of it right in the middle of his own reckoning with his deployment at the Berlin Wall is especially significant as the whole text, fragmented as it is, casts serious doubt on his ability to produce a coherent analysis of his role and 'the tear in the world' (16) it represents for him. Following the completion of his military service, Saeger's immediate aim had been to encapsulate his experiences in writing, in order to present their 'contemptible nature more clearly' (16). Yet his efforts continually foundered on his inability to settle on the form best suited to rendering his account. He is desperately unhappy with the prose version he eventually produces, which is in any event rejected by the publishers, and the only extant version is a screenplay adaptation, included in its entirety as one of myriad documents that comprise *The Night After and the Morning*. Compared to the considerable emotional force of 'Grodek', however, Saeger's efforts to convey his experiences are found wanting by the author himself. At the time, therefore, he abandoned any hope of achieving his aim.

Saeger's citation of Trakl and 'Grodek' comes at the point in *The Night After and the Morning* when the author realises that the collapse of the Wall, and the resultant exodus, cannot ever exonerate him from his complicity with a regime that employed a shoot-to-kill policy at the border. Watching those who would formerly have been deemed 'the fugitives, the traitors, the enemies of the state' (193) leaving the GDR in December 1989, Saeger remarks first that 'the Wall is my trauma' (191), but then goes on to identify himself directly with Trakl: '[The Wall] was my Grodek' (193). When one considers the fate that befell Trakl, as well as the context of his poem, this juxtaposition might appear an inappropriate one. Whilst Saeger's experiences at the border were by no means as traumatic as Trakl's at 'Grodek', they are linked nevertheless by the psychological impact they are shown to have had on both men. By drawing the comparison after the Wall has fallen, Saeger effectively uses Trakl and his poem as a cipher for his own deep shame. 'Grodek' thus provides an orientation point, allowing him to reflect more expressively on his anguish not only at having served at the Wall but also for never having considered an unequivocal 'opposition or rejection of the conditions' (193). Saeger suggests that he might even have considered suicide, had it not been for the fact that he drank to get through his posting. In the end, though, he feels ashamed at his feeble, ineffectual response, which contrasts starkly with the elegiac 'Grodek'. Where Saeger fled, by his own admission, into drunken self-pity, Trakl encapsulated his despair in a powerful piece of writing that ultimately reaches beyond the individual and touches those whom the poet feared lost, the generations yet unborn - future generations to which Saeger, of course, belongs. Thus inspired, the author finally tackles his own personal trauma.

In view of Saeger's bitter self-criticism, it is easy to overlook the fact that with *The Night After and the Morning* itself he has taken his first, admittedly erratic, steps towards an analysis of his role at the Berlin Wall. In this way, it would appear that at the height of the *Wende*, when joyous scenes at the Wall fill him only with guilt, Saeger was able to derive inspiration from the spirit of Trakl. If the Wall was his Grodek, then surely *The Night After and the Morning* might in some way be seen as his 'Grodek'. No matter that Saeger's hybrid text lacks the concision, coherence and aesthetic qualities of Trakl's poem, it can still be viewed as an effective literary depiction of personal turmoil. It affords insights into the complex constellation of emotions surrounding the *Wende* and the assessment of the GDR's legacy, and anticipates with remarkable prescience the fading euphoria after reunification when western and eastern Germans alike were faced with the ramifications of such a dramatic historical transformation.

In particular, the long, hermetic poem that Saeger includes in the text hints at the problems ahead. The complex linguistic patterns deployed throughout - so typical of the poets of the Prenzlauer Berg scene - reflect the difficulty that Saeger has in finding words to describe what is happening in the autumn of 1989, when language has for so long been shackled by ideology, whilst the frequent employment of oxymoron reflects his mixed feelings at the rapidity of the changes sweeping the GDR. But it is Saeger's use of imagery and motifs reminiscent of Trakl's work that is so striking in the context of our investigation. The whole piece is underpinned with a mournful tone, and the presence of the blackbird recalls Trakl's poem 'Decay'.[7] Indeed, Saeger's poem is replete with images of decay, although these are principally ecological in nature - reflecting the GDR's desperate pollution - rather than spiritual as in Trakl's poetry. Despite the lack of any formal correlation between Saeger's poem and the work of Trakl, it is as if the latter has in some fashion helped the former begin to find the means by which to express the hitherto inexpressible.

Whilst *The Night After and the Morning* rarely feels anything more than inchoate due to the amalgamation of different literary documents it embodies, that it exists at all arguably stems from the author's having been stimulated by the example of Georg Trakl, and the realisation that even the darkest despair can find meaningful literary expression. Faced with his complicity with a state that imprisoned its citizens behind a border he himself had guarded, Saeger ultimately found orientation from Georg Trakl and the most painful poetry he knew.

NOTES

[1] Uwe Saeger, *Die Nacht danach und der Morgen* (Munich: Piper, 1991). Page references will appear in the text in brackets. All translations are my own.

[2] Philippe Lejeune, 'The Autobiographical Pact', in *On Autobiography* (Minneapolis: University of Minnesota Press, 1989), pp. 3-30.

[3] Georg Trakl, *Werke – Entwürfe-? Briefe*, ed. Hans-Georg Kemper and Frank Rainer Max (Stuttgart: Reclam, 1984), p. 251. All translations of text from this volume are my own.

[4] The extant German version is reproduced in *Werke - Entwürfe - Briefe*, p. 112.

[5] Patrick Bridgwater, 'Georg Trakl and the Poetry of the First World War', in *Londoner Trakl-Symposium*, ed. William E. Yuill and Walter Methlagl (Salzburg: Otto Müller, 1981), pp. 96-113 (p. 107).

[6] The full letter is included in *Werke - Entwürfe - Briefe*, pp. 248-49.

[7] Ibid., p. 39.

'Ungeist' in East and West: Representations of Ceauşescu's Romania and Pre-Unification West Germany in Two Works by Richard Wagner

David Rock (Keele)

'TURNING ON the radio in the morning means exposing yourself to words that have been mutilated' ['Am Morgen das Radio aufdrehen, heißt, sich inmitten der vergewaltigten Wörter begeben'][1] - this statement was read aloud by Richard Wagner at a literary circle attended by fellow Romanian German writers, held at the University of Bucharest towards the end of the 1970s. The ensuing discussion on ideology and the abuse and manipulation of language was brought to a swift conclusion by a conformist colleague whose personal biography made her particularly vulnerable to the insidious pressures exerted by a totalitarian regime. The incident was cited by Wagner to show how fear was the 'predominant emotion' ['beherrschendes Gefühl'] in Ceauşescu's Romania, leading to continual compromise, with many writers not 'writing in order to write, but writing in order to live'. 'I would not like to have written her books', added Wagner. ['Sie schrieben nicht, um zu schreiben, sie schrieben, um zu leben [...] Ich möchte ihre Bücher nicht geschrieben haben'].[2]

Wagner and his then wife, Herta Müller, left Romania in 1987 and are now recognised as the two most prominent contemporary representatives of Romanian German literature which, as Robert Elsie has claimed,[3] came to an end after five centuries of existence with the emigration of almost all of its writers during the 1980s. This was a decade during which Romania had become a living nightmare of fear, repression and abject poverty. Though only a few were allowed to do so (after being bought out by the West German government), most Germans living in Romania were desperate to leave a country driven into a state of economic ruin and cultural and political isolation by a repressive dictator who was becoming increasingly divorced from the wretched everyday reality that his citizens were being forced to endure.[4] And so when the Ceaușescu regime finally collapsed in December 1989, there was a mass exodus of Romanian Germans to the Federal Republic of Germany, with 100,000 leaving in the first few months of 1990.[5] Wagner has described this as a journey from the periphery to the centre,[6] with Romanian Germans returning from the remote regions of the Banat and Transylvania ('Siebenbürgen') where they had settled earlier centuries to the land of their ethnic and cultural origins. But what awaited them in West Germany, the promised land of their expectations, was a rejection of their Romanian German identity, and assimilation into the mainstream that their forbears had originally left.

The experience of the Romanian German 'Aussiedler' [emigrant] is a central concern of the first two stories written by Wagner after coming to the West, both published in 1988. As their titles suggest, *Ausreiseantrag* [application to leave] and *Begrüßungsgeld* [welcome-money][7] have as their theme his departure from Romania in 1986 and his arrival in the West, culminating in the acquisition of German citizenship. Both feature the same central characters drawn from Wagner's biography: a journalist and writer called Stirner, and his German-teacher-wife, Sabine, who both lose their jobs in Romania as a result of their refusal to conform. The first story is also Wagner's first attempt at 'writing about and attacking the political crimes in this century' ['über und gegen das politische Verbrechen in unserem Jahrhundert zu schreiben'].[8]

Ausreiseantrag gives an anecdotal, discontinuous account of events narrated in the third-person yet from the exclusive perspective of a writer no longer able to publish, emphasising both his isolation and his disconnection from the world around him. The story, set in a town in the Banat in the 1980s, records the effects of the Ceaușescu dictatorship on everyday life which eventually drive Stirner and his wife to leave the country. The narrative charts Stirner's increasingly aimless wandering as he roams the streets in a vain search for some sense in his existence, only to confront instead the submissive lethargy which 'Ungeist' and repression have produced in the Romanian people, so contaminating their minds that they can now only 'say yes to everything' and utter 'Banalitäten': 'He had sought the meaning of the world in the streets and in so doing discovered the gutter in people's minds' ['Er hatte den Sinn der Welt auf der Straße gesucht und dabei die Gosse in den Köpfen entdeckt', A, 75]. Wagner 's story shows the effects of the relentless flood of ideological slogans and bureaucratic orders ['Anordnungen, Unsinn'] coming from Bucharest: 'it was oriental aggression which was killing off all independent thinking' ['Es war die orientalische Aggression, die alles unabhängige Denken tötete', A, 128].

The decline of the world around Stirner is accompanied by his complete isolation and inner paralysis. Faced with the interminable monotony of each day, he too gradually loses his ability to think and to write, feeling 'paralysed' by the 'emptiness' ['Leere', A, 28] around him. Wagner also shows how Stirner's capacity for recalcitrance (his name is a pun on the idiom 'jemandem die Stirn bieten') is eroded by the cumulative effect of a repressive totalitarian society, the 'pressure of the system' ['Druck des Systems', A, 105]: anonymous threats and the awareness of constant surveillance reduce his life to a mere 'struggle for survival' ['Kampf ums Überleben']. The final straw comes when he loses his job as journalist, 'his only possibility of being able to go on in this country' ['die einzige Möglichkeit, weitermachen zu können in diesem Land', A, 15].

In *Ausreiseantrag*, Wagner also demonstrates the inability of writers to make any headway at all during the later Ceauşescu years in terms of a meaningful contribution to Romanian society. The reasons for this failure were explained by Wagner in a short essay published in 1994.[9] Under communist dictatorships there were three categories of authors: those who were encouraged and supported, those who were tolerated and those whose work was banned. Censorship and repression thus created a false sense of importance for the writer - false because literature gained a significance not through itself, through its inherent value as literature, but because it became the only arena where there could be some discussion of political issues, albeit 'between the lines' of published literary texts. As a result, 'Many authors no longer gave themselves up to literature, they exploited it' ['Viele Autoren setzten sich dem Schreiben nicht mehr aus, sie benutzten es'][10] and fame or notoriety became the goal. Yet the powers that be still controlled literary activities through a combination of the carrot and the stick, through privilege and punishment. And so writers knew that they could afford to give the appearance of being subversive as long as they did not go too far. Stirner realises that he too has become 'infected' by this situation in his own writing, and 'that when he is writing, self-censorship is the worst thing. [...] Self-censorship is a virus, you carry it inside you' ['Daß beim Schreiben die Selbstzensur das Schlimmste ist. [...] Die Selbstzensur ist ein Virus, man trägt es in sich', A, 76]. He realises, too, that he will have to learn how to write all over again in order to 'liberate' ['befreien'] himself from this virus. He is only able to do this, gradually, after his arrival in the West. However, the (albeit feeble) dissident tendency of Stirner's writing (and in this he is representative of young German writers in Romania at that time) does mean that he is able to avoid what was for Wagner the greatest danger, and one to which, in his view, most ethnic Romanian writers had succumbed by the mid-80s: that of engaging in the current ideological discourse through which the totalitarian state sought to impose its single interpretation of reality: 'If you use the discourse of the regime, you are lost'. ['Hat man den Diskurs des Regimes, ist man verloren'].[11] Romanian writers were also at a linguistic disadavantage in so far as the regime's dominance extended to language itself, the 'Staatssprache', through which the regime sought to preclude alternative meanings:

> Under a regime that has occupied the language, you cannot express opinions. If you wanted to write realistic literature and said so, you would already find yourself on the regime's terrain. For the regime too called for realistic literature. And the regime determined what was realistic. What you yourself saw as realistic was then considered to be unrealistic, it was inimical to the state and antisocialist. Words were two-sided. [In einem Regime, das die Sprache okkupiert, kann man nicht Meinungen äußern. Wollte man eine realistische Literatur schreiben, fand man sich bereits auf dem Terrain des Regimes. Denn auch das Regime forderte eine realistische Literatur. Was man selber als realistisch ansah galt dann als unrealistisch, es war staatsfeindlich oder antisozialistisch. Die Wörter waren doppelgesichtig. A, 41]

In *Ausreiseantrag*, Wagner offers a striking concrete illustration of such a discourse in which a single meaning prevails in his description of Timisoara before the impending visit of the dictator (A, 17): the 'President' cannot bear the sight of churches, and so the view of the cathedral is obscured by flags and slogans lifted high into the air by hydraulic cranes, a metaphor for a reality saturated with the signs of a discourse which seeks to deny all alternative meanings.[12]

Wagner's next story, *Begrüßungsgeld*, follows Stirner and his wife to West Germany. It recapitulates the first six months that they spend after arriving at the transit camp in Nuremberg and then later in Berlin, portraying the process of migration to Germany, above all in terms of its psychological effects upon the German *Aussiedler* from Romania. Stirner experiences a crisis of identity that stems from cultural and linguistic disorientation. The contrast between the fluid, transient arbitrariness of the West and the world of single meanings in the dictatorship, the 'Eindeutigkeiten' of the points of reference which he has left behind, threatens him with loss of his intellectual identity. Symptomatic of this is the increasing discrepancy which he experiences between the 'centre' and the 'periphery', between the German language spoken every day in the Federal Republic and the German which he speaks and writes. He had expected to feel linguistically at home in Germany, but in Germany he becomes more aware of the Romanian part of his identity than he ever was in Romania. His Banat German accent marks him out as 'someone who comes from outside' ['einer der von außen kommt'], making him appear 'more foreign' ['fremder'] and isolating him from those around him: 'He was now alone with his language' ['Er war jetzt mit seiner Sprache allein', B, 159], comments the narrator.

Stirner's inner turmoil and social disorientation are given striking expression in the form of the work: the sequence of events is sharply broken up, with fragments of experiences and memories intermingled with bits of dialogue, dream sequences and brief reflective passages as the past is interwoven into the present. Frequent flashbacks reveal the deep and lasting psychological scars left by the totalitarian regime. His experiences with Romanian bureaucracy, for instance, make him particularly vulnerable to the insensitive questions of German officials at the reception camp for immigrants: 'Earlier he felt as if he was being exposed to permanent interrogation [...] All this made Stirner helpless when he was faced with the German authorities' ['Früher hatte er das Gefühl, einem permanenten Verhör ausgesetzt zu sein [...] Das alles machte Stirner vor den deutschen Behörden hilflos', B, 246].

In the capitalist, democratic society of the West, too, there are not only such disturbing echoes of the past in Romania, Stirner is also confronted by an oddly familiar form of 'Ungeist'. He finds a grotesque counterpart to the constant ideological pressure and the deprivation of the right to self-determination which he experienced in the totalitarian state: the latent tyranny of 'the economy', which finds its expression above all in the advertising slogans that interminably bombard his senses and remind him of Romania:

> The best anywhere, and even more for your money: the adverts reminded Stirner of earlier political slogans, which promised the best again and again. He saw this ghastly optimism heading his way from both directions. [Überall das Beste, noch mehr für weniger Geld: die Werbung erinnerte Stirner an die Politparole von früher, die immer wieder das Beste versprachen. Er sah diesen schauderhaften Optimismus aus beiden Richtungen auf sich zukommen. B 256]

In other respects, though, the 'Ungeist' of the West is the very opposite of that of the earlier world where things had one centralising meaning in the dictatorship, for in Berlin, he finds himself above all in the capitalist world of advertising and the mass media, where words and images are so manifold and all-intrusive that their fluid, multiple meanings threaten to overwhelm the Romanian-German *Aussiedler*: 'There were too many words around him. Everywhere he was confronted with words [...] He had to get used to the fact that everything was available, images, ideas' ['Es waren zu viele Wörter um ihn. Überall war er mit Wörtern konfrontiert [...] Er mußte sich daran gewöhnen, daß alles zur Verfügung stand, Bilder, Ideen', B, 211-2]. Frequently disorientated by the post-modern world around them, Stirner and his wife sit in their Berlin flat, feeling just as isolated in this teeming Western metropolis as they did in Romania: 'they felt as if they were alone in the world' ['sie kamen sich vor, als wären sie allein auf der Welt', B, 156]. Yet they resist the pressure to adapt and conform: 'We've got to find our own way', said Sabine. From all sides they heard the words "adapt yourselves" and they resisted.' ['Wir müssen uns zurechtfinden', sagte Sabine. Sie hörten von allen Seiten das Wort "Anpassen", und sie wehrten sich dagegen.' A, 156].

The ironic twist in the tail of the story comes in its final scene, for it is at the very moment when Stirner and his wife are formally recognised as German citizens that his split Romanian-German identity becomes most apparent. Yet Stirner does not follow the path of his acquaintances, some of whom have tried to create a new identity for themselves by negating their Banat origins (B, 213), whilst others have attempted to hold on to their past (B, 225). Rather, he accepts his split identity, his Romanian origins and his lonely existence as misfit in Germany, declaring: 'I stand by my biography' ['Ich stehe zu meiner Biographie', B, 226]. And it is this affirmation of his biography that enables him to distil his experiences and so rediscover the ability to write again, which he had lost in Romania: 'He was able to write again, he was capable of observations again. What he saw he was now able to put into some sort of order again'. ['Er konnte wieder schreiben, er war wieder zu Beobachtungen fähig. Was er sah, konnte er jetzt auch wieder einordnen', B, 269].

Stirner's biography is, of course, also his author's. Wagner, too, has experienced the quandary of all Romanian-German *Aussiedler*, articulated in the laconic words of his protagonist Stirner in *Begrüßungsgeld*: 'In Romania, they always said: You German, said Stirner. Here I am the Romanian'. ['In Rumänien haben sie immer gesagt: Du Deutscher, sagte Stirner. Hier bin ich der Rumäne', B, 205] Richard Wagner is, then, a German writer in a unique sense, which he briefly defined thus: 'I sat there in my isolated Banat region and constructed for myself a periphery out of words. [...] My origins in a minority in the East describe my relationship to language and to the world as periphery. My German origin makes it possible for my gaze from East to West to be a longing for the centre' ['Ich saß in meiner isolierten Region Banat und baute mir einen Rand aus Wörtern. [...] Die Herkunft aus einer Minderheit im Osten beschreibt mein Verhältnis zur Sprache und zur Welt als Rand. Die deutsche Herkunft ermöglicht mir den Blick von Ost nach West als Sehnsucht nach der Mitte.'].[13] Yet he has been forced to recognise the danger of this longing for the centre and the need to maintain distance: for a writer such as himself, it is a linguistic danger: 'But whoever reaches the centre ceases to write: leaves the language of literature and finds the linguistic strait-jacket of society' ['Doch wer die Mitte erreicht, schreibt nicht mehr. Er verläßt die Sprache der Literatur und findet die Sprachregelung der Gesellschaft.'].[14] Thus for Wagner, the journey from the Banat periphery to Berlin, his German cultural centre, has, paradoxically, been a journey back to the periphery in the recognition that, in modern western societies such as that of the new Germany, the writer, especially a German one from Romania, frequently remains on the fringe as critical observer and outsider : 'Literature, the periphery of reality' ['Literatur der Rand des Wirklichen'].[15]

NOTES

1. Cited in: Richard Wagner, ‚Die Bedeutung der Ränder oder vom Inneren zum Äußersten und wieder zurück' in: *neue literatur: 'Ideen in Not'*, vol.1 (1994), 33-49 (p .33).
2. Ibid., p. 34.
3. Robert Elsie (ed.), *The Pied Poets: Contemporary Verse of the Transylvanian and Danube Germans of Romania*. (London and Boston: Forest Books, 1990), pp. viii-xiii.
4. See: Thomas Kunze, *Nicolae Ceauşescu: Eine Biographie*. (Berlin: Ch. Links Verlag, 2000).
5. Annemarie Schuller-Weber, 'Nationale Identität im kulturellen Wandel. Bedürfnis nach kultureller Selbstbestätigung: die Rumäniendeutschen', in: *Zeitschrift für Kulturaustausch - 'Migration und kultureller Wandel'*, 45, (1995/1), 55-59.
6. Richard Wagner, 'Die Bedeutung der Ränder ...', pp. 44-5.
7. Richard Wagner, *Ausreiseantrag. Begrüßungsgeld. Erzählungen*. (Darmstadt: Luchterhand, 1991), hereafter abbreviated to A and B followed by the page numbers..
8. Susanne Broos (Interview with Richard Wagner),'Richard Wagner: Politik ist immer eine Dimension in meinem Schreiben' in: *Börsenblatt*,.87, 2 (November 1993), 18-20, (p. 18).
9. Richard Wagner, 'Kulturbrief aus Berlin', in: *Literatur und Kritik*,. 283/4 (April 1994), pp. 11-2.
10. Ibid., p. 11.
11. Richard Wagner, 'Die Bedeutung der Ränder ...', p. 44.
12. See also Graham Jackman, '"Alone in a crowd": The Figure of the "Aussiedler" in the Work of Richard Wagner', in David Rock and Stefan Wolf (eds.), *Coming Home to Germany? The Integration of Ethnic Germans from Central and Eastern Europe in the Federal Republic.* (Oxford/New York: Berghahn, 2002), pp. 157-170 (p. 165).
13. Richard Wagner, 'Die Bedeutung der Ränder oder vom Inneren zum Äußersten und wieder zurück', pp. 36 and 37.
14. Ibid., p. 36.
15. Ibid., p. 46.
16. Richard Wagner, 'Die Bedeutung der Ränder oder vom Inneren zum Äußersten und wieder zurück', pp. 36 and 37.
17. Ibid., p. 36.
18. Ibid., p .46.

'Er klammerte sich an alle Gegenstände': Büchner, Peter Schneider and the Uses of Germanistik

Rhys W Williams (Swansea)

KEITH SPALDING'S vehement opposition to the more strident features of the Student Movement of the late 1960s and early 1970s was predicated on his own earlier experience of the rise of National Socialism. For him, any attempt to subvert the rule of law, any failure on the part of the civil authorities to confront those who advocated direct action, was deeply suspect. It was the failure to act, he maintained, which had brought about the end of the Weimar Republic. The following brief contribution to a volume of essays in his honour (and sadly now in his memory) is an attempt to bring out that other side of the Student Movement, one with which he would undoubtedly have had more sympathy.

Intertextuality has ever been a feature of literary production. But the early 1970s witnessed a particularly urgent need to reappraise and reinvigorate the German literary tradition. Examples abound: Peter Schneider's expropriation of Büchner's *Lenz* (1973); Ulrich Plenzdorf's 1973 reworking of Goethe's *Werther* in *Die neuen Leiden des jungen W.* in the GDR; even Heinrich Böll's *Die verlorene Ehre der Katharina Blum* (1974) with its echo of Schiller's *Der Verbrecher aus verlorener Ehre*; Uwe Timm's *Heißer Sommer* (1974) with its citing of Hölderlin, and his later *Kerbels Flucht* (1980) with its allusions to Kleist. There are parallels in the poetry of the period: Jürgen Theobaldy's volume *Blaue Flecken* (1974) has an epigraph from Hölderlin and opens with a poem 'Abenteuer mit Dichtung', obviously stimulated by a Goethe quotation: and albeit slightly older Peter Rühmkorf makes his own literary antecedents clear in his volume *Walther von der Vogelweide, Klopstock und ich* (1975). This list offers simply a few examples, but the essays and writings of the

228

student generation of 1968 seem to be particularly sensitive to literary antecedents. Several factors may be adduced to account for this phenomenon: the two-hundredth anniversary of the Sturm und Drang movement offers one explanation for the popularity of both Goethe's *Werther* and writings of Jakob Michael Reinhold Lenz. 1970 also saw the two-hundredth anniversary of Hölderlin's birth, which was celebrated by a major exhibition at the Deutsches Literaturarchiv in Marbach. A year earlier Pierre Bertaux's *Hölderlin und die Französische Revolution* had stimulated a heated debate about Hölderlin's political radicalism, a debate which seems to have inspired Peter Weiss's play *Hölderlin* (1971), in which the poet is involved in a fictitious debate with the young Marx. In the GDR, of course, the motive was all too often to wrap up in historical guise an unpalatable political point about the present, as in Christa Wolf's evocation of Kleist and Günderrode in *Kein Ort. Nirgends* (1979). Publishing history also plays a part: it is largely the young Goethe, Hölderlin and Büchner whose ghosts hover over the literature of the Student Movement. The first volume of Büchner's works in the Hamburger Ausgabe, edited by Werner R. Lehmann, appeared in 1967 and the second, containing *Der Hessische Landbote* in 1971. The primary stimulus for renewed interest in these figures is, however, political. Young intellectuals in the early 1970s were seeking in the German literary tradition evidence of radical political views even as they sought to buttress their own rebellion against what they perceived as the stuffy values of the 'Ordinarienuniversität'. Younger academics, for their part, were keen to point to traditional examples within the established canon of works which had contemporary political relevance and seized enthusiastically on modern examples of the appropriation of these canonical texts as evidence that 'Germanistik' could speak to a new generation of students. The speed with which texts like Schneider's *Lenz* found their way into the curriculum bears eloquent tribute to the needs of teachers and students alike.

The Student Movement was a heady mixture of Marx and Freud, viewed through the prism of the Frankfurt School in general and Herbert Marcuse in particular. The category of the aesthetic seemed to bring together the spheres of the private and the political, the individual and the social, in vindication of a German tradition which went back to Schiller's *Briefe über die ästhetische Erziehung des Menschen*. Literature could become an arena in which the urgent claims of the new sexual revolution could be played out against the equally pressing claims of commitment to a romanticised third-world socialism, as remote from Western capitalism as it was from the state-run communism of the Eastern bloc. The utopian visions are either contemporary, but geographically remote: Che Guevara's Latin America, Mao's China or Ho Chi Minh's Vietnam; or they are geographically closer to home, but remote in time, not tempered by contemporary political realities. And where they are closer to home, it is in the lives of writers into which they are projected or out of which they are read. Lenz, Hölderlin and Kleist share a psychological complexity and lability which can be read as a product of the deformations which their society imposed upon them. The 'Innenwelt' is, to employ Handke's term, a reflection of the 'Außenwelt'; the personal, as Marcuse insists, is the political.

In the early Berlin sections of *Lenz* Peter Schneider employs Büchner's text almost exclusively to reinforce Lenz's disturbed mental state; direct allusions are not found later than the twenty-eighth of the forty-three sections. Once Lenz begins to encounter Roman society, even before his move to Trento, depictions of extreme mental agitation are less in evidence. In the eighth section, Lenz wakes in the night and, obsessed by images of L. (who operates, like Friederike for Büchner's Lenz, as a trigger for his disturbed state), wanders around the city: 'Then he began to run.... When Lenz returned his anxiety had gone, he felt light' ['Dann fing er an zu rennen.... Als Lenz zurückging, war die Angst weg, er fühlte sich leicht'] ,[1] lines which supply an obvious echo of Büchner's lines: 'He was seized by a nameless anxiety.... He leaped up and flew down the mountainside.... He saw lights and he felt lighter ['Es faßte ihn eine namenlose Angst.... Er riß sich auf und flog den Abhang hinunter.... Er sah Lichter, es wurde ihm leichter'].[2] The twelfth section depicts an incident in which Lenz wanders alone along a Berlin canal in the twilight. The gradual loss of contours, the disappearance at dusk of the 'boundary between the roofs and the sky' ['Grenze zwischen Dächern und Himmel', p. 18] prompt in him first an attempt to control his sense-impressions by throwing stones into the canal so as to shatter the reflections of the houses in the water, and then a feeling of utter desolation: 'and everything was so cold, so stony. He was dreadfully lonely. He was alone. He wanted to talk to himself, but he couldn't. He scarcely dared to breathe' ['und alles so kalt, so steinern. Es wurde ihm entsetzlich einsam, er war allein, er wollte mit sich sprechen, er konnte nicht, er wagte kaum zu atmen', p. 18]. The quotation from Büchner's *Lenz* here is verbatim. Apart from two brief quotations: 'he had quite forgotten himself' ['er hatte sich ganz vergessen', p. 22], when Lenz is drawn into a political debate in the factory, and 'he calmed down' ['er wurde ruhig', p. 23] after Marina offers him sexual gratification, the direct Büchner allusions are confined to a section in which Lenz observes a group of window-shoppers eagerly examining the latest Volkswagen models. Again it is his sense of social isolation which is stressed:

'He walked on, he was ill at ease, he felt excluded. A strange anxiety seized him, that he wanted to chase the sun. He clung on to all objects, figures rushed past him, he pushed his way towards them. He screamed, he sang. He wanted to make himself smaller.'

[Er ging weiter, es wurde ihm unbehaglich, er fühlte sich ausgeschlossen.... Eine sonderbare Angst befiel ihn, er hätte der Sonne nachlaufen mögen. [...] Er klammerte sich an alle Gegenstände, Gestalten zogen rasch vorbei, er drängte sich an sie. Er schrie, er sang, er wollte sich kleiner machen, p. 33]

The last three sentences of this passage are direct quotations.[3] Only once in the Italian sections of the story is the Büchner model referred to, a reference which characteristically occurs right at the beginning of the Italian journey. In the Albani hills, Lenz experiences a sudden sense of alienation and loneliness: 'he ran down the mountainside. He felt as if the hills were rising and falling' ['er lief den Hang hinunter, es war ihm als ob die Hügel sich hoben und senkten', p. 56]. There is a faint echo here of Büchner's lines: 'everything melted into a single line, like a rising and falling wave' ['es verschmolz ihm alles in eine Linie, wie eine steigende und sinkende Welle'].[4] While mountainous scenery triggers heightened states of awareness for Büchner's Lenz (echoed in Schneider's text) it ceases to provoke crises for Schneider's central character, even though mountains form the backcloth for the whole Trento episode. As Schneider's Lenz advances towards his recovery, the Büchner model gradually disappears from the text.

What is striking from a detailed examination of the two texts is how intrumentalised the Büchner model is, for although Schneider employs Büchner quotations to telling effect to convey Lenz's emotional crisis, he simultaneously limits their relevance by offering socio-political factors as an explanation for events. It is the oscillation between the psychological and the political, between the subjective and the objective, which is Schneider's concern throughout, a concern which critics have been slow to appreciate. While the first sections portray a character struggling and failing to mediate between these possibilities, the end of the story brings successful mediation (or at least its promise) a step nearer. This interpretation may be illustrated with reference to another way in which the Büchner text serves as a model. Schneider's text is the more easily divided into sections because each section tends to begin with an adverb or adverbial phrase of time: 'in the mornings' (p. 5), 'on another day' (pp. 8, 10, 14, 23), 'the next morning' (p. 9), 'in the middle of the night' (p. 11), 'at half past eight in the morning' (p. 13), 'one weekend' (p. 16), 'the next morning' (p. 20, 51, 79), 'one afternoon' (pp. 22, 31, 41), 'on a Tuesday evening' (p. 27), 'one Saturday evening' (p. 37), 'a few days later' (p. 46), 'the next day' (p. 47), 'in the evening' (p. 50); 'a week later' (p. 56), 'a few days later' (pp. 58, 90), 'in the night' (p. 64), 'later' (p. 70), 'one morning' (p. 88), 'at noon' (p. 89). Significantly, of the first twenty-five sections before Lenz leaves for Rome, nineteen begin thus, whereas only eight of the following eighteen sections do. The device is derived from Büchner's *Lenz*, indicating the origins of that text in Oberlin's diary. While the adverbial phrases of time are not used explicitly to introduce sections, they are employed by Büchner to mark changes of mood. Schneider's decision to make far more striking and consistent use of the device in his narrative produces some unusual effects. It suggests that the narrative is, like Büchner's narrative, based on a diary, which establishes a claim to at least subjective authenticity for the experiences recorded; secondly, while appearing to offer a precise chronological framework, the narrative is effectively lifted out of history. Nowhere does Schneider give specific dates for events, even if it is possible from some internal events and from external evidence to locate the action between the spring and late summer of 1970. Time in Schneider's *Lenz* becomes pure succession, at least as far as the Berlin sections are concerned. Lenz is portrayed as being temporarily trapped not only in his own subjectivity but also in his own time, though the reader is invited by the political debate which is part of the text to set this subjectivity in context, to supply a historical framework. Despite the dehistoricising process, Schneider goes out of his way to place the action in a recognizable Berlin and to relate the subjective difficulties to objective problems, involving both the German past (located in Lenz's childhood) and the German present (the anti-Springer and anti-American demonstrations and the Maoist ideas of the early 1970s). While Lenz's emotional crisis, his subjective self-absorption, tends to dehistoricise the action, Schneider is at pains to permit the reader to locate incidents in a specific historical, geographical and political situation, as if to supply a vantage-point outside Lenz's subjective experience, signalling through this device the inter-relationship of the private and the political which is his theme.

The quotation in the title of this essay exemplifies the use to which Büchner's text is put. Schneider implies that Lenz's alienation from normal German consumers, whose own consumer fetishism is focussed on the design changes of the latest Volkswagen model, expresses itself in a quest for contact with 'real' objects, things in themselves, as it were. Here, the sense of social alienation from a capitalist consumer-driven world emerges as a modernist sense of alienation from reality, an echo of Hofmannsthal's so-called *Chandos-Brief* or the *Briefe des Zurückgekehrten*. While Büchner's Lenz desperately seeks physical contact with empirical objects as a means of warding off what Maurice Benn called 'the gradual disintegration and destruction of his mind',[5] Schneider's Lenz has had his fill of consumer products, of objects of alienated labour. The objects which he seeks are alternatives to consumer products, some kind of essential reality which remains when the trappings of bourgeois society are stripped away. It is clear from Schneider's text that radical political ideals are insufficient for Lenz; he yearns for a kind of intensity of experience which will satisfy an inner need, and it is between psychological needs and political ideas that the text and its central character oscillate. Büchner's Lenz offers a ready-made cipher for the dangers which Schneider's character will finally succeed in banishing. For Schneider's Lenz (and one surmises for Schneider himself) Germanistik will prove to have had its uses.

NOTES

[1] Peter Schneider, *Lenz*. (Berlin: Rotbuch Verlag, 1973), p. 12. Subsequent references are from this edition and page references appear in brackets in the text.

2 Georg Büchner, *Sämtliche Werke und Briefe*, Historisch-kritische Ausgabe, ed. Werner R. Lehmann (Hamburg: Christian Wegener Verlag, 1967ff.), I, 80. Subsequent references refer to this edition.
3 Büchner, I, 82.
4 Büchner, I, 89-90.
5 Maurice B. Benn, *The Drama of Revolt. A Critical Study of Georg Büchner* (Cambridge, CUP: 1976), p. 189.

Spinoza and Postmodernism: Some Reflections on Gianni Celati's *Adventures in Africa*

Laura Rorato (Bangor)

BORN IN SONDRIO, in northern Italy, in 1937, Celati studied at the University of Bologna where he graduated having written a thesis on James Joyce. Subsequently he returned to Bologna University to teach Anglo-American literature. During the 1970s and 1980s, however, he also had several visiting professorships in the United States. Celati travelled extensively throughout Europe and America. In the mid 1980s he stopped lecturing and moved to the United Kingdom where he continues to write both fiction and critical essays, and to translate works from French and English.[1] The importance of his fiction has been recognised by various literary prizes, but it is his work as a scholar and, particularly, as a translator that persuaded me that he represents an ideal choice for the present volume. As Trinh T. Minh-ha points out, 'translations mark the continuation of the original culture's life', but during the process of translating 'the translator transforms while being transformed'.[2] This implies a concept of tradition as something fluid that is 'always being reconstructed'.[3] And, indeed, the reconstruction of tradition plays a prominent role in Celati's fiction. The most obvious example is his prose version of Matteo Maria Boiardo's fifteenth century chivalric poem *Orlando Innamorato*. However, for this short essay, I decided to look at the 'birth' of Ridolfi, a Spinozist character in *Adventures in Africa*, to whom Celati would later devote an entire short story entitled 'Cevenini e Ridolfi' in the collection *Cinema Naturale* (Milan: Feltirnelli, 2001).

As Rebecca West illustrates, Celati's interest in Spinoza is probably linked to his life-long admiration for Melville. In 1991 Celati translated Melville's 'Bartleby the Scrivener' and wrote a critical foreword which, according to West, shows signs of having been influenced by the Italian post-metaphysical theorists of 'weak thought' (such as Vattimo and Rovatti), as well as by the writings of Deleuze, who greatly admires Spinoza and lists him among his favourite thinkers (West, 41). Bartleby, however, had already served as a model for one of Celati's short stories, 'Baratto' published in 1987 as part of *Quattro novelle sulle apparenze*, but written many years before, as the author himself says, at the time when he was living in Paris (West, 24). Although a direct reference to Spinoza in connection with Melville only appears in the recently re-written version of that foreword, about to appear in a collection of essays entitled *Studi di affezione* (West, 41), it is obvious that there are many aspects of Spinoza's philosophy that might appeal to a writer like Celati. From the idea of the 'incommensurate singularity of every individual', which is clearly visible in Melville's Bartleby and in many of Celati's stories, to the notion of 'divine inertia' that stresses the futility of seeking 'some secret by trying to plumb the depths of a way of being because manifested presence is absolute in being simply what it is' (West, 44), the seventeenth-century Dutch philosopher seems to enable Celati to express his own philosophical considerations on society and human nature.

Like the theorists of 'weak thought', Celati believes that it is no longer possible to present a set of values as universally positive or negative. It is therefore not surprising to discover that in *Adventures in Africa* Celati alludes to Spinoza's *Ethics*, a work that in Deleuze's view represents an overthrowing of the system of judgement: 'Ethics, which is to say a typology of immanent modes of existence, replaces Morality, which always refers existence to transcendent values' and, 'the opposition of values (Good-Evil) is supplanted by the qualitative difference of modes of existence (good-bad)'.[4] Spinoza's idea of a single substance that is characterised by two or more attributes[5] also seems to support Celati's relativist approach to reality. As Roger Scruton points out, 'to say that there are two attributes is to say that we can know the world completely in two incommensurable ways'.[6] Possible comparisons, however, do not end here. For instance, when reflecting on Spinoza's concept of a body as something that is not defined by form or functions but by a 'complex relation between differential velocities' (Deleuze, 123),[7] Deleuze remarks that 'it is by speed and slowness that one slips among things, that one connects with something else. One never commences; one never has a *tabula rasa*; one slips in, enters in the middle; one takes up or lays down rhythms' (ibid.). According to Luigi Ghirri, a photographer with whom Celati worked in the 1980s and whose ideas influenced his own literary production of that period[8] and are still visible in his more recent works, this statement seems to capture what Celati considers to be the essence of photography. In his introduction to a book containing a collection of photographs by Ghirri,[9] Celati emphasises how Ghirri is able to go beyond the monumental approach, presenting things and phenomena as they manifest themselves. Through his 'atmospheric vision', Ghirri tries 'to displace the glance and open up the landscape' (PN, 11 settembre), thus forcing the viewer to embrace the horizon, that place where 'the open becomes world' (PN, 4 ottobre). To use Deleuze's words once more, Ghirri, like Spinoza, seems to invite us to take up or lay down rhythms (Deleuze, 123). According to Celati, this implies giving up one's individual point of view and all abstract ideas, and learning to look at things from the perspective belonging to a specific form of life. Spinoza's theory of 'common notions' as general, but not abstract, ideas common to all things and representing a unity of composition between two or more bodies (Deleuze, 54)[10] appears to have a resonance here as well as in Celati's last two fictional works. In the *Ethics*, Spinoza also points out that 'what is common to all things [...] does not constitute the essence of any singular thing' (Part II, P37, 54). Such a concept would greatly appeal to Celati who is convinced of the impossibility of grasping any aspect of reality in a final and universally satisfactory way, thus pushing Spinoza's views a step further and questioning the very notion of essence.

Adventures in Africa[11] (first published in 1998) is the diary of a trip to West Africa that took place in 1997 when Celati accompanied his friend Jean Talon through Mali, Senegal and Mauritania to investigate 'the possibility of making a documentary about the healing methods used by the Dogon healers' (AA, xiii). In true post-modern style, Celati does not give the reader a clear and linear account of his travels. Instead, he tries to capture the impressions that the apparent chaos of African life, and of its landscape, make on him and his friend. In so doing he also presents his reflections on the significance of writing in our times and on the representability of reality. To counterbalance the feeling of displacement caused by the journey and the unfamiliar environment, Celati has to keep writing, as if he were at home (AA, 4), because work is the only element capable of giving the individual a sense of purpose and the illusion of stability. Apart from the notes containing 'names of places, lists of things seen on the street' (AA, 11), Celati is also sketching ideas for stories he intends to write, and this is how we are introduced to the characters of Cevenini and Ridolfi:

> Cevenini is half deaf, Ridolfi is blind in one eye and nearsighted in the other... Ridolfi is very cultured and, for this reason, always has to be right, and can't stand to be contradicted. So Cevenini always tells him that he is right ... When they were at home [...] it would so happen that every three months Ridolfi would go crazy [...] One day Cevenini read in the newspaper about a famous Professor Paponio, who had erected a centre for medicine in a place in Africa where they cure insanity with magical methods of the African healers. So, he decided to take his friend Ridolfi to have him cured by magic... (AA, 73)[12]

Later we are told that Ridolfi is a 'Spinozist' (AA, 96) and, after the meeting with a very elegant African woman, we discover his idea of the absolute as something residing 'within that which is nothing special at all, which is absolutely necessitated' (ibid.).

Before comparing Ridolfi's notion of the absolute to that of Spinoza, it is worth mentioning that the physical inadequacies of these two characters seem to express 'the natural conditions of our existence insofar as we do not have adequate ideas' (as Deleuze points out concerning the problem of knowledge in Spinoza; Deleuze, 82). Therefore, we judge things according to the disposition of our brain and accept affections of the imagination as things (*Ethics*, Part I, Appendix, 30). This explains why the two friends have difficulties in communicating with each other. As a consequence, during their trip to Africa they never seem to be in control of the situation and lose their way (CN, 188-9). Cevenini and Ridolfi, however, like Bartleby or Baratto, are also comic figures and, as Rebecca West says, when talking of Celati's analysis of Melville's hero, in them we can see 'Spinoza's concept of divine inertia' which implies that 'every individual and every presence in the world is an incommensurable singularity that expresses in its attributes the anteriority of an infinite essence about which one can say nothing' (West, 44).

As for Ridolfi's idea of the absolute as 'that which is nothing special at all' and yet which is 'absolutely necessitated' (AA, 96), it appears to be in line with Spinoza's definition of God (*Ethics*, I, D6) but also with his notion of 'mode' (*Ethics*, I, D5) and with what he expresses in his postulate 22 where he claims that 'whatever follows form some attribute of God, insofar as it is modified by a modification which, through the same attribute, exists necessarily and is infinite, must also exist necessarily and be infinite' (*Ethics*, I, P22, 17). At first it is surprising to find such a view in a post-modern work, as it seems to be in contradiction with Celati's anti-foundational and post-metaphysical approach to reality, and one might be inclined to consider Ridolfi's statement as an example of that ironic use of tradition that, according to Umberto Eco, is typical of postmodernism.[13] When considered more carefully, however, the emphasis on something that is 'nothing special at all' and yet 'absolutely necessitated' can be seen as an indication of Celati's anti-monumentalism and minimalism. As Rebecca West points out, 'minimalism is seen at least in part as an oppositional countering of mimetic maximalism' and, 'a dictionary definition of the term defines it as "being or offering no more than what is required or essential"' (West, 64). Despite the fact that minimalism (which is often used negatively) is too restrictive a label to do justice to Celati's complex poetics, the above-mentioned definitions, although not entirely satisfactory, imply an attitude towards writing, in particular, and the world, in general, that can be easily associated with Celati. According to West, his work can in fact be seen as 'a long and patient process of chipping away, as he unendingly subjected the solid foundations of historically and rationally determined literary narrative forms to dismantlement, arriving finally to the skeletal, essential, yet ultimately complex question' of what is narrative. Celati's answer, as West illustrates, is 'modest, minimal, even' as he considers narrative as 'a way of organising experience' (West, 89).

Ridolfi's insistence on something 'that is nothing special' is also reminiscent of an essay that Celati wrote for the journal *Quindi* in 1983, in which the term 'adventure', that significantly appears in the title of the book we are currently analysing and is frequently used in the short story devoted to Cevenini and Ridolfi, is defined as 'the opposite of a search for the fulfilment of a tangible and localizable desire'. It is a journey into otherness that can take place 'only in common routine, in that which is the same for everyone, and it is that which no one notices because it is not sensational'. When this does not happen 'the other is replaced by simply another geographic, historical or touristic horizon' (West, 86). This is what Celati and Talon learn from their voyage through Mali, Senegal and Mauritania, which explains why their planned documentary was never produced. As West reminds us, for Celati the 'obvious' is our only kingdom (West, 86), but it is precisely this ability to relate to the obvious that we have lost in western societies where we are forced to live through a permanent documentary 'of total newness', where there is no place for anything precarious or 'rejected by destiny', a documentary 'on global simulation' (AA, 170). The ending of the book is an encouragement to ignore the sensational stimuli to which we are constantly exposed, to break all barriers and return to simplicity, to a more direct contact with the natural world. To recover the ability to experience a true adventure in the obvious, we need to abandon the protective glass with which we are equipped because, 'when one is left behind a window', one becomes aware of 'not needing anything at all, except some of the nothing that cannot be bought, some of the nothing that does not correspond with anything, the nothing of the sky and the universe, or the nothing that the others have who do not have anything' (AA, 170).

The emphasis on nature is the thread that holds together many of Celati's intertextual references. Vattimo, for instance, views ontological difference in terms of a reappraisal of 'nature as the natural basis/background/ungrounding of culture'.[14] Ghirri's 'atmospheric vision', on the other hand, which Celati tries to apply to his own writings, represents 'a celebration of natural phenomena, compared to which each historical document becomes a vanity of knowledge' (PN, 6 settembre). Finally, Ridolfi's idea of the absolute is in line with Spinoza's pantheistic world view as expressed in the *Ethics* (Part I, P14, 9). What I hope to have demonstrated through this short study of a particular aspect of *Adventures in Africa*, is how an author, whether consciously or unconsciously, directly or indirectly, is in permanent interaction with his sources and the endless potential of tradition that, like human life is never static, but constantly evolving.

NOTES
1 Rebecca West, *Gianni Celati: The Craft of Everyday Storytelling*. (Toronto: University of Toronto Press, 2000), pp. xi-xiii.

2 Trinh T. Minh-ha, 'Other Than Myself / My Other Self' in George Robertson, Melinda Mash, Lisa Tickner, John Bird, Barry Curtis and Tim Putnam, eds., *Travellers' Tales. Narratives of Home and Displacement.* (London: Routledge, 1940), pp. 9-26, on p. 18 and 24.
3 Madan Sarup, 'Home and Identity' in *Travellers' Tales*, op. cit., pp. 93-104, on p. 97.
4 Gilles Deleuze, *Spinoza: Practical Philosophy.* (San Francisco: City Lights Books, 1988), p. 23.
5 Cfr.: Benedict De Spinoza, *Ethics.* (London: Penguin Books, 1996), p.1 (Part I, D 3, D 4, D 6). All further references will be to this edition.
6 Roger Scruton, *Spinoza.* (Oxford: Oxford University Press, 1986), p. 42.
7 Cf. *Ethics*, PII: A1, A2 and L1, L2 (p. 41); PI-VI (p. 44).
8 See *Narratori delle pianure* (1985), *Quattro novelle sulle apparenze* (1987) and *Verso la foce* (1989).
9 Gianni Celati, 'Commenti su un teatro naturale delle immagini', in Luigi Ghirri, *Il profilo delle nuvole.* (Milan: Feltrinelli, 1989). Abbreviation: PN.
10 As Deleuze explains, according to Spinoza, 'each existing body is characterised by a certain relation of motion and rest and when these relations corresponding to two or more bodies adapt themselves to one another, the two bodies form a composite body having a greater power' (Deleuze, p. 54).
11 Gianni Celati, *Adventures in Africa.* (Chicago and London: University of Chicago Press, 2000; translated by Adria Bernardi). All quotations are from this edition. Abbreviation: AA.
12 This passage, of course, is also reminiscent of Beckett, an author to whom Celati devoted an entire essay in his *Finzioni Occidentali* (Turin: Einaudi, 1975, 1986).
13 Stuart Sim (ed.), *The Icon Critical Dictionary of Postmodern Thought.* (Cambridge: Icon Books, 1998), pp. 286-7.
14 Gianni Vattimo, *The Adventure of Difference. Philosophy after Nietzsche and Heidegger.* (Cambridge: Polity Press 1993), p. 156.

Uneasy Journey into the Past: Bernhard Schlink's *Der Vorleser*

Jo Desch (Bangor)

AS WE GROW older, images of the past reaffirm themselves, albeit from different perspectives. Depending on our predisposition we may talk of the good old days, or of bygones that had best remain bygones. How do we perceive our own past? Would we have it all over again? Most of us would, but perhaps not quite in the same way.

Take the young lad whose father decides that at 16 he is old enough to explore the wider world and broaden his cultural horizon. His choice falls on Munich where he lodges with a 40-year old widow who, having put her children to bed, comes to sit on the side of his bed, listening to him telling her about the day's exploits and furtively stroking his hand. Though he was none too young to understand the open invitation, misguided pride and confused ideas about the difference in age leave him unmoved and cold, 'kalt und ohne Mitleid und [ich] nenne mich noch jetzt einen Esel'.

It is none other than Keith Spalding who recalls this episode somewhat wistfully in his autobiography *33 – alles umsteigen*.[1] We all change trains at some stage and move on, and the journey back into the past is often one of bewilderment and disbelief, as if it were into another country. Sometimes, as in this case, we can record it with bemusement and the wisdom of a more mature age. At other times, however, it can be unsettling and disturbing, as in Bernhard Schlink's novel *Der Vorleser*.[2]

Like Keith Spalding and like many of us, I guess, the 15 year old Michael Berg enjoyed a traditional upbringing. But he did not allow himself to fall victim to any such scruples. Waking up, like most adolescents do from nightly excursions into the realm of carnal pleasures he soon got the better of his pangs of conscience: 'Ich erfuhr Tag um Tag, daß ich die sündigen Gedanken nicht lassen konnte. Dann wollte ich auch die sündige Tat.' (p. 21). That pragmatic decision threw the doors wide open to a tempestuous love affair with a woman also more than twice his age.

But that in itself did not trouble him. Indeed, it rather enhanced his self-esteem when comparing himself to his peers, made him grow from a timid teenager to a self-confident young man and secured his success in school. He accepted what seemed to be Hanna's whims and occasional violent outbursts with some bewilderment. In order to conceal his illicit liaison from family and friends he contrived lies and the occasional theft from *Karstadt* - with ease, as the lawyer-to-be later recalls. There is no room here for wistful reflection in later life on opportunities lost and pleasures denied. He exploited them to the full. But then that was the fifties, when our parents had no credibility in upholding traditional values that were without currency after the war to end all wars, and youngsters had grown up and were growing up in an atmosphere of hidden promiscuity with *Onkelehen*,[3] *Hausfreunden*,[4] *Fräuleins*,[5] *Besatzungskindern*, pin-ups and 'off limits' nightclubs.

Bernhard Schlink's novel is not, as Stuart Taberner put it somewhat provocatively, about the morality of loving a concentration camp guard[6] - though that may well be a fascinating precept for a wide-ranging exploration of the book, as indeed he intended. Nor does it attempt to analyse in depth the unequal sexual relationship,[7] the Holocaust, or the widely debated conundrum of victims versus perpetrators, an issue deemed by some to 'undermine ethics entirely'.[8] The author takes no moral stance, which is one of the book's many virtues and makes it a deeply moral tale. It is also what many of his critics have condemned who would have perpetual remorse and penance implanted in the German gene.[9] Indeed, Schlink does not meet the expectations of collective penitence of a whole nation for atrocities too heinous even to comprehend. His focus is on just one protagonist coming face to face with memories he thought he had long left behind, as one leaves behind a town when the train moves on (p. 82). But forced to revisit his own past, Michael Berg finds himself implicated in the collective past of his nation more intrinsically than he could imagine and more existentially than those critics would concede. That is the only aspect out of a host of related themes, all well rehearsed, that I am addressing in this essay.

The narrator protagonist unfolds his tale in retrospect, like a detective story. But he does not so much recall the events as explore them. On almost every page there are questions that remain unanswered. Adopting a technique reminiscent of the stream of consciousness, he tries to fathom his past, a past from which he had detached himself when his blissful, carefree 'Gleitflug unserer Liebe' (p. 66) came to an abrupt ending with Hanna's sudden und inexplicable disappearance. That was to have a decisive influence on his future life. For a while he would blame himself for betraying her. But eventually a sense of self-protection prevailed and he repressed his own feelings, presented himself consciously and deliberately as one 'den nichts berührt, erschüttert, verwirrt' - to the extent even of rejecting his grandfather's blessing. 'Dieses Nebeneinander von Kaltschnäuzigkeit und Empfindsamkeit war mir selbst suspekt.' (p. 64) He had, as he says, 'die Erinnerung an Hanna zwar verabschiedet, aber nicht bewältigt.' Although he had come to terms with it, the past had remained '*unbewältigt*' and it was to remain so for the rest of his life. A door had closed. What stayed behind had not been tidied up.

What is it that makes us sad when trying to recall past happiness? 'Ist es das Wissen, was danach kam und daß alles danach nur ans Licht kam, was schon da war?' (p. 38) What is this guilt that, unacknowledged at the time, poisons happy memories? In Michael's case it is his failure to acknowledge Hanna at the poolside, a seemingly trivial incident that nevertheless crystallises his half-heartedness over the last few months (p. 80). He had tried to persuade himself that it wasn't Hanna, but he knew only too well: 'Sie stand da und sah - und es war zu spät.' (p 81) However, such remorse about personal failings pales into insignificance compared to what was yet in store.

'Aufarbeitung! Aufarbeitung der Vergangenheit' (p. 86) was the students' slogan in the sixties. 'Daß verurteilt werden müsse, stand für uns fest'. Michael Berg's generation sentenced their parents to shame - wholesale, and with little tangible evidence, indeed even against such evidence. Michael's father, for example, had suffered himself. He had lost his professorship because of non-compliance with the Nazi doctrine. 'Wie kam ich dazu, ihn zu Scham zu verurteilen? Aber ich tat es.' (p. 88) It is the hubris of a generation that felt itself untarnished by the past, benefiting from what Helmut

Kohl called the 'Gnade der späten Geburt', outraged by collusion, unchanged authoritarian structures, an antiquated status cult, and ex-Nazis in high offices. But they were by no means immune themselves. Having accepted his guilt of betrayal Michael was yet to discover that he had been and still was intimately involved in more than one sense.

'Ich sah Hanna im Gerichtssaal wieder.' (p. 86) Like lightening strikes out of a blue sky, that instant recognition flashes up his long forgotten past, as much out of context as the blunt, isolated phrase that records the plain fact. It shatters his self-image, and the implications are immediately clear. But as we wait for the thunder to end the suspense, the narrator first launches into a lengthy recapitulation and assessment of the righteous indignation felt by his generation, before he can return to the uncomfortable truth six (!) pages later: 'Ich erkannte sie, aber ich fühlte nichts. Ich fühlte nichts.' (p. 90) His senses are numbed, he is unable to comprehend this astounding truth, even catches himself accepting Hanna's imprisonment as just - not because of her crime, but because it puts her out of his reach, out of his world, far away like a distant memory (p. 93). His past has caught up with him and demands to be recognised but he refuses. Unable even to recall their tender moments together he records them as one would record mundane facts, without emotion (p. 95). The strangely unfamiliar past that confronts him causes him to question his identity, as if it were someone else's past, 'als sei es ein anderer, der sie geliebt und begehrt hatte.' (p. 97) The past is another country. They do things differently there. L P Hartley's wonderful opening line to *The Go-between* encapsulates that breach between then and now perfectly and could serve as a *leitmotif* to Schlink's novel.

Try as he may, though, Michael cannot detach himself emotionally from his past. Why else should he choose the more humane explanation for Hanna's crime and refute the equally plausible suggestion of callousness or brutality on her part? (pp. 126ff.) Why should he be haunted by dreams that conjure up vastly contrasting images of Hanna, those from his youth and others concocted in his subconscious mind from what he now knows about her life? Most alarming were those 'in denen mich die harte, herrische, grausame Hanna sexuell erregte', causing him 'Angst, wer ich eigentlich sei'. (p. 142) That existential fear far exceeds his betrayal, and it can no longer be banished to someone else's distant past. The disturbing mixture of yearning, shame and indignation is all *his*, and it is here and now, inextricably linked to the past as it is to the present. What was it that he and Hanna had - and maybe still have - in common? Was it indeed her latent violent nature that had excited him, that had caused him to love her so passionately in his youth - in which case he is equally culpable? Not guilty of causing her departure, yet still guilty of betrayal, he now finds himself also guilty by implication, simply because he had loved a criminal, 'weil ich eine Verbrecherin geliebt hatte.' (p. 129). He, the squeaky-clean sixties rebel, discovers that his own past is manifest in the present, calling him to account.[10]

That past also presents him with an invidious challenge, namely to sit in judgement over Hanna. For it is in his power to influence the outcome of the trial decisively. He, and only he knows that her confession is false. Is he to acquiesce to a miscarriage of justice and allow her sentence to be based on false evidence - which makes him guilty both in law and morally - or should he disclose to the presiding judge what he knows, thereby securing a just, i.e. reduced sentence under the law but infringing Hanna's right as an individual to protect her dignity - which makes him equally guilty? The dilemma is Hanna's just as much as his, and once again their destinies seem inextricably intertwined. Neither his father's philosophical excursus on human dignity and personal freedom (pp. 134ff.), nor the down-to-earth pragmatic approach of the judge who in his career has 'done everything right', can provide guidance, and Michael takes the easy way out. He does nothing and lets the trial take its course. It is an act of non-action that at least allows him to return to live an ordinary everyday life (p. 155) where he, like the judge, has done and will do everything right in an everyday fashion, right down to executing her will and visiting her grave - for the first and only time.

His motives for 'sentencing' Hanna by remaining passive are obscure. As he hovers between his desire to understand her, outright condemnation of her crimes, and the danger of renewed betrayal by deciding one way or the other[11] he cannot find a firm moral standpoint. He wants her in prison indefinitely, but it is not clear whether this is for reasons of just punishment or his own self-preservation. He keeps sending her tapes but shuns any form of contact, thus giving her hope and encouragement as well as causing distress, despondency (p. 195), and possibly, as the warden indicates, her death (p. 197). It is only after her death that he allows the past back into the present when he sees the radiant flush of youth in her face. Why had he not seen it before?[12] Once again, it is too late.

Michael's uneasy association with his past remains unresolved, '*unbewältigt*' like his early memories of Hanna. He has 'made his peace' (p. 205) and 'come to terms' with it, an arrangement that allows him to function normally in his everyday world, but he has not become master of it. The English phrase conveniently disguises the real predicament implying, as it does, acceptance and resignation rather than active conquest and control. '*Etwas bewältigen*' conveys a sense of accomplishment; but 'coming to terms' is yielding to the inevitable. Michael has not conquered. His past is still and will always be another country, never his home; frequently explored, mapped and revisited, but never owned. Or, as Bernhard Schlink put it: 'Wir müssen unsere Biographien immer wieder neu schreiben, um uns dessen zu vergewissern, wer und wo wir sind. Das heißt, wir müssen durch die Vergangenheit immer wieder durch.'[13]

NOTES

[1] Keith Spalding, *33 – alles umsteigen - Eine Autobiographie*. (Lübeck: edition outline / Weißenhorn GmbH, 1992.
[2] Bernhard Schlink, *Der Vorleser*. (Zürich :Diogenes, 1995), p. 40.
[3] Open relationship of a young mother whose husband had not (yet) returned from the war and whose children would call her live-in lover 'uncle'.
[4] The traditional term acquired a new meaning in the late forties and fifties when it was used for a man who was a regular visitor in the home of a young woman with whom, it was implied, he had a sexual relationship. Since men were in short supply in post-war Germany he could be *Hausfreund* to more than one.
[5] In the forties and fifties this traditional form of address for an unmarried young woman was used by American GIs or British soldiers for their (mostly casual) partners. The term thus acquired a derogatory meaning amongst Germans who pronounced it with an American accent and mocked it in scores of jokes. Thousands of illegitimate children from such relationships with soldiers of the occupation (Besatzung) forces were known as *Besatzungskinder*.

6   'The Morality of Loving a Concentration Camp Guard. Teaching Bernhard Schlink's *Der Vorleser*', *Deutsch: Lehren und Lernen*, 25 (Spring 2002), 3-8.
7   That aspect has attracted a great deal of attention in the Anglo-American world, especially after Schlink's appearance on the Oprah Winfrey show which homed in, *inter alia*, on sexual and emotional abuse and the age gap between the lovers – issues much less under discussion on the European continent. Cf. Schlink's comment in an interview with Tilman Krause, 'Gegen die Verlorenheit an sich selbst', *Die Welt*, 3. 4. 1999.
8   William Collins Donahue, 'Illusions of Subtlety: Bernhard Schlink's *Der Vorleser* and The Moral Limits of Holocaust Fiction', *GLL*, 54,1 (2001), 195-214. Ernestine Schlant's comment that 'illiteracy cannot serve as an explanation for cooperating in and committing criminal acts' is equally misplaced since no such link between illiteracy and some moral deficiency is implied; cf. Ernestine Schlant, *The Language of Silence, West German Literature and the Holocaust*. (New York: 1999), p. 213. Similarly Sally Johnson and Frank Finlay, '(Il)literacy and (im)morality in Bernhard Schlink's *The Reader*', in: *Written Language and Literacy*, 4,2, (2001), 195-214 who confuse causality of events with causality in Hanna's psychological makeup and fight windmills when refuting the suggestion that literacy is related to moral judgement - a notion that has no foundation in the text.
9   The book has received unbounded accolades as well as outright condemnation, depending on the critics' view of how the German nation ought to respond to its past. Two examples may suffice to indicate the scope, both, happily, from pro-Jewish magazines. Under the programmatic headline '*Immorality Play*' Ruth Franklin argues in the ostensibly liberal Washington magazine *The New Republic* of 10.15.2001 that the book is mediocre and pernicious in offering moral shortcuts by 'therapeutically "working through" the problems of the past while in fact remaining comfortably aloof from them'. Referring to Hitler and Goebbels as fans of Wagner and Sharespeare she notes how 'the evidence of history demonstrates that Michael's "confidence in bourgeois culture" is misplaced' - a comment strangely unrelated to the text. On the other hand, Tom Tugend in *The Jewish Journal of Greater Los Angeles*, 31.3 (2000), concurs with Barry Glassner, sociologist at USC, who called the book 'one of the most morally complex novels I have read'.
10 Erika Tunner turns his upside down, suggesting that Michael tries to detach himself 'mit naiv-entwaffnendem Eingeständnis eigener Schwäche' from what she calls the German destiny. Cf. 'Vom Unbehagen beim Lesen eines Bestseller', in: *Zschr. zur politischen Bildung* – Eichholz Brief 36 (1999), H.4, 114-9.

11 Jill Scott calls this his catch-22 situation which, as she argues, leaves him a socially dysfunctional individual, a judgement which, I feel, needs to be more clearly defined in this context. Cf. her conference paper 'Consuming Confession: Producing - Convenient Memories in Bernhard Schlink's *Der Vorleser* (The Reader)', held at the University of Manitoba, Oct 2001, http://www.umanitoba.ca/faculties/arts/english/media/workshop/papers/scott/scott_paper.pdf, p.7.
12 P.197. In his laudatory address on occasion of Bernhard Schlink receiving the WELT Literature Prize, Christoph Stöckl referred to this moment, delicately poised between past and present: 'seine in einem Nebensatz versteckte posthume Vermählung gehört stilistisch zum Raffiniertesten und zugleich Ergreifendsten, was in unserer Zeit über eine solche Grenzerfahrung geschrieben worden ist.' *Die Welt*, 13.11.1999.
13 In: Volker Hage, 'Gewicht der Wahrheit. Ein Roman des deutschen Schriftstellers Bernhard Schlink macht weltweit Furore'. *Der Spiegel*, 13 (1999).

A (Post)Colonial Perspective on the Examination System

Rosemary Chapman (Nottingham)

PART OF THE work of an external examiner is to view the range of examinations set in another educational establishment from a different perspective.[1] This angle allows not objectivity but comparison of (relatively speaking) like with like. To read examination papers from another culture and another period alerts one rather to the contrasts and differences produced by historical and cultural contexts. Since the function of the examination is indeed to examine the curriculum taught, one can often detect the slant, bias, silences of set-texts and the manner in which they have been studied. In this brief analysis of a particular educational context (that of Manitoba, Canada, in the early twentieth century), examination papers and the curriculum will be considered as one very tangible sign of the colonial process in all its complexity.

It is widely acknowledged in the field of postcolonial studies that education has been used as a tool of colonial governance. Within the colonial project education served as a means of creating a cultural elite whose function was to mediate the values of empire, the members of this elite having themselves been ideologically influenced by the values and claims to universality of the colonial culture. The most famously cited evidence of this 'civilizing mission' is the 'Minute on Indian Education' of Thomas Macaulay in 1835 which defines the aim of education in India as being: 'to form a class of persons, Indians in blood and colour, but English in taste, in opinions, in morals and in intellect'.[2] Not only the English language, but also English literature, were taught in order to colonize the minds of the educated elite.[3] If one compares the systems and practices of education in different areas of the world colonized by Britain it is clear that the civilizing mission takes on different dynamics in different contexts. Colonies themselves can be broadly divided into 'colonies of occupation' (in Africa and Asia, for example) and 'colonies of settlement', or 'settler-invader colonies' (such as Australia and Canada).[4]

The picture is further complicated in the case of Canada where both France and Britain colonized the territory. The period of French rule in New France came to an end at the battle of the Plains of Abraham in 1759 but much of the established Francophone population remained and various accommodations with it have since been found, Quebec now being the only majority francophone province, but other provinces having a significant francophone minority. The question of whether the English and French languages should have equal status in Canada has been a source of conflict throughout the history of British rule. Provinces have jurisdiction over education. As each new province entered the Canadian confederation, it had to take a stand on the educational provision for Anglophones and Francophones and as well as for other sizeable linguistic and cultural minorities. Manitoba became a province in 1870, with a confessional, bilingual system of education. Its tradition of bilingual provision dated back to the earliest establishment of denominational schools in the area of modern-day Winnipeg by catholic and protestant settlers in 1818 and 1819 respectively. Although the bilingual, denominational education system was subsequently banned in Manitoba in 1890, by which time the Anglophone population had become numerically superior, a compromise was negotiated in 1896, allowing the continuation of some provision of bilingual teaching and religious education where numbers warranted it. But in 1916 this compromise system was abolished and the provincial government introduced compulsory, non-denominational, English language schooling (though out of hours religious education was still allowed where numbers warranted). So, all languages other than English had to be taught in the same way as a second language, normally introduced from grade IX onwards. Only in 1967 was the bilingual principle once again recognized in Manitoba, after fifty years of organized resistance from the Franco-Manitoban community.[5]

It is usual in all settler-invader colonies that settlers - having arrived at different times, by different routes, from a variety of geographical and social origins - have different degrees and forms of allegiance to the *métropole*, and, as Johnston and Lawson have pointed out: 'these factors produced, in many cases, the feeling of being colonized – of being European subjects but no longer European citizens'.[6] In the case of Manitoba, then, one can say that the Francophone population was doubly colonized, both in their capacity as subjects of the British Empire and as a minority, internally colonized by the Anglophone majority. But, of course, in parallel to this colonization of one group of white settlers by another, larger group, there was a still more blatant form of assimilation, carried out in part by the education system.

When the province of Manitoba was founded in 1870 there was a sizeable Métis population, the product of the particular mode of early colonial contact through the white male guides and traders in the fur trade and related trades (supplies, exchange, etc) employed by the Hudson Bay Company and its rival prior to 1821, the North West Company. These men found partners amongst the indigenous population, many of the resulting families later settling in the Red River valley where Winnipeg was subsequently established. From the outset education for the Métis population in the Red River colony and subsequently for First Nations children, often provided within residential schools on the reserves, was automatically delivered in the language of the colonizer, be it English or French, in keeping with the principles of assimilation - linguistic, cultural and religious. In this Second World context the (predominantly) white settler acted as 'an agent of colonial rule over the proportionally, and usually numerically shrinking indigenous population'.[7]

If in settler colonies education acts as a means of colonizing the mind, it is also true that the education system itself is the site of a set of competing and at times contradictory interests. Looking at the examination system and the curriculum as they were experienced by the Franco-Manitoban minority allows us to consider some of the complexities of the relationship between education and colonization. Evidence will be drawn from examination papers set by the Department of Education, Manitoba, in 1928. By 1928 the use of French as a language of instruction had officially been banned for twelve years, although the teaching *of* French was still permitted from grade IX to grade XII. Given the particular situation of Manitoba, it seems appropriate to consider four related questions.

To what extent does education in Manitoba reflect Canada's place in the British Empire? Can one speak of an enduring influence of the French colonial past? Is education in Manitoba non-denominational (in accordance with 1890 Manitoban legislation, but unlike in Quebec where confessional schooling continued)? What signs are there of a distinctive Canadian nationalism in the material studied?

If one takes the view that British colonialism conforms to a simple centre-periphery model of power whereby not only economic and political, but also cultural power emanates from the centre, then one would expect education in Manitoba to bear the imprint of Empire. Certainly there is evidence within the education system to support this view. Teachers were required to swear an oath of allegiance to the crown, British citizenship was a requirement for permanent and high grade teaching certification, it was a legal requirement that schools fly the Union Jack each school day,[8] maps and globes in the class room reminded pupils of the shape of the Empire, readers used in elementary school featured photographs of the reigning monarch.[9] A close knowledge of British history and English literature were at the heart of the curriculum, from the elementary school readers upwards. At Grade XII, the final year of high school study and the equivalent to the first year of university study in addition to papers on Rhetoric and Prose Literature, Poetical Literature, and Composition, there were two Optional English papers for those wishing to specialize in literature. In 1928, Optional English - A included questions ranging from Chaucer and Milton to Swift, Bacon and Burke. Optional English - B includes questions on Shakespeare and a wide range of nineteenth-century essayists, including John Stuart Mill, Thomas Huxley, Thomas Carlyle and Cardinal Newman. Questions required both a demonstration of knowledge and some degree of analytical thought: 'What is Huxley's main proof of his theory of the origin of chalk? What are his collateral proofs?'; 'State concisely what you consider the essential ideas on the nature of education found in your reading of Arnold, Huxley, and Newman, naming the essays that are the sources of your information. (Two or three essential ideas from each writer will suffice.)'. English literature, then, held a prominent position in the high school curriculum and there is no sign of any Anglo-Canadian or American literature being studied as set texts at this level. And despite the French loss of

Empire in 1759 the teaching of French literature would at first sight seem to be equally strongly dominated by the French *métropole*.

Francophone pupils all took examinations in English alongside Anglophones, and followed the same (British) English curriculum. But they were still able to take in the place of Optional English papers two Optional French papers.[10] The Optional French - A paper covered French 17th Century literature, including Corneille's *Polyeucte* (a play about an early Christian martyr) and Boileau, and some general history of literature questions, and Optional French - B included Molière, Bossuet, Laprade, Lamartine and Déroulède. In comparison with those on the English Optional papers, the questions set seem slightly less demanding, either asking for a narrative account: 'Tracez l'histoire triste du Turco.' [Trace le Turco's sad story] or requiring the candidate to agree with the question: 'Mettez en lumière la sagacité pénétrante de Molière dans sa peinture du caractère de Sosie.' [Elucidate the wisdom and the insight of Molière's characterization of Sosie.] So was French cultural colonialism still alive and well in the Prairies nearly two hundred years after the Conquest? The Department of Education annual reports, which give details of set texts for each grade, reveals that the editions of texts used for the teaching of French language and literature were mostly published in Brussels and Quebec. So rather than keeping closely tied to a traditional French canon (education in French state schools being strictly secular), Manitoban advisors looked rather to Quebec and to Belgium, where most text books and literary anthologies were edited by members of the catholic teaching orders. In addition to this catholic mediation (selection, commentary and censorship) of French literature, there are also signs in the French syllabus of a developing interest in French-Canadian writers, most of whom at the time were conservative and catholic.[11]

In addition to the rather specialized field of the Optional French and English papers, there are other signs of cultural and denominational difference. The topics chosen for Composition papers are revealing. In the French composition question for Grade XI in 1928 the choice was as follows:

'Traitez l'un des sujets suivants:
(a) La reconnaissance aux parents;
(b) Moyens de communication – par terre, par eau et par air;

(c) "Je chante, je pleure." Développez les idées que fait surgir cette inscription sur la cloche d'une église.'
[Discuss one of the following topics: (a) Gratitude to one's parents. (b) Means of communication – by land, water and air. (c) "I sing, I weep." Develop the ideas inspired by this inscription on a church bell.]

Two of the three topics have a moral and/or religious dimension.[12] Yet the range of topics set for a Grade XII Composition Paper in English shows a different tendency. Amongst the ten topics, five are literary or literature-related topics ('Gabriel Oak', 'In the Macgregor Country', 'Thomas Hardy, Last of the Victorians', 'My Favorite Canadian Author' and 'In Praise of Reading'), four relate to modern-day Canada (industry, science, media and careers) and one is an imaginative topic. The space given to English literature here confirms its unquestioned importance within Canadian education. Whereas religious and moral values remain at the core of Franco-Manitoban identity, this source of core values seems to be provided within the English curriculum by English literature.

However, alongside the strong presence of the literature of Great Britain and of France in the curriculum, it is becoming clear by the late 1920s that Canada can also be a subject of study, even if its presence is very minor in the English and French literature papers. In 1928 a new history syllabus was introduced and subsequent Department of Education reports commented on its implementation. So, for example, in the Report for 1930-1, we read that a full year was now to be devoted to the study of Canadian history and that: 'it should be possible for every pupil to get a lasting impression of the development of Canadian tradition and of the achievement of Canadian nationhood within the British Empire and the League of Nations'.[13] In the 1928 British and Canadian History paper for Grade XI there are questions on Henry II, the Stuarts, the English people pre-1066, the British parliamentary system and British colonialism. The questions on Canada begin with European exploration, refer to the French presence only prior to the British Conquest, make no mention of Quebec (the origin of many Franco-Manitobans) and no mention of the First Nations. This emerging Canadian nationhood would seem to be white and Anglophone, the successful product of acculturation, in which the Second World has erased its First Nations.

Such an impression of the construction of Canadian nationhood underway in the late 1920s is supported by a brief look at a final set of examination papers - those set in 1928 for entrance to Normal School, where teacher training was provided. Since these candidates were to be the future mediators of culture, both British and Canadian, in Manitoba, it is instructive to see what was required of them. General knowledge is important, far more than any analytical skills. The papers reveal an image of Canada at the centre of this general knowledge, but a Canada that is defined through its relationships with the Empire and the Commonwealth. From a list of place-names candidates have to underline those which are not in the British Empire. Questions on the Canadian North are only concerned with trade routes and white settlements (the two being synonymous). Candidates have to draw a timeline of Canadian history, which begins with European exploration. Once again English literature is embedded in the Composition paper in two of the questions, candidates being asked to write on 'Any scene from *As You Like It*', or 'How a Cat played Robinson Crusoe'. Like the British Empire, English literature remains an unchallenged universal standard and point of reference in the education system - showing the enduring presence of the colonial relationship.

What this study of examination papers and the curriculum has attempted to show is the ambiguity of the position of settler communities under colonialism, caught as they are between the power, and cultural domination, of the *métropole* and their own emerging desires for nationhood. At this point in Canada's history, competing visions of Canada and different narratives of Canadian-ness are being explored. Anglophone Canadians continued to define themselves in relationship to Britain, but sought to erase linguistic and cultural differences within Canada. The relative strength of the Francophone minority in Manitoba, with its own colonial past, but also resilient ties to other Francophone populations (in Quebec and in Belgium, for example) meant that their cultural difference remained still visible within the education system, despite legislative attacks. But in comparison with the francophone minority, other linguistic and ethnic minorities, notably the First Nations, are largely invisible. As for aboriginal Manitobans, absent from the examination material studied and represented only in a few traditional tales in elementary school readers, the education system seems to have progressed little beyond Macaulay's 'civilizing mission' of 1835.

NOTES

1. I met Keith Spalding in his capacity as External Examiner in the Department of German at Nottingham University which I joined as a Joint Appointment in French and German in 1981.
2. Thomas Macaulay, 'Minute on Indian Education', in Bill Ashcroft, Gareth Griffiths, Helen Tiffin, eds, *The Post-colonial Studies Reader.* (New York: Routledge, 1995), p. 430.
3. On the specific role of English literature as a colonizing tool, see Gaurav Desai, 'Rethinking English: Postcolonial English Studies', in Henry Schwarz and Sangeeta Ray, *A Companion to Postcolonial Studies* (Oxford: Blackwell, 2000), pp. 523-39.
4. For a discussion of the complexities of these two terms see Anna Johnston and Alan Lawson, 'Settler Colonies', in Henry Schwarz and Sangeeta Ray, *A Companion to Postcolonial Studies* (Oxford: Blackwell, 2000), pp. 360-76.
5. For details of the legislation see Jean-Marie Taillefer, 'Les Franco-manitobains et l'éducation 1870-1970: une étude quantitative', unpublished PhD, Department of History, University of Manitoba, 1988. Since then the bilingual principle has extended to include aboriginal and Ukrainian programmes of study in the province's schools.
6. Anna Johnston and Alan Lawson, 'Settler Colonies', p. 363.
7. Ibid.
8. Indeed all teachers had to sign a declaration on the half-yearly returns of attendance that the flag was in good repair and flown daily (these returns can be consulted on microfilm at the Provincial Archives of Manitoba).
9. For example, a photograph of King George V is the frontispiece to *The Canadian Readers. Book III* (Toronto: W. J. Gage & Co.; T. Nelson & Sons, 1924) and one of the young Edward, Prince of Wales is the frontispiece to *The Canadian Readers. Book IV* (Toronto: W. J. Gage & Co.; T. Nelson & Sons, 1923).
10. In order to be able to continue teaching the same curriculum to the same standards at high school, the Franco-Manitoban community responded to the 1916 abolition by organizing a clandestine parallel curriculum, secretly continuing to teach in French alongside the official curriculum.
11. Influential set-texts, used throughout the period under discussion were *Précis d'histoire littéraire – par une Réunion de Professeurs, III-V* (Montréal: Frères E.C.), E. Procès, *Modèles français: extraits des*

    meilleurs écrivains avec notices (Brussels: Albert Dewit) and, for the French-Canadian dimension, Camille Roy, *Manuel d'histoire de la littérature canadienne française* published in Montreal in successive editions.

12 Taillefer has commented on the prevalence of a moralizing tone in many of the French passages set for study and in examination questions in the first decade of the century (see Taillefer, 'Les Franco-manitobains et l'éducation 1870-1970: une étude quantitative', p. 201).

13 Report of the Department of Education, Manitoba, 1930-31, p. 66.

The Cultural Component in Foreign Language Teaching

Witold F Tulasiewizc (Cambridge)

CALLS FOR TEACHING the culture of the people whose language one is studying have in the last few years become more frequent, prompted in part by the large number of documents emanating from the offices of the European Community and its member states insisting on the importance of international communication. To be sure, these demands do not seem to take account of the fact that, at all levels of general education, foreign language teaching has always included what has become known as the cultural dimension.

In secondary and tertiary education there exists the opportunity for studying the history or literature, indeed the cuisine, of the relevant nation, while the foreign phrases learned by beginners usually include a song or poem and the practice of some everyday customs. The giving of French or German names to learners or encouraging dressing up in foreign clothes and eating foreign food confirms the presence of a 'cultural' element also at the beginner's level.

So integrated are these activities in language courses that teachers and learners are not immediately aware of the fact that at the time of drilling the words and phrases they are being exposed to foreign culture even if we accept that, in Williams' terminology, it is the 'minor' variety of culture. Though they may have become less frequent for budgetary reasons, the exchanges and secondments, many of them sponsored by the EU, are further indicators of the presence of culture in modern foreign language teaching.

Terms like 'multiculturalism', cultural background and 'culture' itself have meanwhile become superseded by the more popular 'intercultural' and 'intercultural education' which emphasize the attitudes, the interaction involved in the process of learning foreign behaviour in the context of the growing number of multi-cultural and multi-ethnic classrooms.

A relatively recent curricular innovation, which owes much to the demands for a revised programme of foreign language teaching by bringing in the concept of language awareness (Hawkins etc), has been to teach culture through the study of the language, achieved by emphasizing language as an integral part of a nation's culture. Whereas a poem can convey a cultural, artistic or declarative message, the words themselves transmit culture in the form of language.

The form of language as much as its meaning is acknowledged as the medium for transmitting a nation's values, its identity. In the case of younger learners the language may be no more than a simple phrase such as the Chinese greeting 'have you eaten yet?', which, like the French phrase 'bon appetit' in France, indicates the Chinese concern for their speaking partners' physical wellbeing which is given more prominence than in other cultures relying on an undefined adjective such as 'good' in 'good morning'.

In classrooms throughout Europe and beyond pupils have been drilling phrases such as 'guten Tag' accepting them as equivalent to 'bon jour' and to 'good day'. This understandable acceptance of interchangeability because of similarity can be explained by the undue concentration in the teaching of the foreign lexis on the performing skills. Repetition alone, with only small variations of the phrases or structures drilled, does not allow time to reflect on the language that has been learned or one that is, often unsuccessfully, being learned.

The resulting divisions of the day in the formal daytime greeting may look linguistically identical, but often they are not used as such. 'Guten Morgen' may have an exact English equivalent in 'good morning' but the teaching of it usually takes no notice of the absence in everyday formal conversation of a French 'bon matin', the absence of the term seeming to extend the length of the French 'jour' itself. The Greek 'kalimera' does the opposite, the 'morning' being referred to throughout the day.

While it is possible to wish a particularly good morning ('bon matin' in French) to a special partner there is no formal equivalent in French to the English 'good morning'. The time when 'good afternoon' takes over from 'good morning' in formal greetings in

English is not often given much attention by users or learners of English, and may be another example of the failure to refer to the learner's first language when learning another, or indeed to teach elements of more than one language at the same time.

The Language Awareness movement has addressed such interchange and other language issues, for example explaining figurative language to young learners eager to play with language. The presentation of 'Hauptbahnhof' and 'headteacher' but 'central' or 'main station' in the same lesson exemplifies the advocation of a 'contrastive' approach in language learning (James, 1980) which consists of including the study of more than one language understood as capable of improving the motivation for the study of language and thus to help in the study of language media.

The formal greetings above, as well as the times of the clock 'half four' 'halb vier' meaning 'half past four', were among topics taught in a series of Language Awareness assisted lessons in years three and four of a number of primary schools in the home counties of England and the state of the Rhineland Palatinate in the Federal Republic of Germany over a term of six weeks in the year 2000 and repeated in 2001.

The topics were introduced as part of language education lessons which, in the case of the programmes agreed on was the language of instruction, likely to be most of the pupils' first (or principal second) language: English and German respectively, with comparisons being made, as part of a deliberate exposure to the foreign element, with the same phrases or their equivalents in other languages introduced in the course of the lessons where appropriate.

The Language Awareness movement - awareness of language itself documented for the first time as German *Sprachbewusstsein* in the German dictionary of the brothers Grimm, though not used in exactly the same educational sense as the English word - appropriated the term to refer to a type of language education which could help improve users' first language and facilitate the learning of foreign languages (Hawkins, 1984). Under the name of Knowledge about Language, the study of language achieved through talking about it in the process of learning it, envisaged a similar concern with language in a language education as opposed to literature was recommended in the Cox Report of 1989 on the teaching of subject English in the National Curriculum. This actually followed the pioneering approach of the Kingman Report of 1988 which had suggested earlier that the study of English in England and Wales must not be restricted to English but embrace a wider, general acquaintance with language.

Hawkins' famous 'bridge' (1974, 1992) conceived as a curriculum element spanning users' first and other languages, while probably still in the process of being defined, can be said to consist of a contrastive approach to language study in the process of acquiring the usual communicative skills seen as a priority objective of learning a language. The language awareness approach consists of involving the cognitive dimension more substantially in the process of learning language patterns (their forms and functions) for using as skills as well as providing a more general language education to enhance the users' emancipation when using their own first language and for facilitating the study of a modern foreign language (Encyclopaedia of Language) by referring and grouping the similarities and differences between the first and the target foreign language.

If these are not confined to examining the language forms but concentrate on their meanings and the way the meanings are expressed the contrastive study can entail not just a comparison of the form of words and phrases but also an analysis of their functions. In turn, as in the case of 'bon appetit', these words and phrases are checked, their use of language examined with reference to use made of their language by its users as their first language and by others. This is the cultural element of studying the language for its cultural uniqueness, a comparison between the French 'passe partout' and the English 'master key' using the language for discovering its culture.

The above outlined comparative study of language is the principal element of what in this paper is accepted as a study of users' language as an integral part of their culture which makes up their cultural identity.

The intercultural element adds a new emphasis to the study of modern foreign languages, particularly in a context where their use in communication, as in England, in view of the challenge posed by the pervasiveness of Global English, as the lingua franca of communication, is finding less of an uptake. Including the pupils' first language in the contrastive study to improve their command of it, makes the time spent on language doubly worthwhile, in terms of raising first language standards and facilitating the learning of another. This can also make anglophones aware of the need to adapt their first language in such a way as to place them in a better position to understand foreigners speaking their own non-English first language and to cope with their germanized or frenchified versions of English.

The linguistic education is reinforced by what has been termed as 'intercultural education' where the common language study can bring different people closer together in recognizing a common need and using a similar remedy, an important consideration for inclusion as an element in the study of both English and Modern Foreign Languages.

The language learning and acquisition priorities have in the past thirty years or so been acknowledged as part of language awareness assisted study of language, providing a language education not confined to the exclusive study of one language or one langue at a time (Language Awareness journal). Its benefits were those of raising the standard of the first language and to improve the motivation for learning another.

It could be argued that with English the lingua franca, especially in England itself, the foreign language is a redundancy, especially when considering the learning of which to recommend. On the other hand an intercultual education based on language study could go some way to temper the arrogance of monoglot speakers of English, as well as enable them to pick up some foreign vocabulary in the process.

This approach reconciles the need for intercultural understanding while cultivating the teaching of indispensable skills. The recent arrival of Intercultural Education has added the cultural dimension to all language study, which, by taking language itself as the object of study, has transformed cultural knowledge (cultural background) into a more dynamic education process capable of being used as an instrument of language sensitivity making a contribution to international understanding.

Just as Intercultural Education is not intended to be confined to concern with one culture, so the language awareness approach is directed to the study of more than one language, their study mutually reinforcing cultural knowledge and behaviour. In this process the purely communicative skills take second place to the cultural and intercultural understanding that the knowledge of the language can provide.

The language used in the approach is that used in topics that are part of the school curriculum, formal and informal greetings, telling the time, eating customs, instruction on how to play games in the early years of primary schooling. Some, like those involving greetings in different European languages for example, were used in the language teaching programmes in the schools participating in language awareness sessions coordinated by the author.

The aim of teaching the topics, whether from the fine arts or customs and behaviours, was to provide an educational experience, which would be accessible to enable the sharing of it to bring people together in intercultural harmony.

The school teaching programmes or sporting activities, like other parts of the curriculum, were primarily educational, introducing a new experience, the post school level topics would deal with work experience to make EU employment mobility easier, for example bringing in language on how to deal with a customer or to set about preparing a meal.

In each case the language learned was for both purely communicative purposes and for preparing for the behaviour expected in given situations. Language sensitization was intended to prepare for the cultural experience enabled by awareness of language, on the principle: if you can begin to like the language you end up by becoming interested in the people who use it.

Using language for locating the cultural elements was intended for encouraging interculturally acceptable skills and behaviour which required the introduction of language that was appropriate in the behavioural context aimed at. The aim of learning the culture was to enable cultural reconciliation achieved by mutual linguistic knowledge and the behaviour that goes with it. With the growing use of a lingua franca the linguistic skills may give way to the cultural abilities in which language is fully involved in intercultural transmission.

The formal greeting exercices were intended to improve the understanding of others and the facility to speak to them in a fully understood medium. For this purpose authentic materials were introduced and used in the exercises practising the skills.

What is attempted to be understood is a knowledge of the people involved, it being understood that another language arises on its own, a process which determines language behaviour in which there is no one to one relationship between the words and phrases.

BIBLIOGRAPHY

C. Brock and W. Tulasiewicz, ed., *Education in a single Europe*. (Routledge, ^{2}2000).

J. Bruner, *Child's Talk. Learning to use language*. (Oxford University Press, 1983).

M. Byram, 'Foreign Language Teaching and Multicultural Teaching', in King and Reiss, op.cit., pp. 173-86.

M. Byram and P. Doye, 'Intercultural competence and foreign language learning in the primary school', in P. Driscoll and D. Frost, ed., *The Teaching of Modern Foreign Languages in the Primary School*. (Routledge, 1999), pp. 138-51.

S. Gass and L. Selinker, *Language Transfer in Language Learning* (John Benjamin, 1991).

E. Hawkins, *Awareness of Language*, (Cambridge University Press, 1984).

E. Hawkins, 'Awareness of Language/Knowledge about Language in the Curriculum in England and Wales', in *Language Awareness*, 1:1 (1992), 3-9.

C. James, *Contrastive Analysis*. (Longman, 1980).

A. King and M. Reiss, ed., *The Multicultural Dimension of the National Curriculum*. (The Falmer Press, 1993).

I. Oomen-Welke and E. Karagiannakis, 'Language Variety in the Classroom', in *Curriculum & Teaching*, XI. 2 (1996), 45-52).

Report, *Language Awareness from Theory into Practice 2001*, prepared by W. Tulasiewicz, and T. Longhurst, on 'an action research teaching programme'. (University of Cambridge, 2001).

B. Troyna and B. Carrington, *Education, Racism and Reform*. (Routledge, 1990).

W. Tulasiewicz, 'The European Dimension and the National Curriculum', in King & Reiss, op.cit., pp. 240-58.

W. Tulasiewicz, 'Language Diversity: Implications for International Communication and Language Education', in C. Beck and A. Sofos, ed., *Neue Medien in der paedagogischen Kontroverse*. (Logophon, 2001), pp. 170-84.

W. Tulasiewicz and J. Zajda, '(Language Awareness Symposium) Editors' Introduction' *Curriculum & Teaching*, XI.2 (1996), 33-6.

R. Williams, *Culture*. (Fontana, 1981).

The Contributors

Dr Elizabeth Boa, Emeritus Professor of German, The University of Nottingham.

Dr Charmian Brinson, Director of Humanities Programme and Reader in German Studies, Imperial College London.

Dr Alan Busst, Emeritus Professor of French, The University of Wales, Bangor.

Dr Anthony Bushell, Professor of German and Head of Department of Modern Language, The University of Wales, Bangor.

Dr Rosemary Chapman, Senior Lecturer in French, The University of Nottingham.

Dr Jo Desch, retired as Lecturer in German, The University of Wales, Bangor in 1996.

Dr Owen Evans, Lecturer in German, Department of Modern Languages, The University of Wales, Bangor.

Dr Lothar Fietz, Emeritus Professor of English, The University of Tübingen; German Lektor at UCNW, Bangor 1959/60.

Dr John L Flood, Emeritus Professor of German, University of London, Senior Research Fellow University of London Institute of Germanic Studies; delivered first Keith Spalding Lecture in 1994.

Dr Hans-Joachim Hahn, Emeritus Professor of German, Oxford Brookes University, Lektor at UCNW, Bangor 1967-9.

Rev Dr John Heywood Thomas, Emeritus Professor of Theology, The University of Nottingham, Honorary Professor of Theology, The University of Wales, Bangor.

Dr Ian Hilton, retired as Senior Lecturer in German, The University of Wales, Bangor in 1998.

Peter Jentzsch, Professor (i.R.) für Fachdidaktik am Staatlichen Seminar für Schulpädagogik (Gymnasien) Tübingen, Lehrbeauftragter am Deutschen Seminar der Universität; 1960 Austauschstudent in Bangor.

G L Jones, Emeritus Professor of German, The University of Wales, Aberystwyth.

W Gareth Jones, Emeritus Professor of Russian, The University of Wales, Bangor.

Peter Leighton-Langer, retired. Author of *X steht für unbekannt*, a history of the 10,000 Germans and Austrians who served in the British forces.

Harry Long, retired. Former fellow student at The University of Birmingham 1934-38.

Dr Hans Heinrich Meier, Emeritus Professor of English Philology, Free University Amsterdam; member of the Langenscheidt editorial staff in 1954.

Dr T R Miles, Emeritus Professor of Psychology, The University of Wales, Bangor.

Idris Parry, Emeritus Professor of Modern German Literature, The University of Manchester, Verdienstorden der Bundesrepublik Deutschland; Lecturer in German at UCNW, Bangor 1947-63.

Dr R J Pascall, Professor and Head of Department of Music, The University of Wales, Bangor; Emeritus Professor of Music, The University of Nottingham.

Dr Tom Paulin, Poet and Critic, G. M. Young Lecturer in English at Hertford College, Oxford.

Dr S S Prawer, Emeritus Taylor Professor, The University of Oxford, Fellow of the British Academy.

Peter Prochnik, retired as Lecturer in German, Royal Holloway College, University of London in 1998; student of German Department at UCNW, Bangor 1954-9.

Dr J H Reid, Emeritus Professor of Contemporary German Studies, The University of Nottingham.

Dr Hans S Reiss, Emeritus Professor of German, The University of Bristol, Verdienstorden der Bundesrepublik Deutschland, Member of the Freie Akademie der Künste, Mannheim.

David Rock, Senior Lecturer in German, Department of Modern Languages, University of Keele; former student of German Department at UCNW, Bangor 1964-70.

Dr Laura Rorato, Lecturer in Italian, Department of Modern Languages, The University of Wales, Bangor.

Dr Horst Dieter Schlosser, Professor am Institut für Sprache und Literatur II, Fachbereich Neuere Philologien, Johann Wolfgang Goethe-Universität, Frankfurt am Main.

Dr Hinrich Siefken, Emeritus Professor of German, The University of Nottingham, Honorary Professor of Modern Languages, The University of Wales, Bangor; German Lektor UCNW, Bangor 1967-8.

Dr Witold F Tulasiewicz, retired, Fellow of Wolfson College Cambridge Emeritus, currently Visiting Professor of Language and Comparative Education in Bialystok / Warsaw, advisor EU Committee of the Regions.

Dr Carol Tully, Lecturer in German, Department of Modern Languages, The University of Wales, Bangor.

Dr Walter Voigt, Leiter (i.R.) der englischen Redaktion des Langenscheidt-Verlags.

Dr George A Wells, Emeritus Professor of German, The University of London, Humanist Laureate and Member of Academy of Humanism.

Dr Rhys W Williams, Professor and Head of German, The University of Wales, Swansea.

Dr Dietmar Wünschmann, Studiendirektor i.R., Research Assistant and German Lektor at UCNW, Bangor 1964-6.

Dr W E Yates, Emeritus Professor of German, The University of Exeter, Österreichisches Ehrenkreuz für Wissenschaft und Kunst 1.Klasse, Fellow of the British Academy, Corresponding Member Austrian Academy of Sciences.